DATE DUE

MAR 6	2009		
4/10/09			

Twayne's English Authors Series

EDITOR OF THIS VOLUME

Kinley Roby

Northeastern University

Evelyn Waugh

TEAS 301

Evelyn Waugh

EVELYN WAUGH

By CALVIN W. LANE

University of Hartford

TWAYNE PUBLISHERS
A DIVISION OF G. K. HALL & CO., BOSTON

Copyright © 1981 by G. K. Hall & Co.

Published in 1981 by Twayne Publishers,
A Division of G. K. Hall & Co.
All Rights Reserved

Printed on permanent/durable acid-free paper and bound
in the United States of America

Frontispiece photo of Evelyn Waugh by Yevonde, by arrangement
with Camera Press, London

Library of Congress Cataloging in Publication Data
Lane, Calvin Warren, 1923 -
Evelyn Waugh.

(Twayne's English authors series ; TEAS 301)
Bibliography: p: 176 - 85
Includes index.
1.   Waugh, Evelyn, 1903 - 1966—Criticism and inter-
pretation.   I.   Title.
PR6045.A97Z72   1981   823'.912   80-22498
ISBN 0-8057-6793-2

In grateful memory
of
Joe Lee Davis

Contents

About the Author

Calvin W. Lane received his B.A. from Amherst College in 1947, and the Ph.D. from the University of Michigan in 1956. During World War II he served in the U.S. Navy. Since 1956 he has taught at the University of Connecticut, Chatham College, the University of Cincinnati, and for the past twelve years at the University of Hartford, where he is Professor of English. From 1971 - 75, he was Director of the Interactive Studies Program, the University of Hartford's experimental venture in humanities-oriented, interdisciplinary courses. Dr. Lane has published articles on Evelyn Waugh's book reviewing and radio and television broadcasts. His teaching interests include twentieth-century British fiction and poetry, nineteenth-century American literature, the Agrarian writers, in particular the novels of Robert Penn Warren, and Baroque art and literature.

Preface

This study of Evelyn Waugh can be traced back to that time when a harried graduate student first delightedly happened upon Waugh's early novels and took immense pleasure in their combination of uproarious farce and satiric thrusts, a pleasure that has remained undiminished.

Throughout, in outlining major thematic concerns in Waugh's writings, I have attempted to encourage both students and the general reader to discover Waugh on their own. While, hopefully, scholars may find some new insights and fresh material in my reading of Waugh's published work, the book is not primarily intended for them, but for the general reader.

Extended critical interest in Waugh's accomplishment began with Frederick Stopp's pioneering study, *Evelyn Waugh: Portrait of an Artist*, published in 1958. Since that time, several studies have appeared, including brief monographs by Paul Doyle and David Lodge, to more lengthy studies by James Carens, and Christopher Sykes, the latter writing the official biography. I have made occasional references to these and to other Waugh studies, but followed a general practice of not reading too widely in secondary sources until I sorted out my own reflections, for I wanted to approach Waugh's writing from a viewpoint not subtly conditioned by my predecessors. When my evaluative judgments concur with those of other critics it represents a fortuitous conclusion reached independently of other Waugh scholars.

I have discussed only those works that seem to be of major significance in Waugh's long writing career. Because it is quite likely that Waugh's future reputation will be based on his standing as a writer of satiric fiction, I have reluctantly omitted any detailed consideration of the travel accounts, biographies, and the first volume of the planned three volume autobiography. As the source books for several of Waugh's novels, the travel accounts demonstrate how an artist shapes his observations to the needs of fiction, but are peripheral to an understanding of the novels. The biographies of

Rossetti, Edmund Campion, and Ronald Knox are models of Waugh's graceful, clear style. With the exception of the Campion study, they are not especially noteworthy. Although *A Little Learning* (volume I of the projected three-volume autobiography) and *The Diaries of Evelyn Waugh* provide evidence for the strongly autobiographical tone of the novels, they are not the experience of the fiction itself.

Waugh was a truly protean author in his ability to move in a seemingly effortless fashion from fiction to biography to travel books. In a highly varied writing career, he remained amazingly consistent in his views of humanity, some would say dogmatically so, but a wide experience of life from Oxford to the jungles of South America, to the battlefields of World War II confirmed his pessimistic, satiric attitude toward the often absurd, witless foibles of mankind. In tracing out these views, I have made several arbitrary divisions in chapter headings. Chapter 1 considers those biographical elements that so richly contributed to his pessimistic outlook, from prep school life to the unshakeable ennui that clouded Waugh's later years after World War II. Chapter 2 begins with consideration of anarchy and farce in *Decline and Fall*, and then examines how the farcical tone begins to shift to a darker mood, especially in *A Handful of Dust*. Waugh increasingly implies that he was living in a world that had lost all common sense and all traditional sanctions—a world in which the grotesquely abnormal blandly passes for the normal, and in which betrayal becomes commonplace. For him, the long tradition of Catholic doctrine provided a stay against the chaos of the modern world. Chapter 3 points this out in considering those features of Waugh's religious belief (most notably in *Brideshead Revisited*) that diluted the satiric edge. Chapter 4 considers as a single unit the three novels of Waugh's involvement in the Second World War (*Officers and Gentlemen, Men at Arms*, and *Unconditional Surrender*), published as *Sword of Honour*. Waugh traces the progression of his antihero, Guy Crouchback, from romantic idealism to bleak pessimism in the years 1938 - 1945. Confronted with the disillusioning realities of warfare on a global scale, Crouchback discovers, near the end of the trilogy, that only the individual redemptive act can provide solace in a nearly totally secular world. Waugh always distrusted formal literary criticism, and never wrote out an extended credo in the fashion, say, of E. M. Forster and Henry James, writers he highly admired.

Nevertheless, he expressed consistent and strong opinions about what fiction could or could not do, opinions scattered throughout his book reviews, articles, and interviews. Chapter 5 draws on this material in summing up his views on the craft of fiction. Chapter 6 evaluates Waugh's achievement as a satiric novelist, and especially his command of a precise and varied style that modulates from ambiguous detachment to extravagant burlesque. Throughout the text, page references to Waugh's novels are to the revised edition, excepting those novels not included in the revised edition.

The book could not have been completed without the generous assistance of many individuals and institutions. I am especially indebted to the University of Hartford for financial support, including a grant allowing me to use library resources in England. The staff of the Mortensen Library at the University of Hartford also deserve thanks for their willing cooperation.

For their invaluable assistance along the way, I would like to thank Professor Frank Chiarenza, former Dean of the College of Arts and Sciences, Professors Lee Yosha and Robert Logan of the English Department, Professor Craig Daniels, Charles Condon, and Dean James Vinson, and Bernice Berman and Jean McNamara.

Professor Paul Doyle, editor of the *Evelyn Waugh Newsletter*, kindly lent me his first edition of *Work Suspended*. Professor Charles Linck's doctoral dissertation, "The Development of Evelyn Waugh's Career: 1903 - 1939," an important record for all Waugh scholars, was a highly valuable source. I want to thank Ms. Alice Phalen and Christine Lamb for their editorial patience, and Professor Kinley Roby, field editor of the Twayne English Authors Series, for his suggestions. Finally, I cannot begin to acknowledge what I owe to my wife, whose long encouragement and discerning reading of the manuscript made the study become a reality.

CALVIN W. LANE

University of Hartford
West Hartford, Connecticut

Acknowledgments

I would like to thank the following for permission to quote from copyrighted material:

Excerpts quoted from *The Loved One, The Ordeal of Gilbert Pinfold, Love Among the Ruins, Ronald Knox, Tourist in Africa, Sword of Honour, Decline and Fall, Vile Bodies, Black Mischief, A Handful of Dust, Scoop, Robbery under Law, Put Out More Flags, Work Suspended, Brideshead Revisited, Scott-King's Modern Europe, Waugh in Abyssinia,* and *Edmund Campion* reprinted by permission of A. D. Peters and Company.

Quotations from *The Private Diaries of Evelyn Waugh,* ed. Michael Davie reprinted by permission of A. D. Peters Company on behalf of the Evelyn Waugh Estate.

To Little, Brown and Company for permission to quote from *Helena, Tactical Exercise,* and *Basil Seal Rides Again.*

To Duckworth and Company, Ltd., for permission to quote from *Rossetti, Labels, Remote People, Ninety-Two Days,* and *When the Going Was Good.*

To Associated Book Publishers for permission to quote from Terence Greenidge, *Degenerate Oxford.*

To David Higham Associates, Ltd., for permission to quote from Harold Acton, *Memoirs of an Aesthete.*

Chronology

1927   Three-week employment on the *Daily Express*. Gossip
        columnist, the *Weekly Dispatch*. Engaged to Evelyn
        Gardner.
1928   *Rossetti: His Life and Works* (biography), followed by
        Decline and Fall, first published novel. Marriage to Evelyn
        Gardner.
1929   Articles on the younger generation in the *Evening Stan-
        dard* and the *Spectator*. Travel in the Mediterranean.
        Breakup of first marriage.
1930   *Labels* (travel account). *Vile Bodies* (novel). Converts to
        Catholicism under the instruction of Fr. Martin d'Arcy.
        Correspondent for *The Times* to report coronation of Haile
        Selassie.
1931   Further travel in Africa. *Remote People* (travel account
        based on African journey).
1932   To the West Indies and British Guiana. Short stories for
        Harper's Bazaar, Life and Letters. Black Mischief (novel).
        Begins book reviewing for the *Spectator*.
1933   Controversy over *Black Mischief* in Catholic journal, the
        Tablet.
1934   Summer, exploring party to Arctic. *Ninety-Two Days* (ac-
        count of South American trip). *A Handful of Dust* (novel).
1935   Reports the Italo-Ethiopian War for the *Daily Mail*. *Ed-
        mund Campion* (biography of Jesuit martyr).
1936   *Mr. Loveday's Little Outing* (short stories). *Waugh in
        Abyssinia* (travel account). Awarded the Hawthornden
        Prize for *Edmund Campion*. Annulment of first marriage.
1937   Marries Laura Herbert, granddaughter of the Earl of Car-
        narvon, and settles at Piers Court, Gloucestershire. Book
        reviewing for *Night and Day*. Becomes a director of Chap-
        man and Hall Publishing Company.
1938   Trip to Mexico. *Scoop* (novel).
1939   *Robbery Under Law* (account of Mexican journey). Of-
        ficer's commission in the Royal Marines.
1941   With No. 8 Commando Forces in the Middle East.
1942   Transfers to the Royal Horse Guards. *Put Out More Flags*
        (novel). *Work Suspended* (fragment of partially completed
        novel).
1943   Injured during parachute training.
1944   With Randolph Churchill, joins British Military Mission to
        Yugoslavia.

1945   Demobilized, returns to Piers Court. *Brideshead Revisited* (novel, Book-of-the-Month Club selection in the United States).

1946   *When the Going Was Good* (material from earlier travel accounts). Attends war crimes trials at Nuremberg.

1947   *Scott-King's Modern Europe* (novella occasioned by trip to Spain). Trip to Hollywood to discuss filming of *Brideshead Revisited*. Honorary degree from Loyola College, Baltimore.

1948   *The Loved One* (novella). Lecture tour to Catholic universities in the United States.

1949   *Work Suspended and Other Stories Written before the Second World War* (revision of *Work Suspended*).

1950   *Helena* (historical novel).

1951   Journey to Jerusalem. Candidate for the Lord Rectorship of Edinburgh University.

1952   *The Holy Places* (essays), *Men at Arms* (novel). Wins James Tait Black Memorial Prize for *Men at Arms*.

1953   Publicly objects to Marshal Tito's visit to England. *Love Among the Ruins* (novella).

1954   *Tactical Exercise* (short stories). Voyage to Ceylon—suffers hallucinations.

1955   *Officers and Gentlemen* (novel).

1956   Moves to Combe Florey, Somerset.

1957   *The Ordeal of Gilbert Pinfold* (thinly disguised autobiographical novel).

1959   *Ronald Knox* (biography).

1960   *Tourist in Africa* (travel account). Writes series of articles on contemporary customs and travel, "Passport into Spring" for the *Daily Mail*.

1961   *Unconditional Surrender* (published in the United States as *The End of the Battle*, novel).

1963   "Basil Seal Rides Again" (short story, also published in signed, limited edition).

1964   *A Little Learning* (autobiography, first volume of projected three volume series).

1965   *Sword of Honour* (the final version of the war novels: *Men at Arms* (1952), *Officers and Gentlemen* (1955), and *Unconditional Surrender* (1962)).

1966   Dies at Combe Florey on Easter Sunday, April 10, 1966, after attending Mass.

CHAPTER 1

The Artist and His World

A T the time of his death on Easter Sunday, 1966, Evelyn Waugh had increasingly retreated within himself, more and more at odds with a social order that appeared to him to have nearly limitless depths of imbecility. After unquestioning military service to the Crown in the war years of 1939 - 45 he had survived through the "Attlee-Cripps regime when the kingdom seemed to be under enemy occupation,"[1] only to have his cherished comfort in the medieval ritual of the Church shattered when the vernacular was substituted for the Latin of the Mass. In self-defense against the world at large, he occasionally appeared in public as a ferocious John Bull, and when confronted by bores, resorted to a large and probably useless Victorian ear-trumpet. Like the guises assumed by so many of his characters in a long succession of novels, it was a mask that concealed a highly sensitive being often amused, often appalled, by the irrational behavior of mankind. Yet it had not always been this way, for according to his own account in *A Little Learning* (1964), he spent a happy childhood in the afterglow of the Victorian era.

I *Childhood: Family and Religious Ties*

Waugh seems to have most resembled his great-great-grandfather, Lord Cockburn, described in the *Edinburgh Review* of January 1857 as having "large lustrous, and in repose rather melancholy eyes, which, however, when roused by energy or wit, sparkled like a hawk's."[2] In considering the parade of lawyers, soldiers, and clergymen that constituted his family background, Waugh wondered how these individuals could have produced himself and his brother Alec (like Evelyn, a novelist) and concluded that heredity can only be compared to a poker hand (*A Little Learning*, 26).

His father, Arthur Waugh, hard-working, genial, and something of a hypochondriac, was the senior editor of Chapman and Hall publishing house. His Dickensian moods and his reading aloud from Dickens in the evenings help account for the large number of amiable eccentrics in Evelyn's fiction, including Augustus Fagan (*Decline and Fall*), Lottie Crump (*Vile Bodies*), Uncle Theodore (*Scoop*), and Peregrine Crouchback (*Unconditional Surrender*). He also enjoyed reading to his family selections from Shakespeare, Tennyson, Browning, Trollope, Swinburne, and Wilde. The evening readings cannot be underestimated in attempting to understand Evelyn Waugh's development as a creative writer, for their emphasis on "the cadences and rhythms of the language" was so pleasurable that young Evelyn "never thought of English Literature as a school subject, as matter for analysis and historical arrangement, but as a source of natural joy" (*A Little Learning*, 72).

In Waugh's novels, father figures are often merely a bundle of crotchets (Colonel Blount in *Vile Bodies*, for example), but in one novel, *Officers and Gentlemen*, Mr. Crouchback is a truly civilized, humane being, and surely represents Waugh's belated recognition of another side of his own father's nature. It was Arthur Waugh who was largely responsible for the shaping of his younger son's code of ethics, despite Evelyn's rebellious undergraduate years at Oxford. The senior Waugh's reflections on the values of the Victorian middle class, outlined in *Tradition and Change*, rather accurately describe many of the values held by his younger son, and especially so as Evelyn advanced into middle age:

It distrusted passion, deprecated haste, was afraid of rebellion. . . . It loved its country blindly, was somewhat insular in outlook, and believed in that steady, premeditated kind of reform, which made its ground good before it ventured to advance. . . . It was terribly afraid of democracy, which it recognized at work all around it, and which it regarded as the harbinger of anarchy in thought and life; its creed was founded on a complete trust in the necessity of Law and Order, as much in Art as in Morals. And, although we have, most of us, broken free from some or other of these spiritual captivities, we are all the creatures of our birth. . . .[3]

As a young boy rather excluded from the close bond between his father and Evelyn's older brother, Alec, he later established his own

hard-won claim to his father's affection, and came to share his distrust of the anarchic impulse in democracy, especially as epitomized
in his fictional army officers Hooper (*Brideshead Revisited*) and
Trimmer (*Officers and Gentlemen*), opportunistic and graceless
representatives of plebeian democratic society.

Of his mother, a quiet, retiring woman who loved to read, we
know little, other than that Evelyn was devoted to her. The picture
of his parents and of family life Waugh draws in *A Little Learning*
is that of a very solid, protected childhood, with the sprawling outer
fringes of London only beginning to intrude on the quiet of
Hampstead Heath.

Perhaps most significant in Waugh's childhood was a precocious
interest he began to develop in Anglo-Catholicism at age eleven.
This extended to the construction of a shrine in his bedroom before
which he burned incense, an interest that continued into Waugh's
adolescent years, even when he became a professed agnostic for a
short period. There were other portents for the future in Waugh's
editing of the Heath Mount school magazine, the *Cynic*, and his
writing, at age thirteen, of an apocalyptic three-canto vision of war
and death, entitled *The World to Come*, privately printed by
friends of his father.

Following the accepted pattern of their social class, Waugh's
parents sent him off to preparatory school. They decided upon Lancing, a High Church institution, rather than Sherborne, attended by
both his father and by Alec. The latter had so scandalized the ad-
ministration at Sherborne with his first novel, *The Loom of Youth*,
an exposé of homosexuality in prep-school life, that the school was
ruled out for Evelyn. By the time he had enrolled at Lancing he had
read widely and indiscriminately in his father's library. Among his
favorites were Malory's *Morte d'Arthur* and Compton Mackenzie's
Sinister Street, a curious blend of romantic interest in the feats of
chivalry and an attraction to what was then a rather modern avant-
garde novel. The campus at Lancing, dominated by a large Victorian chapel built in the style of the Gothic revival, provided the
perfect setting for Waugh's absorption in the medieval, an absorption that dated back to the wallpaper decorated with medieval
figures in his nursery and to the volume of aquatint plates of
Froissart's *Chronicles* he had owned as a child. Hetton Abbey, in *A
Handful of Dust* (1934), strongly suggests the Lancing chapel.

Waugh's experience at the school (1917 - 1921) was not a happy

one, but he disguised it under a generally pugnacious attitude. In
The House Is Gone, Dudley Carew recalls Lancing and his
friendship with Waugh: "Evelyn showed the same passive exterior,
the same innocence of the intent to be amusing as later characterized his books. Besides, he had a cherubic face."[4] To compensate
for his being an outsider and to make a name for himself he wrote
for the school magazine, helped found the Corpse Club (a haven for
literary-minded but precociously bored students), and took part in
debating. In his last two terms at Lancing, Waugh competed for
and won the Prize Poem written in Spenserian stanzas on the set
subject of an incident from Malory's Arthurian tales. Waugh chose
"the nostalgic disillusioned musing of Sir Bedivere after the death
of Arthur" (*A Little Learning,* 137). His choice was perfectly in
character with thematic statements to be developed in his fiction,
and surfaced years later in Tony Last's obsession *A Handful of Dust*
(1934) with an idealized chivalric past.

II   Oxford: The Reasonable Diehard

He enrolled at Oxford in January 1922, having won a scholarship
to Hertford College. During the early 1920s Oxford was in a tran-
sitional stage, for the veterans of the First World War who had
returned to the university were now graduating, and another
generation of undergraduates, restlessly aware that it had not
fought,[5] was just beginning to assert itself and to develop its own
code of ethics, a development made all the more difficult by the
seeming breakdown of ethics during the war. Eventually, Waugh
sought out and associated himself with this latter group of deter-
minedly nihilistic students in rebellion against the mores of their
fathers, but in his first months at Oxford he held to the routine
freshman pattern rather like that followed by the dimly circumspect
Paul Pennyfeather, the hero of Waugh's first novel, *Decline and
Fall* (1928). He learned to smoke, got drunk a few times, did
enough studying to get by, and joined in the debating at the Union.

In one report of Union activities it was drily observed that "Mr.
E. A. St. J. Waugh tried his best to be that inconceivable creature,
the reasonable Diehard."[6] Nearly a year later, when the question
was raised whether or not a more friendly attitude ought to be en-
couraged toward the German people an account of the debate in the
Oxford Magazine stated: ". . . He [Waugh] unfolded a strong

docrine of patriotic hate. His line throughout was that he was the only man in the street present among the precocious intellectuals of Oxford. Mr. Waugh has considerable possibilities."[7] Aside from its casual prophesy of Waugh's possibilities, the attribution to Waugh that he was "the only man in the street present" indicates his sensitive awareness of the gulf that separated him from many of the socially prominent students with whom he was beginning to mingle.

In addition to his rather indifferent debating activities, Waugh began to write light verse and stories for several of the undergraduate magazines (*Isis, Cherwell,* and the *Oxford Broom*). His first story, "Antony Who Sought Things That Were Lost," was printed in the June 1923 issue of *Broom,* edited by one of Waugh's new friends, Harold Acton. Unremarkable in its mixture of Byron, Poe, and James Branch Cabell[8] it sounds the note of betrayal so often repeated in the novels, and features a hero who "seemed always to be seeking in the future for what had gone before,"[9] suggesting, if lightly, an attitude of misdirected romanticism to be given full emphasis in *A Handful of Dust.*

Waugh's social life more than kept pace with his academic routine. In the boisterous activities of the Hypocrites Club and in the more respectable Carlton and Chatham Clubs, Waugh discovered others of like temperament. Of the first group, he remarked: "The Hypocrites, like Gatsby's swimming pool, saw the passage, as members or guests, of the best and the worst of that year [1923]. It was the stamping-ground of half of my Oxford life and the source of friendships still warm today" (*A Little Learning,* 181). Although social in origin, Waugh's beer and wine drinking friendships also involved a leaven of genuine literary interest, for many of this coterie later developed very solid reputations as novelists, critics, editors, and writers of belles-lettres. A partial listing would include Peter Quennell, Christopher Hollis, Harold Acton, Patrick Balfour, Cyril Connolly, Alfred Duggan, Douglas Woodruff, Anthony Powell, and Terence Greenidge. A slight acquaintance with Graham Greene developed into a long-lasting friendship after the Oxford years. A sprinkling of the aristocracy was numbered among the group, in particular, Hugh Lygon (son of the seventh Earl of Beauchamp) with whom Waugh planned to share rooms during his final term at Hertford College. Waugh's detractors always held it against him that he was a snob and social climber. Granting an element of truth in the charge, certainly he could have done worse than to associate with a group of such creative promise.

He went up to Oxford ostensibly to tutor in history, but gravitated more and more toward the partying and drinking set, and did not get along at all well with his dean and tutor, C. R. M. F. Cruttwell, whom he drove into a paroxysm of rage when, lamentably, he admitted that he did not know that the Rhine emptied into the North Sea. Waugh had his revenge for this lapse in geographical knowledge: again and again in his novels some of his more odious characters are named Cruttwell. On the other hand, the social and literary horizons opened up for Waugh by his new undergraduate acquaintances proved to be his real education. In *Memoirs of an Aesthete*, Harold Acton recalls Waugh's distinctive appearance during the university years:

An almost inseparable boon companion at Oxford was a little faun called Evelyn Waugh. Though others assure me that he has changed past recognition, I still see him as a prancing faun, thinly disguised by conventional apparel. His wide-apart eyes, always ready to be startled under raised eyebrows, the curved sensual lips, the hyacinthine locks of hair, I had seen in marble and bronze . . . on fountainheads all over Italy. . . . Whatever he did had a firm style of its own, a recognizable signature that set it apart from its surroundings. I have met other fauns, but none with such artistic integrity.[10]

It was Acton who introduced him to T. S. Eliot's *The Waste Land*, only recently published, and made him aware of a world of free spirits that included the Sitwells, Bernard Berenson, and Gertrude Stein. He also discovered E. M. Forster, especially his work on Alexandria, *Pharos and Pharillon*, and Max Beerbohm's university novel, *Zuleika Dobson*. In his casual reading at Oxford and later, a precise, lucid style was what most impressed Waugh, particularly in the work of such disparate writers as Wodehouse, Firbank, Hemingway, and Elizabeth Bowen.

Looking back on the Oxford years (recreated with romantic nostalgia in *Brideshead Revisited*) Waugh noted, in comment both realistic and romantic, in the *Sunday Times* of November 7, 1965, that only a small minority of those who attended Oxford "are captivated by her genius. Those few are likely, for good or ill, to remain life long votaries of what has always been largely an illusion. It is the illusion of youth suddenly freed from the shackles of school, not yet shackled by the responsibilities of maturity, living for three or four years in isolation in what was once the most beautiful city in the kingdom. . . ."[11]

III   *The Restless Years*

The illusion of youth came to an abrupt end, for Waugh was barely scraping along academically and was encumbered with debts when his despairing father terminated the Oxford experiment in June of 1924. There followed a long downward curve in his career. He lived at home on increasingly irritable terms with his family, meanwhile attending Heatherley's art school in the hopes of making a living as a commercial artist. Bored by suburban London, he drifted back to Oxford on weekends and took up the partying where he had left off. Desperate for money, he taught in private schools, first at a grandly unorganized institution in Wales and later at a school for backward children of the rich in Buckinghamshire. As Waugh later recalled this nearly totally bleak period in his life, he vaguely contemplated suicide, and one dark night swam out to sea at the beach near the school where he was teaching, only to be thwarted by the intense stinging of jellyfish, an appropriately absurd Waugh conclusion to the episode.

During his short career as a teacher he continued to write, including an unfinished novel. His first commercially published story, "The Balance: A Yarn of the Good Old Days of Broad Trousers and High Necked Jumpers," appeared in *Georgian Stories* (1926), edited by Alec Waugh. He also began to frequent London salons and occasionally shared in the extravagant antics of the fashionable younger set, whose elaborate costume parties were publicized in the London tabloids.[12] Waugh's diary entries for this period suggest an almost continuous round of partygoing, yet the diary provides evidence that Waugh always remained an acute observer rather than an active participant in the frenetic milling about of his contemporaries, soon to be pilloried in *Vile Bodies*.

In 1927 Waugh became involved in two interrelated situations, both destined to alter the course of his life. He met and fell in love with the Honourable Evelyn Gardner, daughter of Lord Burghclere, and was commissioned by Duckworth's to write a biography of Dante Gabriel Rossetti. Inspired by the need to qualify as a respectable son-in-law, Waugh turned to and finished off the book in a matter of weeks. Although the biography emphasizes Rossetti as painter rather than as poet, it occupies a respectable position in the Rossetti canon. In trying to clear away the rubbish of legend associated with Rossetti he discovered: "The baffled and very tragic figure of an artist born into an age devoid of artistic standards; . . .a mystic without a creed; a Catholic without the discipline or consolation of the Church. . . ."[13] This summation would suggest that the young biographer, whose first novel was yet to be written, was not truly one of the nihilistic "Bright Young Things" of the 1920s, and, perhaps half-consciously, was already beginning to move toward what would be for him the protective haven of the Church.

Waugh noted that in his expression of Pre-Raphaelite art, Rossetti helped promote the distorted medievalism of the mid-nineteenth century, an expression, reflected in the vaulted halls and fretwork of domestic architecture, denoting a specious romanticism ill-equipped to deal with the onslaught of an advancing industrial system. He also saw in Rossetti's romantic love of decay the root of his failure, and that he lacked "the essential rectitude that underlies the serenity of all great art" (*Rossetti*, 226 - 27). Even if hurriedly dashed off, Waugh's observations are perceptive in their understanding of Rossetti and the age in which he lived. Some of his remarks, most notably the strictures on romanticism, would appear again in the novels.

The study received a good press, but this wasn't enough for Lady Burghclere, who doubted Waugh's ability to hold a steady job. Infuriated, he threatened a clandestine marriage and shortly carried out his threat when he and Evelyn Gardner were secretly married. Both Evelyns were eminently unsuited for each other, being equally precocious in nature. The whole business seemed a charade, their friends distinguishing between them by calling one "He-Evelyn" and the other "She-Evelyn." They lived in a tiny flat in Islington, imaginatively described by Harold Acton: "Blake's *Songs of Innocence* belonged there, and *Alice in Wonderland* and a cage of twittering canaries."[14] But it wasn't all a charade, for *Decline and Fall*, a seemingly detached yet wickedly satiric attack on the irrational behavior of the English upper class, contemporary education, and the penal system, had just been published, and the future looked bright when the young couple sailed for the Mediterranean on their first real honeymoon, a honeymoon marred by his wife's near fatal bout with pneumonia.

The social life of the Waughs proved to be too distracting, for Evelyn was now hard at work on *Vile Bodies* (1930). He sequestered himself in the quiet of a country inn to finish the novel, only to discover, a few weeks after doing so, that his wife had been having an affair with a young man employed by the BBC. Feeling horribly betrayed, he went ahead with divorce proceedings. At the time, his despairing remark to his brother Alec—" 'The trouble about the world today is that there's not enough religion in it. There's nothing to stop young people doing whatever they feel like at the moment' "[15]—implies a longing for stability and order that was soon to be reaffirmed, in part, by his conversion to Catholic doctrine.

Vile Bodies concludes amidst the desolation of total war and probably reflects Waugh's own dark mood at the time. However, the severe trauma of Waugh's marital situation did not become fully apparent until the publication of *A Handful of Dust* (1934). In Brenda Last's abandonment of her hopelessly archaic husband, Tony Last, Waugh mixed a compound of irony and pathos in which the satiric tone all but disappears.

Waugh began to take Catholic instruction from Father Martin D'Arcy in the summer of 1930 and became a member of the Church in September of the same year. In 1949 he wrote, ". . .On firm intellectual conviction but with little emotion I was admitted into the Church. . . . I look back. . .with wonder at the trust of the priest who saw the possibility of growth in such a dry soul."[16] While it is likely that his conversion was hastened by a deep personal need to associate himself with an unassailable continuity of traditional belief following the failure of his first marriage, a concern for religious values dates back to his boyhood, although it remained submerged in his early adult years. The absence of a coherent value system in the aimless lives of the central characters in *Decline and Fall* and in *Vile Bodies* (as well as in the later novels) clearly suggests Waugh's awareness of a conservative standard of belief shoved aside or ignored in the world Waugh knew.

With the breakup of the marriage, he traveled almost continuously from 1929 to 1937. His journeys took him to the Mediterranean, to North Africa, twice to Ethiopia (the first trip in 1930 to report the coronation of Haile Selassie for *The Times*, the second in 1935 to cover the opening stages of the Italo-Ethiopian War for the *Daily Mail*), to South America, where he undertook, mostly alone, an especially arduous trek through the jungles of British Guiana and Brazil, and to the Arctic on a dangerous and amateurish expedition with Hugh Lygon and another companion. Always on the move, he chronicled most of these journeys in several travel books in which he figures as a highly observant but antiheroic traveler. Certainly he helped to popularize the 1930s vogue for accounts of travel in exotic places, but unlike his contemporary Richard Haliburton, who crossed the Alps on an elephant in emulating Hannibal's exploits, Waugh's travels were always unostentatious affairs. If, rather in the pose of Mark Twain in *Innocents Abroad*, he satirizes the naive tourists, "trapped and mangled in the machinery of uplift,"[17] he also warns against the cult of the antique for antique's sake. When an American lady gushes about the antiquity of the Dardanelles and imagines quinqueremes laden with cargoes of ivory and sandalwood, Waugh remarks, "I could not, but with a little more imagination I think I might easily have seen troopships, full of young Australians, going to their deaths with bare knees (*Labels*, 139).

He was always sharply observant of incongruities resulting from contact between highly divergent cultures, and especially so in his two accounts of his travels in Africa, *Remote People* (1931) and *Waugh in Abyssinia* (1935). On his first trip to Addis Ababa, a city caught up in the throes of instant European modernization, the air fragrant with the smoke of cooking fires, and tom-toms incessantly drumming, Waugh was reminded of *Alice in Wonderland:* ". . .It is in Alice only that one finds the peculiar flavor of galvanised and translated reality, where animals carry watches in their waistcoat pockets, royalty paces the croquet lawn beside the chief executioner, and litigation ends in a flutter of playing cards. How to recapture, how to retail, the crazy enchantment of those Ethiopian days?" (*Remote People*, 29). Amidst the frantic chaos of the coronation preparations, the diminutive Haile Selassie could be seen being chauffeured around the city in regal splendor, the butt of a submachine gun sticking out from under a plush shawl held by a guard riding with the driver. In all of these observations (quite unlike the pedestrian reports of his fellow journalists), Waugh delighted in the rich spectacle of intermingled primitive and modern cultures.

When he turned pundit in these two books in generalizing on the political situation, he became less sure, and made several observations that brought down on him the anathema of liberal critics in England. Although critical of European destruction of African folkways, he developed a lame apologetic for colonialism in Africa, his main arguments contending that all history "has been determined by the movements of peoples about the earth's surface" and the European settlement in Africa will depend "on the ability of the immigrant race to maintain efficiency in an alien climate" (*Remote People*, 180 - 81). Despite these distressing generalizations, Waugh was alert to African - East Indian racial tensions, and scornful of those Europeans whose "sanity gently oozes away on putting on a topee" (*Remote People*, 190). Similarly, while *Waugh in Abyssinia* is an apologia for the Italian presence in Africa, it is not fascistic, as Rose Macaulay implied, nor does it entirely justify European aggrandizement. As usual, Waugh was his idiosyncratic self, both defender and critic of European civilization, sometimes the latter, when he writes of nineteenth-century colonialism: "France, Germany, and Belgium were the more ruthless; we the more treacherous. We went into the shady business with pious expressions of principle. . .we preached on, blandly and continuously" (*Waugh in Abyssinia*, 6).

Although Waugh did not hide his prejudice against the Ethiopian government, the opening pages demonstrate comprehensive knowledge of the internal struggle for power in Ethiopia, a struggle that is not yet resolved. Later, when he wrote his last travel book, *Tourist in Africa* (1960), Waugh became even more pessimistic toward the corrupting effect of European institutions, for he felt three wars in Africa "on a far larger scale than anything perpetrated by marauding spearmen, waged by white men against white, and a generation which has seen the Nazi regime in the heart of Europe had best stand silent when civilized and uncivilized nations are contrasted" (American edition, 180). Uneven though they may be, the travel books are a mirror reflection of observations given imaginative substance in the novels. Many of the situations recorded are often grimly fantastic, but in Waugh's view of life, mankind's plight has seldom been otherwise.

Beyond their immediate topical interest, the accounts of Waugh's African travel provided both the situation and background for two of his most brilliantly malicious satires, *Black Mischief* (1932) and *Scoop* (1938). *Black Mischief* is a merciless study of an emerging African nation whose young leader, Emperor Seth, desperately and unsuccessfully attempts to refashion the kingdom of Azania in accord with the most advanced European notions of civilization. Its swaggering raffish hero, Basil Seal, is the most outrageously attractive figure in all of Waugh's fiction. He appears again in *Put Out More Flags* (1942), and is revived once more in the short story "Basil Seal Rides Again" (1962). In *Scoop* Waugh returned to an African setting, but this time in a more genial mood, he describes the misadventures of the bemused William Boot, a diffident country gentleman writer of a nature column, suddenly and mistakenly ordered to cover a revolt in Ishmaelia.

Although he spent much of his time in the 1930s in almost constant traveling, he continued to write steadily and prolifically. Between 1930 and 1936 alone he published nine works, including fiction, travel accounts, and biography, plus many book reviews and an occasional article. *Ninety-Two Days* (1934), complete with a photograph of Waugh the intrepid explorer in breeches and boots, records an excruciatingly uncomfortable trip to the interior of British Guiana and Brazil that Waugh undertook by himself. As was true of his visits to Ethiopia he had been initially attracted by the prospect of observing at first hand an area of the globe in a transition stage between the barbarous and the civilized. The journey turned out to be a nightmare of mud, lonely jungle wastes, and rivers apparently leading nowhere, and also included an encounter with a slightly manic trader who claimed to have religious visions. In *A Handful of Dust* the trader reappears as Mr. Todd, the most sinister of all the madmen scattered throughout Waugh's fiction.

His quietly dramatic biography of the recusant martyr Edmund Campion earned him the Hawthornden Prize (an award made to promising young English writers) in 1936. Although Waugh generally kept within the limits of historical fact, Campion's life, leading inexorably to martyrdom, readily lent itself to the dramatic scope of the novelist. On the whole, the critics were favorably disposed toward the book, but a few did take him to task for playing down Catholic political maneuvering during Elizabeth's reign. Such statements had little effect on Waugh, for he disclaimed the role of a formal historian in ingenuously noting in the preface to the work: "All I have done is select the incidents which struck a novelist as important, and relate them in a single narrative. It shall be read as a simple perfectly true story of heroism and holiness."[18] The Campion biography was followed by a collection of short stories, *Mr. Loveday's Little Outing* (1936), that emphasized, in one form or another, the irrationality of English social customs and attitudes passing as rationality.

IV   *The Settled Observer*

With his first marriage annulled by the Church in 1936, Waugh settled down for good in 1937 (excepting his military service in World War II) when he married Laura Herbert, a member of the gentry and ironically enough a distant relative of Evelyn Gardner. The marriage proved to be quite happy and reconciled Waugh to his father, who felt that Laura was a steadying influence on his younger son. As if to put the seal on his changed, more fixed status, Evelyn adopted the coat of arms of Waugh of Midsomer Norton. A snobbish act? Perhaps. But the motto he adopted for the coat of arms: "Industria Ditat" (Hard Work Pays), bluntly indicates his pragmatic yet workmanlike devotion to the craft of writing. In 1938, the Waughs bought Piers Court in Gloucestershire, a run-down estate large enough, in the next few years, for a family of six children.[19]

His new domesticity in no way impaired his gimlet-eyed observance of English social and political life, especially the latter. As always, he spoke his mind, without any thought to the popularity of the views he expressed. Although he had praised the imposing of Italian order in Ethiopia during the Italo-Ethiopian War, he stated in 1937 that "Fascist policy is consistently and essentially opportunist."[20] In the same year, on reviewing *Vain Glory* (memoirs of World War I, edited by Guy Chapman) he astutely evaluated the mood of Nazi Germany on the eve of the Second World War: ". . .It is a book that is badly needed almost everywhere but in England. Germans will not be allowed to read it, and I think the editor has. . .severely impaired the usefulness of his own work by yielding to the temptation to score points against the Nazi regime. We have no need in England to be reminded of the intolerable injustice of that regime. . . . There is again the appalling danger of a generation growing up who look upon it [war] as a glorious vocation to be followed for its own sake."[21] His critics chose to ignore statements such as these, for what really raised their hackles was the stand he took in a poll conducted by the *Left Review* (1937) concerning the attitude of English writers toward the Spanish War. As one of the five writers who supported Franco (against over one hundred who supported the government), he tersely remarked that if he were a Spaniard he would be fighting for General Franco, but that "as an Englishman I am not in the predicament of choosing between two evils. I am not a Fascist nor shall I become one unless it were the only alternative too Marxism. It is mischievous to suggest that such a choice is imminent."[22] Two years later, Waugh again became embroiled in political controversy upon the publication of *Robbery Under Law* (1939), which describes a brief visit to Mexico. It is a blend of astute political observations and intemperate attacks on the anti-Catholic policy of the regime in power. Because he recognized that it had been hastily written, he did not include it in the one-volume compilation of his travels, *When the Going Was Good.* Despite some ill-considered remarks in the work, he observed, as he did in *Remote People* and in *Waugh in Abyssinia,* a precariously fragile surface stability that masked hidden instability.

V   *Participation in World War II*

His lifelong suspicion of politics and politicians notwithstanding, when war was declared he immediately tried to enlist for active service, even though he was overage, and spent month after month in a futile effort to join up. Finally, in December of 1939, he was commissioned in the Royal Marines. This twilight period of terrible inactivity he mockingly recorded in *Put Out More Flags,* published in 1942. Waugh took to soldiering with great zeal, but he never could or would adapt himself to the routine of army life, was a terror to the enlisted men in his platoon, and a bedeviling irritant to his superiors. His courage was never in question, but he could be recklessly contemptuous of authority when arrogantly or stupidly exercised. Eric Linklater describes Waugh's military bearing: ". . .a rather short, square-shouldered, stiffly held man with a red face, a resolute jaw, and a soldierly keen eye. . . ."[23]

In 1941 he volunteered for service with No. 8 Commando in the Near East and took part in several abortive raids on the North African coast. Then, in May of that year, he was among the detachment of troops ordered to Crete in a futile effort to shore up the British forces attempting to fight off the German paratroop invasion. Despite the bloody chaos of the battle, Waugh maintained a voluminous diary in which he unsparingly recorded the horror of both officers and enlisted men going to pieces under the German pounding and being reduced to an animallike struggle for survival. Waugh's detachment, under the command of Lt. Col. Robert Laycock (much admired by Waugh for his soldierly qualities), was finally evauated after days of nearly incessant fighting. A great deal of the Cretan action observed by Waugh appears later in *Officers and Gentlemen,* especially the study of Major Hound, a spit-and-polish paradeground officer whose whole being disintegrates under the stress of combat. Hound's model was an officer whom Waugh had closely observed during the fighting.

The next couple of years were generally frustrating ones for Waugh, despite the publication of *Put Out More Flags* and *Work Suspended* (1942), a thinly disguised autobiographical fragment begun in 1939 concerning the artist both living in and isolated from the society in which he finds himself. Left behind in 1943 when Laycock's Special Services Brigade went to North Africa, Waugh felt a great sense of futility. His father died in June of 1943, perhaps further increasing his despondency. However, early in 1944, his career as a writer took an unexpected and quite fortuitous turn. Waugh had twisted his knee in December of 1943 during parachute training near Manchester and while on leave of absence wrote *Brideshead Revisited,* the most explicitly Catholic of all his novels. Although he had to sit out the invasion of Europe, he finished the rough draft of *Brideshead* in June of 1944.

At this moment of inactivity he was rescued by Randolph Churchill, who invited him to join the British military mission to the Yugoslavs. At the outset it was nearly all up for both Waugh and Churchill, for the plane carrying them to Yugoslavia crashed and burned. Following this ominous beginning, the British staff soon found itself mired in political intrigue in its efforts to maintain communication with the Communist-dominated Yugoslav partisans. This activity was personally distasteful for Waugh because, as he later saw it, the British accommodation to the Russians in Yugoslavia and elsewhere represented the final sell-out of principle in achieving the Allied goal of winning at any price. Like Guy Crouchback (Waugh's central character in the *Sword of Honour* trilogy) Waugh had traversed the entire arc from idealism to disillusionment in the years from 1941 to 1945.

VI *Postwar Disillusionment*

Demobilized, he returned to Piers Court and to his family in 1945. He had done his duty as a soldier, but he had no longing for military or political glory and remained steadfast in his loyalty to writing. At the time, he noted in his diary, "I regard the greatest danger I went through that of becoming one of Churchill's young men, of getting a medal and then standing for Parliament; if things had gone as then seemed right, in the first two years, that is where I should be now. I thank God to find myself still a writer and at work on something [*Helena*] as 'uncontemporary' as I am."[24]

With the publication of *Brideshead Revisited*, Waugh's audience was suddenly trebled, especially in the United States, where the novel was named a Book-of-the-Month Club selection. This was incongruous, for Waugh had always been truculently nationalistic in his anti-American bias, but his attitude was indicative of an increasingly dour view of the modern world. In 1947, after a brief trip to Spain with Douglas Woodruff to take part in celebrations honoring the memory of the Dominican theologian Francisco deVittoria, Waugh wrote a novella of life in a dictatorship (*Scott-King's Modern Europe*). In it he described the visit to Neutralia of Scott-King, a dim English pedant and teacher of classics at Granchester, to observe the celebration of the poet Bellorius. The Secretary of the Bellorius Association tells Scott-King, "I studied in Zagreb, Budapest, Prague, Vienna—one was free, one moved where one would; one was a citizen of Europe. Then we were liberated and put under the Serbs. Now we are liberated again and put under the Russians. And always more police, more prisons, more hanging."[25] Duped into attending a ceremony extolling the Neutralian dictatorship, Scott-King becomes entangled in the ambiguities of political machinations, and finally escapes (disguised as an Ursuline nun) in company with other refugees, all fleeing from somewhere to a nameless somewhere else. Safely back at Granchester, when asked by the headmaster if he would be willing to teach more modern subjects such as economic history, Scott-King bravely refuses on the ground that " '. . .it would be very wicked indeed to do anything to fit a boy for the modern world' " (*Scott-King's Modern Europe*, 89). Certainly Waugh himself felt increasingly out of touch with the modern world and less and less a citizen of Europe at the end of World War II.

This revulsion from contemporary society also made itself felt in his nonfiction. Writing in 1947 on the work of Mrs. Trollope, Chesterton, and Arthur Koestler, he wondered if the morally innocent, Edwardian Chesterton would have continued to write in the same fashion ". . .if he had lived to see the Common Man in arms, drab, gray and brown, the Storm Troopers and the Partisans, standard bearers of the great popular movements of the century; had he lived to read in the evidence of the War Trials the sickening accumulation of brutality inflicted and condoned by common men, and seen, impassive on the bench, the agents of the other criminals, vile, but free and triumphant?"[26] This was no idle expression of disgust by a writer uttering diatribes from a snug rural retreat, for Waugh was present at the Nuremberg Trials. For him the trials were a terrible extension of the illogic he had observed during the war, particularly during its latter stages. Distrustful of what the new age had wrought in the political and social institutions of Europe and of England, he was equally horrified by the despoliation of the English landscape: "German bombs have been but a negligible addition to the sum of our own destructiveness. . .our surviving fine buildings and corners of landscape only serve to accentuate the prevailing desolation."[27]

Waugh's involvement in World War II and his complete distaste for the postwar Labour government did not leave much room for the anarchic play of wit that had made his novels so distinctive before the war. Henceforth, whether to be attributed to the more frequent black moods that marked his life or simply to the sobering effect of middle age, he was never to return to the sustained grotesque farce of the early work, except in *The Loved One* and in certain passages of *Sword of Honour*. Unlike P. G. Wodehouse, whom he much admired, and whose naive behavior in World War II while a prisoner of the Nazis he stoutly defended,[28] he was no longer the seemingly uninvolved, detached young novelist of the prewar years.[29] His writing after the war represents a very solid achievement, especially in the continued nurturing of an elegant, beautifully controlled prose style, and in the scope of the war novels, but the spirit of farcical outrage had largely departed, for he did not remain the iconoclast, out to shock an older generation that had generally abandoned the old virtues. He was as troubled as ever, perhaps more so, in his belief that trust, rectitude, and clear thinking had been totally abandoned in the Second World War. As a consequence, the atmosphere of the novels became more somberly reflective.

Following the success of *Brideshead Revisited,* American film producers invited Waugh to come to Hollywood to work out arrangements for a movie adaptation. The negotiations fell through because proposed changes in the script were unacceptable to him, but in the end the journey turned out to be quite productive. He happened to visit the elaborately landscaped, manicured grounds of Forest Lawn Cemetery, and was so horribly impressed by the American funeral mythology he observed at Forest Lawn that on his return to England he wrote a novella, *The Loved One* (1948), satirizing American efforts to gloss over the fact of death. Waugh's interest in U.S. tribal customs lasted for two or three years, including a couple of articles in *Life* magazine and a lecture tour of four Catholic universities in 1948 - 49, in which he discussed Catholic authors Ronald Knox, G. K. Chesterton, and Graham Greene.

He became ever more the settled author, often cranky and captious, slowly elaborating for himself the role of a Restoration country squire suspicious of contemporary fads. Only on infrequent occasions did he command public attention, as when he was named a candidate for the Lord Rectorship of Edinburgh University in 1951, but lost out to Sir Alexander Fleming. Happily, in 1952 he was awarded the James Tait Black Memorial Prize for *Men at Arms*, the first of three novels dealing with World War II. As his "contribution" to the Coronation Year in 1953, he wrote *Love Among the Ruins: A Romance of the Near Future*, a parody of life in a future Socialist state, in which uniformity of behavior leads to such intense boredom that the Department of Euthanasia becomes swamped with requests for suicide. Among other social and legal changes, "it was a first principle of the New Law that no man could be held responsible for the consequences of his own acts."[30] Not much longer than a short story, *Love Among the Ruins* is derivative in its Orwell-Huxley overtones.

Possibly as belated recompense for his involvement with British efforts to placate the Communists in Yugoslavia during World War II, he publicly objected to Marshal Tito's visit to England in 1953. Well aware of his increased peevishness, Waugh remarked in his diary on November 17, 1955: "Resolved: to regard humankind with benevolence and detachment, like an elderly host whose young and indulged wife has asked a lot of people to the house whose names he does not know."[31] In attempting to describe what was happening to Waugh in these years it is easy to go along with the popular view of the Swiftian misanthrope increasingly withdrawn into himself. Writing shortly after Waugh's death, his son Auberon denied this, in maintaining that "those who saw him in the last ten years will know that they were the most mellow and tranquil of his life."[32] The truth probably lies somewhere in-between, for the testimony of Lady Diana Cooper, Christopher Sykes, Arnold Lunn, Peter Quennell, and others strongly indicates a growing sense of boredom, disgust, and alienation. Whatever glaring façade he maintained against the world at large, he never fooled himself.

VII   *The Ordeal of Evelyn Waugh*

Troubled with insomnia and with occasional lapses of memory, he became careless of his health; the combination of alcohol and sleeping pills brought on hallucinations that he tried to shake in a long voyage to Ceylon in January of 1954. The hallucinations gradually disappeared and his horrifying experience was recorded in the thinly disguised autobiographical novel *The Ordeal of Gilbert Pinfold*, published in 1957. The description, in the opening pages, of a radio interview reluctantly agreed to by the novelist Pinfold has its source in an interview with Waugh conducted by three BBC interrogators on November 11, 1953, in which his questioners, blandly malicious, did their best to goad him into intemperate answers. The questions ranged from inquiries about his personal life to art, capital punishment, and the welfare state. Although deliberately provoked, Waugh retained his composure, for his replies were crisp and courtly in manner. When asked, "Why do you write?" he answered, "I wish to make pleasant objects, works of art exterior to myself." The remark was quite in keeping with his reticence in discussing his own work. Equally typical was his response to "Do you like the human race?" to which he dryly responded, "Liking the human race is a prerogative of God."[33]

Intrusion on his privacy by newspaper reporters further roused Waugh's ire, for in 1955, at the time of publication of *Officers and Gentlemen*, he became involved in an unwanted newspaper interview that ended in the law courts. This incident concerned the efforts of *Daily Express* reporters Nancy Spain and Lord Noel Buxton to interview him at his home. The affair illustrates his fierce desire to safeguard his privacy and also had overtones of the high comedy of *Decline and Fall* and *Vile Bodies*. Passersby were well acquainted with the notorious sign he had posted on the gates of the entrance to his estate: "No Admittance on Business." But this stern admonition was apparently no deterrent to the prospective interviewers who showed up, uninvited, at Piers Court to try to interview him. According to Waugh's account, published in the *Spectator*, Lord Buxton cryptically announced himself: " 'I'm not on business. I'm a member of the House of Lords.' These moving and rather mysterious words were uttered on my doorstep the other evening and recorded by the leading literary critic of the Beaverbrook press."[34] In his diary entry Waugh wrote: "I remained tremulous with rage all evening."[35] The matter did not end at this point, however, for Nancy Spain revenged herself by writing a newspaper column in which she attacked Waugh as a literary "has-been." In turn, he instituted and won a libel suit against the *Daily Express*. Waugh was justifiably resentful of the two newspaper writers barging in on him, but the incident also provides further sad evidence of increasing testiness in his later years.

VIII   *The Last Years: Interview and Opinions*

In the summer of 1956, the Waughs sold Piers Court and moved to Combe Florey, Taunton, where Waugh spent the remaining years of his life. Although there was certainly a diminution of his circle of friends, partially the result of Waugh's irritable behavior, Frances Donaldson confirms that many writers visited the Waughs, including "Graham Greene, Henry Green, Ronald Knox, Anthony Powell, L. P. Hartley, Christopher Sykes, Cyril Connolly, Christopher Hollis. . . .It is difficult to see from whom he cut himself off except the journalists who invented these fictions. . . ."[36] But many of the old friends did drop off one by one, or were dropped, and, with the exception of Randolph Churchill, were not taken back into the fold.

He found writing a more arduous business than it had been earlier in his career[37] but his grasp of style remained sure, if more and more markedly Victorian in manner. When asked in a television interview, " 'Do you regard your life's work as over?' " Waugh resignedly answered, " 'I wish I could say so. . .writers have to go on and on until they drop.' "[38] He completed his biography of his old friend Ronald Knox in 1959. Meticulously detailed and quite successful in recreating a sense of the late Edwardian period in Knox's undergraduate years at Oxford before World War I, it is a rather colorless study, possibly reflecting the cloistered nature of

Knox's academic and religious life. When writing *Edmund Campion*, Waugh made full use of his skill as a novelist in dramatizing the events that led to Campion's martyrdom, but he could not do the same thing in writing about Knox, and, as was true of the Rossetti study, his biography does not allow the reader to see the man in any depth. But perhaps Ronald Knox would have been a difficult figure for any prospective biographer. Almost totally dedicated to the life of the mind, and never subjected to the rigors of a parish priest, he was a diffident person, despite his eclectic writing interests that included belles-lettres (*Essays in Satire, Let Dons Delight*), four detective novels, and a new translation of the Vulgate Bible. With characteristic restraint, in describing Knox's fatal illness, Waugh simply relates that two friends accompanied him to Torquay in an effort to improve his health, and that one of these friends accompanied him to Sidmouth, in yet another change of scene. The friends were Evelyn and his wife—a charitable act quite in keeping with the many acts of private kindnesses engaged in by the Waughs, and certainly at variance with the public image of Waugh.

Tourist in Africa (1960), an account of a totally unadventurous journey along the east coast of Africa to Capetown, largely aboard ship, was the last of Waugh's travel books. Although far removed from the dogmatic vigor of *Remote People* and *Waugh in Abyssinia* it contains many sharply observant vignettes of an Africa that had radically changed since the 1930s. Portions of the book, notably the description of the Genoese nineteenth-century equivalent of Forest Lawn Cemetery that Waugh visited in company with "Mrs. Stitch" (Lady Diana Cooper), light up with the old Waugh verve; others, including details of shipboard life, and impressions of East Africa, are undistinguished. In form, *Tourist in Africa* consists of a series of diary entries, not unlike Ludovic's gloomy brooding in *Sword of Honour*, and moves effortlessly from the world of train conductors and Mrs. Stitch to racial tensions in Tanganyika. In a turn of phrase Laurence Sterne might have written in *A Sentimental Journey*, Waugh remarks: "As happier men watch birds, I watch men. They are less attractive but more various" (18). He did not rate *Tourist in Africa* very high and did not include it in the uniform edition. One can agree with the writer of the dust jacket blurb that "it is impossible for Evelyn Waugh to write uninterestingly," and disagree with the thought that the book "is refreshingly unorthodox," for

Waugh's observations of the changing cultural and political scene in Africa represent limited praise, guarded optimism, balanced against strongly held conservative views that characterized all of his travel writing.

Apart from the flat tone of the Knox biography, Waugh's dry wit was as astringent as ever, and often at his own expense. This is especially evident in his diary notations; for example, he writes on December 8, 1960: "I must have given my hat many hundreds of times to the old porter at the Ritz. The other day when I came to leave after luncheon he was not on duty, so I went behind his counter and collected my belongings. In my hat he had put a label with the one word 'florid.' "[39]

Unconditional Surrender (1961), published in the United States as *The End of the Battle*, brought to a close the series of closely linked novels on Guy Crouchback's progressively disillusioned involvement in World War II. The completion of the trilogy (brought together in one large volume entitled *Sword of Honour*, published in 1964) represents a major literary achievement in its panoramic magnitude, an achievement that has not yet received the full recognition due it despite the praise of such critics as Walter Allen, Andrew Rutherford, and Anthony Burgess. In its all encompassing, slow development it resembles the novels of Trollope. In tracing out the vagaries of Guy Crouchback's career from the beginning of the war to its inglorious conclusion, Waugh maintains a sustained interweaving of military, civilian, and political aspects of the struggle as they affect the plight of his outmoded, romantic idealist.

In 1962, Waugh's last piece of fiction, "Basil Seal Rides Again," was printed in the *Sunday Telegraph* and in *Esquire* and then published in a signed, limited edition of five hundred copies, dedicated to Mrs. Ian Fleming. No longer the saturnine blackmailer of the earlier fiction, but middle-aged and corpulent, Basil like Waugh himself "had scorned to order his life with a view of longevity or spurious youth" (2). But a spark of the old Basil still persists. When Basil's daughter is about to marry an especially repulsive hippie reincarnation of her father, she is tricked into believing that her suitor is her half-brother, the product of an indiscreet affair in Basil's youth. The result: an end to the affair and the disappearance of the unsavory youth. It is a slight story, dependent on its shamelessly trick ending, but it rounds out the cast of characters in Waugh's fiction and, similar to *The Ordeal of Gilbert*

Pinfold, contains merciless self-parody: "His voice was not the same instrument as of old. He had first assumed it as a conscious imposture; it had become habitual to him; the antiquated, worldly-wise moralities which, using that voice, he had found himself obliged to utter, had become his settled opinions. It had begun as a nursery clowning for the diversion of Barbara; a parody of Sir Joseph Mannering; darling, crusty old Pobble performing the part expected of him; and now the parody had become the persona" (24 - 25).

Waugh's settled convictions became more and more apparent in several radio and television interviews and in travel articles written for the London newspapers. In a television interview in June 1960, conducted on a far more friendly level than the one in 1953 which figured so prominently in *The Ordeal of Gilbert Pinfold*, he freely answered questions about his life and writing career. His remarks on the Oxford years were brief and contained none of the gamy confidences that appeared in the diary excerpts first published in the *Observer* in 1973. As to his conversion, he said that it was a matter of "conversion to Christianity rather than conversion to Catholicism." When asked, "Would you discourage us into reform?" he briskly retorted, "No, I am just trying to write books," and said that it wouldn't occur to him "to sit down and write about gangs." In answer to concluding questions concerning his withdrawn seclusion at Combe Florey, he asserted that he "got bored largely because of deafness," that he did not miss the literary world, had not "the smallest interest in country life," and was "much more at ease with fellow Catholics. . .than with heathens or Protestants."[40]

In 1963, in remarking on the occasion of his being admitted to membership in the Royal Society of Literature, he delivered a highly witty, graceful speech in which he told his audience that most authors are "simply hard-working writers who have done nothing but write all our lives and tried to learn our difficult trade as best as we can in solitude."[41] He wrote a series of feature articles for the *Daily Mail* in 1960 and again in 1962 on contemporary mores and travels (the Riviera, Athens, Monaco, Venice, and South America) whose general tone echoed a favorite line of Uncle Theodore in *Scoop:* " 'Change and decay in all around I see.' " Monaco and Venice were pockets of haute cuisine and high culture, respectively, but in the heat of the summer the Riviera had become "alive as though insects were hatching. From June until October the charabancs come thundering from the north bringing Belgians and Germans and Americans."[42]

Offended by much of what he observed, and forced into the boredom of apathy, his mood in these years is typically represented by what he had to say on "Sloth" in *The Seven Deadly Sins*, a compilation of essays by prominent British novelists, poets, and critics: "All the glittering prizes of success have lately become tarnished. The company in the room at the top has lost the art of pleasing. But Sloth is not primarily the temptation of the young. . . . It is in that last undesired decade, when passion is cold, appetites feeble, curiosity dulled, and experience has begotten cynicism, that *accidia* lies in wait as the final temptation to destruction."[43] On the same subject, Arnold Lunn recalls equally melancholy remarks on Waugh: " 'I have that degree of detachment from the world,' he said, 'which would be very edifying if it led to Christ but is not at all edifying because it merely leads to boredom.' "[44] Although Lunn's attribution may not be entirely accurate, such masochistic self-honesty is perfectly in keeping with Waugh's temperament.

He remained a devout Catholic until his death, but as a lover of tradition he was horrified by changes in the Mass from Latin to the vernacular because he saw these changes as irrational, modish giving in to contemporary attitudes. He publicly expressed his deep concern in writing a letter of protest to the *Tablet:* "All the tongues of Babel are to be employed save only Latin, the language of the Church since the mission of St. Augustine."[45] Of the many speculations attempting to account for Waugh's failure to accommodate himself to these shifts in the attitude of the Church, the most perceptive is Fr. Van Zeller's belief that to a person of Waugh's temperament the post - Vatican Council mood represented "a swing away from the order established in persecution times. When you have written *Edmund Campion* you take these things to heart."[46]

On another matter, though he apparently never made much of it, either publicly or privately, he may well have been disappointed that he never received the official public commendation he so fully deserved. According to Auberon Waugh he refused minor public honors tendered by Prime Minister Macmillan because of the very limited degree of recognition implied.[47] Michael Davie, the editor of the *Observer* diary excerpts, infers that Waugh's negative remarks about Oxford scholars in *A Little Learning* deprived him of an honorary fellowship that had been considered for him.[48] If the inference is true, it was unfortunate that academic recognition was withheld from Waugh, for *A Little Learning*, his last published work, is a remarkably subdued, old-fashioned, and warm evocation of his years at Oxford.

In weighing the effect of these disappointments, disappointments that must have contributed to his increased estrangement from society at large, one must take into account what Alec Waugh has said about Evelyn's declining years. In *My Brother Evelyn*, he reflects: "In later life Evelyn may often have given the impression of being heartless; he was often snubbing, he could be cruel. But basically he was gentle, warm and tender. He was very like his father, and his father's own emotionalism put him on his guard."[49] Alec's remarks are generally corroborated by Graham Greene, who notes: "He had the rare quality of criticizing a friend, harshly, wittily and openly to his face, and behind the friend's back of expressing only his kindness and charity."[50] Although we ought to guard against the popular view of Waugh as the aging misanthrope (a stereotype perpetuated in many of the obituary notices and especially in the account that appeared in *Time* magazine),[51] the evidence found in the diaries suggests that there was, indeed, a core of truth in this conception of a man who had walled off his life from the outside world. Four years before his death, Waugh set down in his diary: "One has heard all the world has to say, and wants no more of it."[52]

Like Jonathan Swift, withdrawn and virtually exiled in Dublin, like the embittered Mark Twain late in his career, Waugh suffered the classic fate of the true satirist: beginning with an uproarious scepticism masking genuine concern for the spectacle of the continued follies of mankind, the satirist's vision often leads either to despair or to resignation. Like Swift and Twain, frequently consorting on familiar terms with the socially and politically mighty, Waugh reserved his most devastating barbs for unthinking wielders of great power, and maintained an even-handed balance between involvement with and detachment from those groups he satirized. As he grew older, he ceased to delight in this literary and personal juggling act. He did not quite sink to the gloomy depths of a Swift, but in turning back to his childhood and youth in *A Little Learning* (rather analogous to James Thurber in *The Thurber Album*) he retreated into reminiscence, no longer concerned with entertaining the world, or with recording its follies.

Stoutly refusing to play the role of a gracefully retired man of

letters, he did not give in to increasing physical ailments, and quietly died at home on Easter Sunday, April 10, 1966, after having
heard Mass spoken in the Latin rite. To the end, he remained a
complex, often difficult, idiosyncratic person who could not and
would not accommodate himself to the temper of contemporary
British life. This was recognized by one of his longtime friends who
spoke on a special BBC broadcast a year after his death: "He was
like no one else, and that was one reason why we loved him through
all the upheavals, all the storms and through the many happy
days."[53]

CHAPTER 2

The Early Novels: Waugh as Satirist

"But I don't want to go among mad people," Alice remarked.
"Oh, you can't help that," said the Cat: "we're all mad here. I'm mad.
You're mad."
"How do you know I'm mad?" said Alice.
"You must be," said the Cat, "or you wouldn't have come here."
Lewis Carroll, *Alice's Adventure in Wonderland*

THE world of Evelyn Waugh is mad, chaotic, and deluded beyond all logic. Its inhabitants, even those we may view with some compassion, such as Tony Last in *A Handful of Dust*, lead a lunatic existence amidst a world in which absurdity posing as reason makes a mockery of rationality. With variations, this preoccupation runs through all of Waugh's novels, from the wildly grotesque parody of the British educational and penal systems in *Decline and Fall* (1928) to the savagely bitter indictment of humanistic values in *A Handful of Dust* (1934), and concludes with a melancholic betrayal of all traditional standards of integrity and honor in the England of World War II described in *Sword of Honour* (1965).

In developing a view of life in which illogic reigns supreme, whether it be in England or in Africa, Waugh presents a long series of antiheroes, passive characters victimized by society at large. There are no Stephen Dedalus - like awakenings to experience in the early novels. Paul Pennyfeather (*Decline and Fall*), Adam Symes *Vile Bodies* (1930), and William Boot *Scoop* (1938), unblinkingly accept whatever outrageous turn of fortune they may encounter. Waugh's narrative structure remains essentially unaltered in these works: it usually contains a main character living in a society from which reason has fled and which thrives on hypocrisy and guile. Only the irrepressible Basil Seal *Black Mischief* (1932), and *Put Out More Flags* (1942) can cope with an irrational environment on its own terms, for most of Waugh's characters are inept creatures whose calm surface appearance is ironically juxtaposed against anarchic disorder in the lives of others, and often in themselves, as in Tony Last of *A Handful of Dust.*

Paul Pennyfeather, Adam Symes, Tony Last, and William Boot are inept to the last degree, but Waugh describes their actions with ambiguous detachment, not with venom or ridicule. He is critical of their naiveté that gets them into such horrible scrapes, yet sympathizes with the plight of these essentially good-natured young men whom, if we except Tony Last, Waugh adroitly rescues from the machinations of the absurd world in which they live. Sean O'Faolain puts it very well in stating that the laughter Waugh evokes in his first six novels is "our happy tribute to the delicate balance he strikes between his detachment from his characters which allows him to satirize them and his affection for them which allows him to pity them."[1]

Most of Waugh's critics only mention in passing the sheer enjoyment derived from reading the novels, whether it be in the dry undercutting of pomposity and untested assumptions, the sharp incongruities of his fantasy world, the upsetting of conventional morality in the escapades of his amoral characters,[2] or in seeing fools hoist with their own petard. His success in creating our enjoyment lies in his manipulation of situation and language, especially the latter, for he is one of the great prose stylists of the twentieth century. Perhaps only Waugh could fill his novels with one grisly death after another, yet force us to accept these deaths with only a passing shudder and even, perhaps against our will, to find them incongruously entertaining. Yet in criticism of his work, the pleasure principle often vanishes, and the injunction of the Author's Note to the first edition of *Decline and Fall,* "Please bear in mind throughout that IT IS MEANT TO BE FUNNY,"[3] is not always remembered by his critics. When Waugh wrote of wine-drinking that the first and most important thing to remember "is that it is something to be enjoyed. The pleasure that it gives is the only test of the vintage . . ."[4] he might just as well have been describing his oft-stated aim in writing: to turn out a well-made art object intended solely for his readers' delectation.

However, if he were only a writer of well-made farce, he would be no more than a sophisticated version of P. G. Wodehouse, a writer whose virtuoso skill he much admired. While Waugh's early novels share "with comedy the knowledge that fools and foolishness have gotten out of hand"[5] they do not fulfill the traditional norm of comedy that right reason will eventually assert itself. Wodehouse's innocents live in a totally imagined, unreal world of imperturbable butlers, dragonlike great aunts, the Drones Club, and Blandings Castle, in which everything comes right at the end with the parceling out of marriages, inheritances, and so on. Waugh's characters are absurd types living in an absurd world, but grotesque though it may be, it is a world whose outlines we recognize. Infrequently, as in *Decline and Fall* or in *Scoop,* the novels conclude with what passes for a happy ending, but more often we end on a desolate battlefield (*Vile Bodies*) or at a cannibal feast (*Black Mischief*).

I Decline and Fall

From his experience teaching school in North Wales came most of the setting and some of the incidents of *Decline and Fall,* Waugh's first published novel, illustrated with his own sketches.[6] He had already tried his hand at writing a novel during his teaching apprenticeship, but when he submitted it to Harold Acton for a critical reading and Acton delicately implied that it was adolescent work, Waugh promptly burned the manuscript. He profited by Acton's astringent remarks, and in gratitude dedicated *Decline and Fall* to him.

Loosely constructed, the plot wildly gyrates from one episode to another. His pants torn off by rioting members of the aristocratic Bollinger Club, Paul Pennyfeather, divinity student, is unjustly expelled from Scone College for indecent exposure, only to be swindled out of his inheritance by his guardian. After his rustication, Paul decides to take up teaching. In a scene recalling a similar passage in Dickens's *Nicholas Nickleby,* Paul is interviewed by the seedily elegant Augustus Fagan, headmaster of Llanaba Castle, an obscure prep school in Wales. Slyly advising Paul "to temper discretion with deceit" (33), Fagan hires him. On arrival at the school, a rambling building elaborately medieval in style, Paul encounters a staff composed of odds and sods including the incorrigible Captain Grimes, Fagan's repulsive daughters Flossie and Dingy, the unhappily respectable Prendergast (a Modern Churchman afflicted with "Doubts"), and the butler, Philbrick, who assumes varying fantastic disguises in following his true métier, that of the con man.

Paul's teaching career reaches its nadir on the day of the annual track meet when the drunken Prendy accidentally shoots little Lord

Tangent in the heel at the start of one of the races. Simultaneously with this disaster, an exchange of insults erupts between the *nouveau riche* brewery Clutterbucks and the grandly arrogant Lady Circumference, the latter a braying horsy type, whose conversation never strays far from matters of drains and fertilizers ("dig it and dung it" [82]). At the height of the uproar, Lady Margot Beste-Chetwynde (English pronunciation: "beast cheating") arrives, accompanied by her American black paramour, a jazz musician, Mr. Sebastian "Chokey" Cholmondley. In a rambling outburst of rhetoric (Waugh parodies the style of Shylock's defense of his humanity) Chokey says "that poor colored man has a soul same as you have. . . . Don't he love Shakespeare and cathedrals. . .same as you?" (97). Waugh's characterization of Chokey and his pretensions may go beyond the limits of outrageous statement that even Waugh's most devoted admirers would allow to him, but he pilloried any artificiality wherever he found it. This scene is social comedy, perhaps even suggesting, if lightly, a note of pathos, for the society of the Chetwyndes and Circumferences is completely self-serving, and has no interest whatsoever in Shakespeare or in cathedrals.[7]

Margot hires Paul to tutor her son, Peter Pastmaster. As Paul drives up the winding road to the estate, the great shade trees appear to him to be symbolic of serenity in a mad world, but at a turn in the driveway he is abruptly confronted with a chromium and glass monstrosity built on the site of an historically important Tudor mansion razed to make way for Margot's latest whim designed by the Bauhaus influenced Professor Silenus, who understands the contemporary problem of architecture as " 'the problem of all art. . .the elimination of the human element from the consideration of form' " (142). Arriving at the start of a houseparty attended by social climbers, politicians, and homosexuals, the bedazzled Paul comes under Margot's hypnotic spell, totally ignorant that underneath her surface beauty she is a drug addict, nymphomaniac, and madam on a grand international scale.

Seduced by and presently engaged to Margot, he is sent off to Marseilles to arrange passage to South America for the girls of her "Latin American Entertainment Company" (unknown to Paul, a chain of highly successful bordellos). Having accomplished his mission, the blissfully unperturbed and innocent Paul is about to marry Margot when he is arrested for trafficking in the white slave trade.

At the trial, upbraided by the prosecution for dragging " 'down to his own pitiable depths of depravity a lady of beauty, rank, and stainless reputation' " (189), Paul takes the rap for Margot and goes to jail. The prison scenes contain the most grimly humorous and horrifying parade of illogic in the entire novel. Adhering to the premise that crime can be cured by aesthetic expression, the rational sociologist-warder of the jail orders that a manic carpenter, a Blake-like religious zealot who has hallucinatory visions to kill and spare not, be provided with tools. Acting on his own inner "logic" the carpenter proceeds to saw off the head of a prison chaplain, none other than poor Prendergast, still trying to find himself.

Margot's influence extending into the prison system, Paul mysteriously receives books, sherry, clothes, oysters. Just as mysteriously, he is abruptly released from jail and sent to a nursing home (through yet another coincidence run by Augustus Fagan) for the removal of his appendix, removed many years ago. A shyster doctor attests to Paul's death on the operating table. Disguised by a mustache, Paul finally returns to the tranquility of Scone College to take up his theological studies once more. Unchanged by all the vicissitudes of fortune he has encountered, Paul resumes his ordered scholarly routine. Perhaps Waugh implies that only by settling for one's own limited, absurd "reality" can we live in a world that, in its absurdity, spills over into fantasy.

No plot summary can do full justice to the wild convolutions of a Waugh novel, to its piling up of one grotesquerie upon another, or to the combination of the unexpected and the satiric. The plot of *Decline and Fall* might have been devised by P. G. Wodehouse, but the genial Wodehouse could never have written the opening scene describing the drunken orgy at the annual Bollinger Dinner:

At the last dinner, three years ago, a fox had been brought in in a cage and had been stoned to death with champagne bottles. What an evening that had been! (13)
It was a lovely evening. They broke up Mr. Austen's grand piano. . .and tore up Mr. Partridge's sheets, and threw the Matisse into his lavatory; Mr. Sanders had nothing to break except his windows, but they found the manuscript at which he had been working for the Newdigate Prize Poem, and had great fun with that (15).

Here, as throughout Waugh's work, the economy of phrasing

creates an explosive effect in the reader's mind, an effect of outrageous farce, and of a wit that never preaches, yet is savagely implicit in its presentation of irrational, inhuman behavior. The
greater the outrage, the more calm becomes the voice of the omniscient narrator.

Waugh possessed the double vision of the satirist in which either
seeming detachment or wild burlesque masks genuine concern for
the absence of reasonableness in our lives. Again and again in the
early fiction one dreadfully incongruous action follows another, actions that his antiheroes take as the accepted pattern of events, and
that do not awaken any moral indignation in them. Ordinary norms
have no more applicability here than in Lewis Carroll's work. In our
recognition of this, the pleasure and the horror (both often
simultaneously experienced by the reader) lie in Waugh's sure skill
in making us abruptly aware of the yawning gulf between *what
appears to be* and *what is*. When Paul goes to jail to cover up for
Margot, he takes it as a matter of course that the appearance of her
respectability be maintained. On the one hand he knew he had
shielded her from criminal prosecution; on the other, his was the
growing conviction "that there was something radically in-
applicable about this whole code of ready-made honour that is the
still small voice, trained to command, of the Englishman all the
world over." Totally unable to envision the glamorous Margot in
prison, ". . .he was strengthened in his belief that there was, in
fact, and should be, one law for her and another for himself" (220 -
21). Paul's attitude is a bleak reminder that some, indeed, are more
equal than others in the real world. In a mildly existential fashion,
his situation reflects life as absurdity, in which our notions of what
ought to be do not apply. The incongruity of these encounters takes
on a horrible, zany logic, for we soon learn that one bizarre action
will most surely lead into another. Like Paul, we end where we
began.

G. K. Chesterton's observations on satire apply to Waugh's preoccupation with the absurd: "The essence of satire is that it perceives
some absurdity inherent in the logic of some position and that it
draws the absurdity out and isolates it, so that all can see it."[8]
Illogic, parading as wisdom, is joined in Waugh's fiction with what
Louis Kronenberger calls "the reversed world," the turning inside
out of society. When Waugh wrote of Anthony Powell that his fictional "world grows larger and becomes more and more anarchic

like the world all of us recognize as we grow older in experience,"[9] he also named the most notable quality of his own work. In his novels, as in the novels of Aldous Huxley, no one communicates, no one listens, thus further heightening the sense of anarchy.

Like Voltaire's *Candide*, Paul Pennyfeather remains a victim, who moves through life a passive observer of the anarchy surrounding him, a hybrid character somewhere between Lemuel Gulliver and Bertie Wooster. Though Paul stoically accepts his fate, we can detect his creator behind the mask, mocking our hypocrisies. Paul's naiveté seems unbelievable, yet Waugh moves the action along with such economy of effect and language that, as in reading Voltaire or Swift, our attention quickly becomes focused on the institutions being dissected rather than on characterization. But this is natural enough for the satirist, primarily concerned with charging whole battalions, rather than with the development of character. The disembodied wraith of Paul Pennyfeather must remain just that, for a more complex, sympathetically portrayed characterization would inevitably lower the highly charged satiric tone of *Decline and Fall*.

In a leisurely digression at the beginning of the second part of the book, somewhat in the manner of an eighteenth-century novelist, Waugh disingenuously informs his readers not to expect any complex characterization. Paul Pennyfeather must remain shadowy, for the entire novel is "an account of Paul's mysterious disappearance, so that readers must not complain if the shadow which took his name does not amply fill the important part of hero for which he was originally cast. . . . Paul Pennyfeather would never have made a hero, and the only interest about him arises from the unusual series of events of which his shadow was witness" (146 - 47). Waugh's digression works, for it extends the outward distance, detachment, that he maintains throughout his early novels. The playing down of character not only helps to emphasize the satire, but also contributes to the absurd discontinuity in the lives of so many of Waugh's central figures.

A totally inert creature, Paul never becomes more than an observer of life. His dilemma is summed up by Professor Silenus, who unexpectedly shows up late in the novel. He compares life to one of those amusement park revolving wheels that everyone tries to jump onto as the wheel spins. At the center there is apparently no movement, " '. . .a point of rest, if one could only find it. . . . It's all right for Margot, who can cling on, and for me, at the centre, but you're static. Instead of this absurd division of the sexes they ought to class people as static and dynamic' " (244 - 45). Paul must remain static, unaffected by all the horrors heaped upon his head; for him to be any more than that, an active agent in his own fate, would be destructive of the tone of the novel, detached and merciless.

In considering the antihero as victim, David Daiches asserts that we are to laugh at Paul Pennyfeather "rather than to pity him, even though the laughter has masochistic overtones. Idealism emerges as mere ignorance, innocence as a dangerous lack of sophistication which makes the virtuous anti-hero the complacent tool of sophisticated vice. . . ."[10] These remarks do not take enough into account, however. While it is true that our laughter grows out of the incredible situations Paul gets caught up in, like Candide he does acquire some limited knowledge of the way of the world. Misplaced idealism, as in the harebrained rehabilitation theories of the prison warden, has consequences as disastrous as out and out villainy. Daiches exaggerates Paul's unawareness, for Waugh simply deploys his main character as a means of recording the idiocies of the society in which he has his being.

Pennyfeather's seismographic recording of every tremor of un-reason that life presents serves as Waugh's major satiric device, but some of the lesser characters are only slightly less important, and es-pecially so in suggesting the ever shifting, fluid unreality of life. First seen as school butler at Llanaba Castle, then as theater owner, shipping magnate, duelist, and author, Philbrick shifts his identity with chameleonlike speed. As he spins wilder and wilder tales about his exploits, the line between fantasy and reality becomes totally blurred. Wanted on a criminal charge, he disappears halfway through the novel, only to reappear at Oxford in the last few pages, riding in a Rolls-Royce. Philbrick's mysterious links with crime and high finance, Prendergast's wig, and Grimes's wooden leg are defenses against an intrusive reality that has no more substance than their own shadowy careers. In an equally fantastic manner, both Pennyfeather and Grimes undergo identity transformations of one kind or another, and escape a world which also assumes various disguises to cloak its irrationality.

Grimes gets along by learning how to outwit the system at its own game. He is always rescued from trouble because he is, for better or worse, usually the latter, a product of the public-schools. He blandly remarks to Paul, " 'There's a blessed equity in the English social system. . .that insures the public school man against starvation. . . . They may kick you out, but they never let you down' " (37). Because he is a product of the establishment, even though a bounder and distinctly not a gentleman, Grimes survives. Faced with a court martial during World War I, he is rescued by a fellow Harrovian and sent to a desk job in Ireland. Momentarily domesticated, he marries Flossie Fagan. He laments that at the end of the honeymoon and flowers await " 'the hideous lights of home and the voices of children. . . . There's no escape. . . . We are just potential home builders, beavers, and ants. . . !' " (121 - 22). But this dread vision doesn't last, for when it is discovered that he is a bigamist, he disappears, apparently a suicide by drowning.

Later, disguised in a red beard, Grimes is hired to manage one of the branches of the Latin American Entertainment Company. Through the crass working of fate, his first wife, a resident of the palais de joie, recognizes her errant husband and has him arrested. Sent to prison at Egdon Heath, his path once more crosses Paul's. In a final burst of glory, he escapes and is listed as being officially dead, but Paul doubts that this is to be the ultimate fate of Grimes, for "he was a life force. Sentenced to death in Flanders, he popped up in Wales; drowned in Wales, he emerged in South America; engulfed in the dark mystery of Egdon Mire, he would rise again somewhere at some time. . ." (232 - 34). The morally dubious Grimes has learned how to survive, like Philbrick, in a world in which form, not substance, matters. Paul is ground under by the Establishment system, and is just as casually rescued by the same system that brought him to grief, but this is not so of Grimes, shamelessly decadent, who blithely escapes the shackles of conventional society. We don't judge him or Philbrick, for they are too fantastic, perversely satyrlike figures, as Waugh suggests of Grimes, in a parody of nineteenth-century aesthetic diction: "Surely he had followed in the Bacchic train of distant Arcady, and taught the childish satyrs the art of love?" (234).

While Grimes rises above all obstacles, Prendergast remains, like Paul, the born victim. Resigned to life, forlorn, obsessed by his religious "doubts," and mocked by his students, he can do nothing right. Prendergast behaves in such a desperately inept fashion that he becomes a figure of ridicule, a theologian in whom Anglicanism has become sterile. When Prendergast recounts to Paul the otherwise totally ridiculous circumstances of his religious crisis and bleakly remarks, " 'I couldn't see why God had made the world at all' " (43), the mask drops. No longer able to accept the Panglossian view that everything is for the best in the best of all possible worlds, Prendergast voices a thematic concern that underlies the succession of grossly irrational acts, some mildly eccentric, some grimly lunatic, everywhere observable in *Decline and Fall*.

Most of the time, however, Waugh achieves the intended effect by a very tight-reined, seeming neutrality of expression. He scores off progressive education in a note Paul receives from Potts: " 'There is a most interesting article in the *Educational Review* on the new methods that are being tried at the Innesborough High School to induce coordination of the senses. They put small objects into the children's mouths and make them draw the shapes in red chalk. Have you tried this with your boys? I must say I envy your opportunities. Are your colleagues enlightened?' " (57).

Beyond the satiric exposures of such Establishment institutions as the educational system, the prison system, and even the Anglican Church there is one undeniable reality, the fact of death. A few weeks after being accidentally shot in the heel at the track meet, Tangent does indeed die of the slight bullet wound. In *The Novel Now*, Anthony Burgess notes the acts of violence that appear in Waugh's fiction. It is Burgess's contention that while we may take the deaths of Tangent and Prendergast as "nursery rhyme deaths—too ritualistic or comic to be true. . .," on the other hand, "if we look below the surface, we shall find that Waugh is recording an age so lacking in roots or ethical convictions that enormities like even cannibalism (in *Black Mischief*) can find no category of judgment, hence no condemnation."[11] The same judgment can be applied to the bizarre death of Agatha Runcible in *Vile Bodies*, Waugh's second novel. So it is in all the early novels that while the deaths themselves are grotesque, the greater enormity is acted out by a morally neutral society in which they could occur.

Illustrated with Waugh's pen-and-ink sketches, *Decline and Fall* fared remarkably well in the book reviews, for the critics realized that here was a work by a fearsomely brilliant young author, although only a few noted its satiric quality. Arnold Bennett asserted in the *Evening Standard* that *Decline and Fall* "is an uncompromising and brilliantly malicious satire, which in my opinion comes near to be quite first-rate. . . . I say without reserve that this

novel delighted me."[12] Writing in the *New Statesman* Cyril Connolly unreservedly praised the author's comic spirit, lifelike
characters, and sparkling dialogue: ". . .One cannot but be
grateful to a writer who for once sets out purely to amuse the reader
and succeeds so well."[13] Two years later, after the publication of
Vile Bodies, Rebecca West boldly stated that she would think
herself "making a good investment if I bought every manuscript I
could lay hands on by Mr. Waugh" and reserved particular praise
for the creation of Captain Grimes in *Decline and Fall*, "one of the
world's great rogues, one of those whose serenity and bloomy sense
of inner rightness almost persuade honest men that there is a strong
moral case for roguery. . . ."[14] Of the contemporary reviewers only
Rebecca West sensed that here was a true satirist, beyond the pure
fooling noted in the mixed review that appeared in the *Times
Literary Supplement*.[15]

Although the critics differed as to whether Waugh was a writer of
farce or satire, they sensed that a refreshingly new, unorthodox
talent had made its appearance. In this first, highly distinctive novel
that set the pattern for all of his novels of the following decade
Evelyn Waugh had at one bound established himself as a biting
critic of post - World War I society and as a satirist of the first order.

II   Vile Bodies

Vile Bodies resembles *Decline and Fall* in its series of outrageously farcical, satiric episodes loosely strung together, in its inclusion of
several characters from the earlier work, and in its unblinking focus
on the grossly absurd, witless behavior of the host of characters who
preen and strut their way through the novel. From the irrelevancies
of Adam Symes and his fiancée, Nina Blount, to the frantic activity
of Agatha Runcible, whose name recalls Edward Lear's "runcible
spoon" in the "The Owl and the Pussycat," to the Neanderthal
rumblings of the Right Honourable Walter Outrage, "last week's
Prime Minister," and to the cheerful hypocrisies of the American
evangelist, Mrs. Melrose Ape, we again find ourselves in a world of
caricature.

The young people who throng this novel are bright, lively, often
silly and careless, and spend their waking hours aimlessly milling
about in their search for the new, for anything that will shock their
parents' generation. Well-to-do children of the pre-Depression era,

they are neither malicious nor destructive in their actions, but their whimsical, sometimes fatal irresponsibility, as in the case of Miss Runcible, can end catastrophically. The whole tone is set by Waugh in lines from *Alice in Wonderland* that precede Chapter 1: "Now here, you see, it takes all the running you can do to keep in the same place." There are no road signs, no trustworthy standards of conduct, no solid earth underneath. Even the stability of social order has become scrambled in a world in which the ex-king of Ruritania has been reduced to accepting handouts at Lottie Crump's hotel, and marquesses and barons have become gossip columnists.

Despite the general similarities to *Decline and Fall*, there are significant differences, particularly in the somber mood of the final pages of *Vile Bodies*. Order, even of a limited, static kind is not reimposed, and the novel ends on a battlefield, with civilization shattered. The bleak tone of the novel's conclusion may be partially attributable to the economic shock waves of 1929, so destructive to the euphoria of the 1920s but it is more likely, as Waugh admitted in the *Paris Review* interview, that the breakup of his first marriage helps account for the bitterness of the closing passages.[16] Further, much of the dialogue of *Vile Bodies* differs in tone from the first novel. By means of staccato, monosyllabic, and fragmentary conversation, chaotic in effect, Waugh's Bright Young Things of the late 1920s create a secret "in-group" society, in casually studied opposition to the stodgy bourgeois society of their parents in which everything is "too bogus."

The novel opens with Adam, Agatha Runcible, and other British counterparts of F. Scott Fitzgerald's aimless children of the Jazz Age aboard ship for the Channel crossing from France. Also aboard is a mystery figure, improbably named Father Rothschild, who functions, in his masked identity, as a Teiresias-like commentator at various points in the novel. Other passengers include the tremulously vague *grande dames* Lady Throbbing and Mrs. Blackwater (puzzlingly alienated from the strange mores of their children), and Mrs. Ape's entourage, including three sexy angels named Faith, Hope, and Chastity. We are brought up short by the last name, expecting "Charity" instead. Part of the fun in reading Waugh derives from spotting his literary allusions. They are encountered everywhere in *Decline and Fall*, and are scattered throughout his novels. Here, it seems likely that Waugh remembered lines from

Comus, Milton's poem to temperate behavior: "O welcome, pure-eyed faith, white handed hope,/Thou hovering angel girt with golden wings,/And thou unblemished form of chastity." The references become even more sardonic in the context of Mrs. Panrast's interest in Chastity. As the ship wallows through heavy weather, the evangelist's "Angels" despairingly sing Mrs. Ape's famous hymn "There Ain't No Flies on the Lamb of God." More pragmatic than her choir, Mrs. Ape heads for the ship's bar, sings hymns with its seasick male occupants, and then passes the hat. Thus in a few caustic strokes, Waugh pillories Mrs. Ape's strident Christianity.

At the end of the voyage, the customs inspectors stop Adam, confiscate his copies of Dante and Aristotle as pornography, and seize his memoirs, meanwhile parroting the demagogic phrase of a cabinet minister that " 'if we can't stamp out literature in the country, we can at least stop its being brought in from the outside' " (25).

At London, Adam salves his indignity by retreating to Lottie Crump's battered hotel,[17] where one can "still draw up, cool and uncontaminated, great healing draughts from the well of Edwardian certainty" (37). Adam wins a thousand-pound bet, phones his fiancée, Nina Blount, to tell her he now has the money to marry her, and gives the money to a drunken Major to bet on a horse, only to have the "Major" suddenly disappear. He appears and disappears in later scenes, much like Philbrick, in *Decline and Fall.* Adam must again phone Nina to tell her the marriage is off. Fortuitous, idle chance rules their lives.

Adam next attempts to borrow money from Nina's father, Colonel Blount, the first of several eccentric father figures in Waugh's novels. Blount's library is a wild mélange of stuffed owls, skulls, and old movie magazines, but his eccentricities are balanced by cunning, for he gives Adam a check signed "Charlie Chaplin." Unaware of this fraud, Adam celebrates by spending the night with Nina at a secluded hotel. The escapade is disillusioning for both Adam and Nina. In an intrusive authorial remark included in the first edition of *Vile Bodies* but omitted from the revised edition, Waugh tells his readers that ". . .like so many people of their age and class, Adam and Nina were suffering from being sophisticated about sex before they were at all widely experienced."[18]

Adam makes one final effort to extract money from the Colonel.

He discovers that the latter has given over his estate to a movie company shooting "an all talkie super-religious film,"[19] a desperately inaccurate version of the life of John Wesley (in one scene Wesley duels with the pious evangelist George Whitefield). Although in later years Waugh felt that the movie scenes took up too much space in the novel, they contain some of its funniest moments, for in their broad parody of the unrealities of movie-making, they suggest a fantasy world that Nathanael West was to develop on a larger, more serious scale in *The Day of the Locust*.

The novel's climactic episode takes place in an auto race. Holding strictly to his dictum to sketch in, but never to explain, and without being too heavily symbolic in his presentation of the racers madly whirling about the countryside, Waugh underscores the aimless lives of Adam, Nina, Agatha Runcible, Ginger Littlejohn—all spectators at the meet. The fragmentary dialogue of the race drivers enhances the chaotic scene:

> ". . .Burst his gasket and blew out his cylinder heads. . ."
> ". . .Broke both arms and cracked his skull in two places. . ."
> ". . .Tailway. . ."
> ". . .Merc. . ."
> ". . .Mag. . ."
> ". . .crash. . . ." (158)

Through a series of chance circumstances and mistaken identity, Agatha Runcible suddenly becomes a driver in the race, charges into the lead only to veer off the track, and ends by smashing into a stone cross in a marketplace miles away. Carried to a darkened room in a London nursing home she has hallucinatory visions of "'driving round and round in a motor race until I was left all alone driving and driving—and then I used to crash and wake up'" (186). This circular image repeats, in slightly altered form, the metaphor of the amusement park wheel in *Decline and Fall*, but this time many of the Bright Young Things are thrown off, and Miss Runcible dies.

Having bought Adam's interest in Nina for seventy-eight pounds sixteen and twopence, Ginger promptly marries Nina. With war imminent, and with Ginger called up by his regiment, Nina lightly abandons her husband to take Adam home with her at the Christmas holidays. This is of slight consequence to Colonel Blount, for, immersed like Laurence Sterne's Uncle Toby in his eccentric hobbies, the world outside his own skin doesn't exist for him; one member of the younger generation is indistinguishable from the next. Secure in their deception, Nina and Adam share in the traditional family pleasures: church, fireplace, presents, carol-singers.

In the midst of the Christmas ceremonies, war is declared. In the novel's epilogue, ironically entitled "Happy Ending," Adam finds himself alone in the mud and desolation of a vast battlefield. Like an apparition out of the past, the drunken Major reappears, now risen to the status of general. He also has one of Mrs. Ape's "Angels" in tow, a forlorn Molly Bloom, now considerably bedraggled from her downward descent to camp follower. When he babbles to himself, " 'Damn difficult country to find one's way about in. No landmarks. . .' " (210), he unwittingly summarizes what has happened in *Vile Bodies*—the destruction of all normal ties, domestic, social, political. Everything has broken up, from the psychic disintegration and death of Agatha Runcible to the disintegration of Western civilization on a symbolic battlefield.

The fragmentation of this unstable, fantastic world is reflected in almost every action or conversation of its inhabitants. Never is there any rational meeting of mind or will. In one passage, the Right Honourable Walter Outrage, "last week's Prime Minister," remarks to Father Rothschild: " 'What war. . . . No one has said anything to me about a war. I really think I should have been told' " (132). Like the scenes at Lottie's Crump's, this has the true *Alice in Wonderland* ring to it, for everyone is at cross purposes.

All distinctions and especially sexual distinctions, become blurred. On the way to the auto races, "Miss Runcible wore trousers and Miles touched up his eyelashes in the dining-room of the hotel where they stopped for luncheon" (152). One of the most sustained images of a world in uneasy transition is contained in the lengthy description of the racing cars constructed of frantic realignments of tires, engines, gear ratios. For Waugh, these racing mechanisms embody the true existential symbols of the twentieth century: "The real cars . . . those vital creations of metal who exist solely for their own propulsion through space . . . these are in perpetual flux; a vortex of combining and disintegrating units; like the confluence of traffic at some spot where many roads meet, streams of mechanism come together, mingle and separate again" (160).

This is not only a world in flux, but a world whose younger generation has lost, perhaps irrevocably, any significant links to its past. When Ginger and Nina fly over England enroute to their honeymoon on the Riviera, Ginger euphorically misquotes lines he once memorized in a poetry book describing " 'This scepter'd isle, this earth of majesty, this something or other Eden' " (196 - 97), but he cannot even identify them with Shakespeare, so dissociated is he from his own heritage. Ironically, what they see from the plane is hardly "this earth of majesty," for beneath them lies "a horizon of straggling red suburbs; arterial roads dotted with little cars; factories . . . emptying and decaying; a disused canal" (196 - 97). A similar image appears earlier, in the description of the drab environment of the Royal George Hotel, and especially "the canal from whose shallow waters rose little islands of scrap iron and bottles" (155). Both passages, in their images of sterility and decay, quite likely reflect similar imagery in "The Fire Sermon" section of Eliot's *The Waste Land,* which Waugh had become acquainted with as an undergraduate.

A seemingly neutral, dispassionate manipulator of cleverly structured black comedy, Waugh skillfully concentrates on the building of each scene so that we read from one page to the next in agreeably horrified anticipation, never disappointed, of the next improbable action. But, as suggested in his use of highly visual, descriptive images of sterility, he does not always maintain this studied neutrality in an uniform fashion, and in such moments, the detached pose vanishes in Waugh's strongly implied judgmental comment on the self destructive lives of the young people who parade through *Vile Bodies.* This is particularly noticeable in Adam and Nina's pursuit of a life of pleasure in attending one round of parties after another. From what Patrick Balfour and Nancy Mitford have written of the social life of the well-to-do young of the mid-1920s, Waugh's picture is not inaccurate.[20] In the preface to the revised edition of the novel Waugh tells us that he was "rather on the fringe than in the centre" of this group, thus accounting for his objective description, tinged with revulsion:

(. . . Masked parties, Savage parties, Victorian parties, Greek parties, Wild West parties, Russian parties, Circus parties, parties where one had to dress as somebody else, almost naked parties in St. John's Wood, parties in flats and studios and houses and ships and hotels and night clubs, in windmills and swimming baths. . .parties at Oxford where one drank brown sherry and smoked Turkish cigarettes, dull dances in London and comic dances in Scotland and disgusting dances in Paris—all that succession and repetition of massed humanity. . . . Those vile bodies. . . .) (123)

On the same evening that Adam and Nina attend a party held aboard a dirigible moored in a dingy suburb, the older generation gather for a more sedate affair at Anchorage House. In his description of the latter, Waugh is gently ironic and nostalgic for a lost way of life. Even the house itself, "lurking in a ravine between concrete sky-scrapers. . .had grace and dignity. . . ." The Stayles, Vanburghs, Throbbings, no matter what the eccentricities of their children, are decent, temperate people, "that fine phalanx of the passing order, approaching, as one day at the Last Trump they hoped to meet their Maker, with decorous and frank cordiality to shake Lady Anchorage by the hand at the top of her staircase" (126 - 27). In this passage and elsewhere, Waugh is simultaneously detached and subjective. It is this characteristic of his work, as Malcolm Bradbury has pointed out,[21] that sometimes baffles both the uninitiated reader and professional critics, for he moves effortlessly from a stinging satiric attack on the witless behavior of the Prime Minister or the calculated deceit of Margot Metroland to the quasi-romanticized scene described above in which the satiric note (equating Lady Anchorage and God with decorous manners) is muted.

Like all satirists, essentially conservative in his values, he never allows to his readers a comfortable untested assumption of their own beliefs and prejudices. When Outrage says of the younger generation that they missed a chance after World War I to save a whole civilization and that all they want to do is have a good time he does not see that it was his generation that had betrayed the young people of the post - World War I years. Waugh's sense of the historical, later to be more fully developed in the *Sword of Honour* trilogy, is mirrored in Father Rothschild's reply to Outrage that people do not want to lose their faith in religion and that young people in particular "are all possessed with an almost fatal hunger for permanence." Warming to his subject, Father Rothschild accurately predicts what actually did happen in Europe and in England in the late 1930s:

We long for peace, and fill our newspapers with conferences about disarmament and arbitration, but there is a radical instability in our whole world-order, and soon we shall all be walking into the jaws of destruction again, protesting our pacific intentions. (131 - 32, 133)

Father Rothschild must not be taken too seriously as political pundit. His very name and vocation suggest an impudently improbable linkage. He appears to be an omniscient figure of international intrigue, like his next reincarnation, Mr. Baldwin, in *Scoop*, yet in his remarks on an unstable world order, he seems to voice his creator's thinking. For a moment, double-edged, ambiguous detachment has been dropped.

Waugh's reading of the restless malaise of his young people was an intuitively aware understanding of the mood of the 1930s. Less understandable is the presence of death in *Vile Bodies*. As is repeated so often throughout Waugh's fiction, the lives of some of the characters are abruptly snuffed out. We are tempted to moralize, to read these deaths as suggesting a macabre, almost medieval preoccupation with the dance of death in the midst of life, but on the other hand, they may simply accentuate Waugh's acutely individual brand of black comedy, or they may be no more than a convenient means of getting rid of a minor character who threatens to loom too large in the novel's structure, as most certainly appears to be the case in several instances in Waugh's fiction, and especially in the abrupt death of Apthorpe, that marvelously rich seriocomic figure of the *Sword of Honour* trilogy. At any rate, beneath the surface froth of *Vile Bodies*, death remains inescapable, unaccountable, and capricious. At a drunken party at Lottie Crump's hotel, one of Judge Skimp's girls falls from a chandelier and is killed, but in the newspaper coverup the harsh facts are artfully concealed as an accident. Lord Balcairn, alias Chatterbox the gossip columnist, is caught gate-crashing at a party given for Mrs. Ape by Margot Metroland (Margot Beste-Chetwynde of *Decline and Fall*), goes home to his flat, writes a highly libelous account of the private lives of those attending, and then commits suicide. Centuries after the romantic glories of Acre and Agincourt, this is how the Balcairns end, totally unfitted to coping in the modern world. As Christopher Hollis points out in his introduction to a British edition of *Decline and Fall* the characters are so two-dimensional and unreal that their death awakens no true compassion in us. Only with the death of John Last in *A Handful of Dust* do we feel a stirring of sympathy.

Lord Balcairn's death is the snuffing out of a butterfly, but Agatha Runcible's death, hastened by a noisy and alcoholic party at her bedside, seems far more symbolic of a high-spirited but aimless younger generation unable to order their own lives.

The capricious jigsaw puzzle of their lives is illustrated not only by how they act, but by how they talk as well. Their abrupt and fashionably jaded conversation is a code language that alienates them from the older generation and also sets the tone for the novel. In the opening pages, when Adam phones Nina to tell her their engagement is off, their conversation seems almost a parody of the language spoken by the sophisticates of Hemingway's early novels:

> "Oh, I say, Nina, there's one thing—I don't think I shall be able to marry you after all."
> "Oh, Adam, you are a bore. Why not?"
> "They burnt my book." (35)

Near the novel's end, their paths once more fitfully recrossing in a brief liaison at a London hotel, their sense of an annihilating boredom is implied by this cryptic exchange:

> "Oh Adam, what *do* you want . . . you're too impossible this evening."
> "Don't let's talk any more, Nina, d'you mind?"
> Later he said: "I'd give anything in the world for something different."
> "Different from me or different from everything?"
> "Different from everything. . .only I've got nothing. . .what's the good of talking'?"
> "Oh, Adam, my dearest. . ."
> "Yes?"
> "Nothing." (190)

The word "nothing" is then repeated, motiflike, a few pages later, in Agatha Runcible's traumatic dream world of racing cars:

> *"Faster. Faster."*
> The stab of a hypodermic needle.
> "There's nothing at all to worry about, dear. . .*nothing at all*. . .*nothing*." (198)

In its description of the naive behavior of the young people who throng the pages of *Vile Bodies*, the novel probably owes something to Wodehouse, and its language may owe a slight debt to the clipped yet ambiguous style of Ronald Firbank, as Waugh acknowledged,[22] and perhaps a slight attribution to Hemingway, but the total effect is unmistakably vintage Waugh.

Unlike *Decline and Fall, Vile Bodies* quickly caught on with the reading public. Many of the critics began to realize that here was a satiric writer of stature. V. S. Pritchett observed in the *Spectator* that "Mr. Evelyn Waugh has written in *Vile Bodies* a hectic piece of savage satire. . . . I laughed until I was driven out of the room."[23] L. P. Hartley shrewdly commented, "If we read this high-spirited book between the lines, and look at its gift horse, humour, in the mouth, we may find that the ground is not solid beneath our feet; we are dancing on a volcano, carousing on the edge of a precipice."[24] Arnold Bennett was less sure, preferring *Decline and Fall.* He felt that *Vile Bodies* contained a few good satirical flourishes, but that (as one might have expected from Bennett) the plot was weak, resulting in "a large number of pages which demand a certain obstinate and sustained effort of will for their perusal."[25]

Although the book has moments of high comedy, especially in the turmoil of the auto racing so directly symbolic of the frenzied activity from beginning to end, the satire is diffuse, as Arnold Bennett suggests, and less concentrated than in *Decline and Fall.* There are may brilliantly handled vignettes such as the seizure of Adam's memoirs, or the scene at Margot Metroland's party when Mrs. Ape's evangelistic fervor is put down by the equally indignant rhetorical fervor of Britannia insulted, Lady Circumference, but such moments are only rather incidentally related to a total pattern.

The disillusioned tone of the closing pages, ending with the loss of all order, may be partially accounted for as an effort to exorcise a world that had treated Waugh rather wretchedly early in the game, but regardless of Waugh's private concern that may have brought about this altered mood *Vile Bodies* vividly records the spiritual hangover which was the heritage of World War I and the subsequent sense of unease that affected English life in the years preceding World War II.

III   Black Mischief

Following his journey to Addis Ababa as correspondent for *The Times* to report the coronation of Haile Selassie in the fall of 1930, Waugh published his impressions in *Remote People* (1931), a non-fiction travel account, and then gave freer rein to this experience in his next novel, *Black Mischief.*

Black Mischief is set in an atmosphere of grimly comic treachery reminiscent of the corruptive tropical settings of Graham Greene's novels. Beleaguered by a rebel force, the Oxford-educated young Emperor Seth of Azania hides from reality by issuing a series of bold, unenforceable proclamations. Like all of Waugh's statesmen, Seth masks his own emptiness behind a smokescreen of abstractions:

"I am Seth, grandson of Amurath. Defeat is impossible. . . . We have the Tank. This is not a war of Seth against Seyid but of progress against barbarism. . . . The whole might of Evolution rides behind him; at my stirrups run woman's suffrage, vaccination and vivisection. I am the New Age. I am the Future." (20)

Although Waugh sympathetically characterizes Seth as a hopelessly ineffective creature trapped in a situation not of his own making, Seth never stops to question his identity or to ask who or what he is. Rather like Joyce Cary's Mr. Johnson, he is caught between two cultures; intelligent enough to sense the primitive, superstitious limitations of his people, he cannot rid himself of them, and imitates every glittering European modernity. At night, the vision of an abstractly ideal European Socialist community vanishes, and a more primordial, sinister vision asserts its potent supremacy as Seth lies awake, "his eyes wild with the inherited terror of the jungle, desperate with the acquired loneliness of civilization. Night was alive with beasts and devils and the spirits of dead enemies. . ." (29 - 30). Later in the novel, the undercurrent of barbarism becomes increasingly menacing, lurking just beyond the vernacular hymn singing of the missions and the jingling bells of the Nestorian monasteries.

The anarchic threat of irrational primitive belief ready to topple the sham civilization of Azania is paralleled by the atmosphere of anarchic physical disorder at the capital city of Debra Dowa, a hodgepodge of native huts and uncompleted modern buildings. On a triumphal progress, Seth's limousine breaks down, and his private train steams away, sans coaches. A wrecked automobile used as a home by a family of natives blocks the main and only tarred road. Symbolic of the jerry-built modernization of Azania, it is still there at novel's end, long after Seth's reign has collapsed.

Early in the novel, the disarray of Seth's world is heightened by the straggling arrival of Seth's victorious troops, laden down with loot. When the mercenary soldier, General Connolly, informs Seth that the Emperor's father has been caught and eaten by a group of Wanda tribesmen (this action forshadowing the novel's grim ending), Seth replies in an unconsciously ironic fashion, " 'I am afraid that as yet the Wanda are totally out of touch with modern thought. They need education. . . . We might start them on Montessori methods' " (46 - 47). In its flat, direct statement and seeming removal of the author's presence, the dialogue of this scene is typical of Waugh's playing off of one incongruity against another so as to pile up an intensified ironic effect. The incongruity of the abstract words, following on the horror of cannibalism jolts the reader, especially in Waugh's refusal to moralize. We make the association, nevertheless; Seth is truly a Jonsonian "humor" character so totally caught up in his crazy mission to civilize his people, that the only way he can respond to the dreadful news of his father's death is with meaningless shibboleths. This isn't all, however, for like any master of the satiric-comic, Waugh builds on the scene, and concludes with a sly jab at Montessori methods of primary education as a cure-all for the ills of mankind.

Having fully established the chaotic quality of life in Azania, Waugh next cuts to London to introduce Basil Seal, twenty-eight, his amoral, lying, certainly ungentlemanly, and engaging hero. Although we first meet him at loose ends recovering from a hangover "on the sofa of a totally strange flat. . .a gramaphone playing," and a man in shirtsleeves shaving himself (70 - 71), Basil still lives in a childlike make-believe world. One moment he may pose as an expert on international diplomacy, the next as a dietary expert. He may visit the blasé Alastair and Sonia Trumpington as they hold court in bed surrounded by dogs, glasses of "black velvet," and a raffish crew of hangers-on, but they spend the evening playing the childhood game of "Happy Families."

Fed up with his empty life, he suddenly decides to observe the Azanian rebellion. His remarks to his out of touch mother (caught up in her own private world of engraved invitations and the nightly glass of hot milk), are indicative of Waugh's wanderlust in the early 1930s: " 'Every year or so there's one place on the globe worth going to where things are happening. The secret is to find out where and be on the spot on time' " (88). He finances the journey with money given him by his mistress, Angela Lyne (she appears again in *Put Out More Flags* and in *Sword of Honour*), and by stealing and pawning his mother's jewels. On the strength of a casual undergraduate acquaintance with Seth, Basil becomes head of the

Ministry of Modernisation, whose aim is to promote modern, progressive notions of life throughout Azania, but which really implies "the right of interference in most of the public and private affairs of the nation" (124).

Aided by his magnificently crooked assistant, the voracious shopkeeper Youkoumian, an adroit practitioner of the art of survival, he proceeds via the "One-Year Plan" instantly to reshape Azanian society along the lines of Soviet political thinking. There is sharp, abrupt irony in Basil's theorizing:

". . . We've got a much easier job than we should have had fifty years ago. If we'd had to modernize a country then it would have meant constitutional monarchy, bicameral legislation, proportional representation, women's suffrage, independent judicature, freedom of the press, referendums. . ."

"What is all that?" asked the Emperor.

"Just a few ideas that have ceased to be modern." (132)

With Basil acting as his Shavian superman, Seth proceeds to modernize Azanian life, including the ordering of boots (over General Connolly's protests) for his shoeless palace guards, who promptly boil and eat them, according to their own appropriate logic of what is proper to the occasion.

Prudence Courteney, the sheltered and overly romantic daughter of the British envoy, becomes the secret mistress of Basil. Most of their assignations take place in Basil's room over Youkoumian's store, in an atmosphere compounded of unwashed laundry and cigar butts floating in a wash basin. Waugh strongly emphasized the sordid, furtive nature of the affair, yet this did not save him from unexpected criticism by a Catholic critic writing in the *Tablet* who misunderstood Waugh's intent and concluded by stating that "on his dunghill no lily blooms."[26]

Upstaged by Basil in the crisis of the boots, General Connolly plots to release the long-imprisoned but true ruler, Achon. The conservative forces rally in opposition to Seth's elaborately planned Birth Control Pageant ("Through Sterility to Culture"). His regime undermined, Seth goes out alone into the streets, and monomaniacally possessed of his vision to rebuild Debra-Dowa, attempts to pull down the Anglican Cathedral, stone by stone. Soon after, he is overthrown by the Achon faction; however, at the precise moment the crown is placed on the head of the half-crazed Achon, the new king dies, and total anarchy holds sway in the capital.

Disguised in native costume, a la Lawrence of Arabia, Basil leaves to search for Seth. What he does not know is that the plane carrying Prudence to the coast and the safety of "luncheons, dances and young men . . . all the easy circumstances of English life" (218), has been forced down in the jungle. Arriving in the back country, Basil finds out that Seth has been murdered. Gathering for the funeral ceremonies, the native mourners wear "necklets of lions' teeth, shrivelled bodies of toads and bats, and towering masks" (228). The descent into barbarism seems complete, but not quite, for after sharing in a tribal feast, Basil recognizes Prudence's red beret set askew on the head of a native chieftain, and learns that he has eaten Prudence in a cannibal stew. It is a moment of horror, similar to Marlow's in Conrad's *Heart of Darkness* when, scanning the distant reaches of the Congo riverbank with his fieldglasses, Marlow discovers the ornaments on the fenceposts of Kurtz's trading station are human skulls.

Chapter 8 serves as ironic epilogue to the grand guignol conclusion of the story. Basil, back in London, seeks out Alastair and Sonia Trumpington. The Trumpingtons don't want to hear about his adventures ("'Keep a stopper on the far-flung stuff'" [234]), though they detect a change in Basil, and Basil's experience, unlike Marlow's, remains locked within himself.

In Azania, Seth's crazily erratic rule has been replaced by the monotonous gray officialdom of the British-French mandate. The broken down lorry is still there, triumphantly blocking traffic. Only Youkoumian, the eternal entrepreneur, survives to profit by yet another sale of boots. In the streets of Matodi, Azania's seaport, a gramophone can be heard playing Gilbert and Sullivan:

> Three little maids from school are we,
> Pert as a schoolgirl well can be
> Filled to the brim with girlish glee—
> Three little maids from school.

Taken in the context of *Black Mischief*, these lines are a sharp commentary on the naive unreality of a British education, and the grim consequences thereof. Basil's officious buccaneering in Azanian politics has come to naught. As in *Decline and Fall*, the novel concludes with surface order restored, but there has been a shift in tone. In Waugh's first novel we can accept and even pleasurably anticipate the way in which one imbecility is piled on another. However, in *Black Mischief*, possibly more than in *Vile Bodies*, there is an undercurrent of revulsion, of mindlessness and barbarism ascendant that makes itself felt in the latter part of the novel, and runs counter to the lively preposterousness of Azanian life described earlier in the work.

With *Black Mischief*, Waugh's reading of our lives as isolated, mad, and absurd, first stated in *Decline and Fall* and repeated in *Vile Bodies*, becomes fixed. It is the pattern, with variations, that was to characterize all of his fiction, with the possible exception of *Helena* and *Brideshead Revisited*. Yet even in these later works, both apologias for Catholic doctrine, the grotesque creatures and situations of Waugh's comic vision threaten to overturn serious commitment to expression of religious principle.

As in the first two novels, no one communicates or listens to anyone else in *Black Mischief*'s half-world of European "civilization" and African "barbarism." If the reader feels uneasy about Waugh's seemingly patronizing attitude toward black Africans awkwardly struggling into nationhood, he soon discovers that Waugh's European types fare no better. The infantile British envoy Sir Sampson Courteney may be quite indifferent to the loss of a codebook, but becomes filled with childish glee on finding a toy sea-serpent in his bathtub. In an equally ludicrous manner his opposite number, M. Ballon, the French diplomatic representative, mistakes the innocent jottings of a game of consequence as a diabolical intrigue by the British. Emperor Seth's blind acceptance of everything modern culminating in the overthrow of Seth at the Birth Control Pageant is farcical, even pathetic, but his European counterparts behave just as foolishly. White or black—all feel the lash of Waugh's scorn. Primitive societies are often childlike and cruel, Waugh implies, but the kingdom of Azania, for all its gaucheries, is only a distorted echo of a European society not worth copying.

Black Mischief has the inconsequential logic of dreams, shifting and fantastic. This is particularly well illustrated in the description of the masked ball held to celebrate Seth's victory over the rebel army. Savage and civilized become one, in a withering description that in its indictment of humanity recalls Swift's race of "pernicious vermin":

Paper caps were resumed; bonnets of liberty, comical dunces' hats, jockey caps, Napoleonic casques, hats of pierrots and harlequins, postmen, highlanders, old Mothers Hubbard and little Misses Muffet over faces of every complexion, brown as boots, chalk white, dun, and the fresh boiled pink of Northern Europe. False noses again; brilliant sheaths of pigmented cardboard attached to noses of every anthropological type, the high arch of the Semite, freckled Nordic snouts, broad black nostrils from the swamp villages of the mainland, the pulpy inflamed flesh of the alcoholic, and unlovely syphilitic voids. (114)

Although Waugh avoids the barely concealed, harsh raging of Swift or Smollett, we sense the revulsion, for the grotesque masks only partially cover a more loathsome reality underneath. That "repetition of massed humanity . . . those vile bodies" reappear, but now in a more concentrated effect of disgust.

One must be careful, however, in reading Waugh not to force his novels into a Swiftean mold of total disgust. His comic spirit is as unbridled, as anarchic as the world he describes, and Basil Seal is just the right character to survive in this milieu, the antithesis of Paul Pennyfeather or Adam Symes. He is also presumptuous, and a thorough fraud, but we overlook these qualities in following his erratic career because Waugh knows how to create delightful, if shocking, suspense, and beckons us to read on in discovering how one outrageous action will be toppled by another.

There is something essentially appealing, something that slips by the censor in most readers in Basil's aristocratically casual, and usually successful avoidance of the Puritan work ethic. Like Comus Bassington of Saki's *The Unbearable Bassington*, Basil gets ahead by conniving manipulation of the right connections, does so with coolly insolent style, and touches a sneakingly responsive nerve in the reader. Obviously delighting in Basil's escapades, Waugh makes it difficult for us to pass moral judgment. Although quite distinct from the passive antiheroes of the preceding novels, like them Basil is also isolated and out of step. His audacity is a measure of the dead weight of the unthinking social and political situations he so frequently outwits. Arrogant yet rather childish-looking, he suggests the young Winston Churchill, as Martin Green has noted.[27] He was one of Waugh's favorite characters, and appears again in a leading role in *Put Out More Flags* (1942) and in Waugh's last piece of fiction, *Basil Seal Rides Again* (1963).

Typical of Waugh's fiction, *Black Mischief* abounds in sharply drawn one-dimensional minor characters. These include the inept, bored Sir Sampson, the finagling Youkoumian, and the pair of myopic do-gooders, Dame Mildred Porch and her companion, Miss Tin. Traveling around the world in the interest of the Cruelty to Animals Commission, they have come to Azania to investigate conditions at the capitol. Blind to the human suffering everywhere surrounding them, they find only what they want to find. Writing home, Dame Porch moralizes: "Fed doggies in market place. Children tried to take food from doggies. Greedy little wretches" (160). In their economy and carefully artless understatement, these lines are representative of Waugh's sly digs at the callousness of the British upper middle class.

Despite the fertility of Waugh's comic inventiveness in describing the collision of European and African civilizations, and his success in creating a whole gallery of minor characters, criticism of the novel was uneven, especially so in the instance of the Catholic writer who felt that no good Catholic could have written the novel. Stung by this unexpected attack from a coreligionist, Waugh immediately responded via a letter to the *Tablet* defending the morality of *Black Mischief*:

The story deals with the conflict of civilization, with all its attendant and deplorable ills and barbarism. The plan of my book was to keep the darker aspects of barbarism continually and unobtrusively present, a black and mischievous background against which the civilized and semi-civilized characters performed their parts.[28]

The Times Literary Supplement reviewer liked the novel, and noted the unique quality of Waugh's special vision of life, but James Agate, writing in the *Daily Express*, said he couldn't make sense of the book, and that the satire was heavy-handed. Agate concluded with the patronizing remark that "the book will be deemed wildly funny by the intelligentsia, and there is always the chance that it is too clever for me."[29] As was to occur with increasing and distressing frequency in reviews of Waugh's fiction, some of the critics had already begun to stray from objective evaluation to ill-mannered attacks on Waugh's private opinions and beliefs.

American reception of *Black Mischief* was generally quite favorable. Reviewers in the *Boston Transcript* and the *New York Times* emphasized the interplay of irony and wit, while William Maxwell, writing in *Books*, remarked on the "strange blending of the comic and sickening" and interestingly, if rather heavy-handedly, compared *Black Mischief* to Jacobean tragedy "wherein the stimulus of horror is used to arouse an audience no longer capable of being moved by the austere tragedy of the mind."[30]

With three novels and two travel accounts (*Labels*, 1930, and *Remote People*, 1931) Waugh had now begun to establish himself as a writer demanding serious critical attention. Like all first-rate satirists he increasingly ran the risk of being misunderstood by the critics, but also appealed to a widening reading audience delighting in his deadpan presentation of the absurd incongruities between unthinking, pompous statements about education, politics, "progress," penology, and so on, and the reality that often exposes our pretensions.

IV   A Handful of Dust

A *Handful of Dust* originated in a short story entitled "The Man Who Liked Dickens," and was first published in serial installments in *Vogue* magazine. This form of publishing, although of long tradition in England, did not do justice to the cumulative effect of the novel, according to Christopher Sykes,[31] and it was not until publication of the novel in its entirety that its power was fully recognized.

Taking as its epigraph Eliot's line "I will show you fear in a handful of dust" (*The Waste Land*), the novel is strongly autobiographical in tone. In no other of his novels is there less distance between the author and his audience, for in the anguish of Tony Last's broken marriage the disillusionment of Waugh's first marriage is transmuted into art. Only in *Sword of Honour* is there an equivalent sense of betrayal and melancholy regret for the loss of traditional values.

Disarmingly simple, the narrative focuses on the outwardly stable marriage of Tony and Brenda Last, and its sudden collapse, brought on by Tony's naive but disastrous role-playing as a country squire. Moderately intelligent, Tony has never escaped from an adolescent preoccupation with a chivalrous medieval past, a preoccupation that is destructive, for it prevents him from assuming the difficult burden of true adulthood. Unable and unwilling to face the truth of Brenda's affair with the insipid John Beaver, he refuses to sell Hetton Abbey so that she can marry Beaver. However, rather than confront a dilemma largely of his own doing, he flees England and rushes to his fate in the jungles of South America, where he falls into the clutches of the mad trader Mr. Todd.

In working out the implications of a novel that might have been no more than sordid domestic tragedy in the hands of a less sure writer, Waugh plays off images of country-city-jungle in developing the complex ironies of the Tony-Brenda situation. Constantly shifting the action back and forth between the city and the country, and later the jungle, Waugh implies that both the pastoral life in the country and the glittering, sophisticated world of the city provide inadequate substitutes for a moral order lacking in the lives of the two principals. Then in the latter pages of the novel, Tony's descent into the pathless jungle is juxtaposed with Brenda's increasing isolation in a city as barbarous as the jungle.

With his customary terse understatement, Waugh begins with a brief description of the opportunistic Mrs. Beaver and her listless son, an idler who sits by the phone all day waiting for last-minute invitations to fill out dinner parties. Having suggested John Beaver's rootless existence, Waugh then describes Hetton Abbey, rebuilt in an overwhelmingly theatrical, medieval style, in 1864. The total effect of Hetton, from the cathedrallike gloom of its great hall to the bedrooms named after Yseult, Lancelot, Galahad, and Guinevere, is markedly Tennysonian.[32] But Hetton is not the real article. Like Llanaba Castle it is make-believe, and its rococo ornamentation is as incongruous as the abstract steel and concrete monstrosity at King's Thursday. Despite the intricate decorative effect, rot has set in: "In order to make an appearance of coffered wood, moulded slats had been nailed in a chequer across the plaster. . .damp had penetrated into one corner, leaving a large patch where the gilt had tarnished the colour flaked away. . ." (18). The anachronistic, fake quality of the house carries over into Tony Last's own existence. The books in Tony's library, including romantic Arthurian tales (*Bevis of Hampton*) and the sterile world of Hemingway's balked heroes (*A Farewell to Arms*) suggest a character who wavers between a yearning for the romanticism of the past and acceptance of the treacherous world in which he must learn to live.

True to the pattern of the medieval knight, Tony follows a monotonous ritual of ceremonious behavior: Sunday church, a visit with his tenants, and a glass of sherry. His church attendance has become an unthinking, meaningless rite. The gently senile vicar wanders on about his days in India; his irrelevancies about life in the East have little to do with the spiritual condition of his parishioners. This is especially true of his customary Christmas sermon, originally written for far-off garrison troops, with its references to "the ravening tiger and the exotic camel, the furtive jackal and the ponderous elephant" (70) which perfectly illustrate the decayed Anglicanism Tony continues to give his allegiance to.

When Tony shows the visiting and bored John Beaver around Hetton, Waugh's low-keyed, ironically romantic description emphasizes the pseudogothic quality of the estate: "Shafts of November sunshine streamed down from lancet and oriel, tinctured in green and gold. . ." (41). The ceremonial showing off of the house is totally deadening for Brenda, who yearns for the cosmopolitan life of the city where she is to maneuver Beaver into an affair with her. It is a sadly dull business that becomes even more horrible through Brenda's cold-blooded appraisal that Beaver is a snob not worth all the tired intrigue involved. But he is also close to the bright lights of London. Rather than play up the latent comedy of the myopic Restoration squire (Tony) and his restive country wife, Waugh continues to develop ironic contrasts in this contemporary King Arthur - Guinevere - Galahad triad. Brenda is a latter-day Guinevere who throws herself away for a worthless Galahad. Unable or unwilling to recognize his wife's adultery, Tony becomes increasingly miserable.

In the next stage of his demoralization, Brenda, Polly Cockpurse, and Mrs. Beaver come down to Hetton from London, Mrs. Beaver with the intent of redecorating the interior of Hetton with walls of white chromium, and thereby boldly assaulting all that Tony holds dear. To cap her increasingly callous betrayal, Brenda attempts to keep Tony occupied through the enticements of one of her friends, a richly comic figure named Jenny Abdul Akbar, whose seductive posturings fail to overcome Tony's reserve.

Events now move rapidly toward a climax in the hunt meet, eagerly looked forward to by Tony's son, John Last. Just before the meet, an American guest, Mrs. Rattery, mistress of Jock Grant-Menzies, arrives by plane; she is rich, denationalized, and a drug addict. Very self-possessed (like Angela Lyne) she momentarily distracts Tony with nursery games immediately after John is accidentally killed, kicked by a startled horse terrorized by a backfiring motorcycle. Appropriately for this novel, the modern, mechanized world has taken its toll. As in the macabre and quite fortuitous deaths of Little Lord Tangent, Agatha Runcible, and Prudence Courteney, a seemingly malignant fate has once again come into play.

At this climactic juncture, Mrs. Rattery's card-playing, with its manipulated, artificially contrived order, is set off against the near total disasters engulfing Tony's life. Recalling Madam Sosostris, the fortuneteller of *The Waste Land,* "Mrs. Rattery sat intent over her game, moving little groups of cards adroitly backwards and forwards about the table like shuttles across a loom; under her fingers order grew out of chaos; she established sequence and precedence; the symbols before her became coherent, inter-related" (127). But even this false sense of order is denied to Tony, for whom no order grows out of chaos. Unsustained by any genuine religious faith, other than his weekly church attendance, Tony is cut off from all his moorings in the death of John.

It does not seem likely that in 1934 Waugh specifically intended to direct our attention, as he does in *Brideshead Revisited*, to the need for firm religious convictions, but the implication is present in *A Handful of Dust*. Secular, fortunetelling efforts to control life were not enough for Waugh. Years later, he remarked in an article for *Life* that *A Handful of Dust* "contained all I had to say about humanism."[33] Jock finds Brenda at a fortuneteller's apartment and tells her that John is dead. At first she believes that it is John Beaver, and not her son, who has died. The scene is brief, yet significant in its several implications. The fortunetelling suggests a shaky reliance on the whims of fate parallel to Mrs. Rattery's card-playing a few pages earlier; Brenda's hesitation as to John's identity implies that both her husband and son have been betrayed; and finally, although Jock's curt, neutral response to her reaction indicates that he has recognized the depth of Brenda's betrayal, we learn at the end of the novel that he has married her. She returns to Hetton, but leaves before the funeral. Chapter 3 ends with the omniscient narrator's laconic remark that Tony ". . .had got into the habit of loving and trusting Brenda" (144).

In Chapter 4, "English Gothic II," the Brenda-Tony situation opens out to make room for Waugh's scathingly satiric attack on the hypocrisy of the English divorce system. Agreeing to a divorce, Tony must go to Brighton with a professional witness and be seen in bed with her so as to provide the evidence needed by the courts. Tony's lawyers solemnly brief him about the masquerade he must assume in order to win a divorce:

"Lately we had a particularly delicate case involving a man of very rigid morality and a certain diffidence. In the end his own wife consented to go with him and supply the evidence. She wore a red wig. It was quite successful." (148 - 49)

The imposture is heightened when Tony discovers that the woman has brought along her whining young daughter for a weekend at the seashore. But for Tony "no new mad thing brought to his notice could add a jot to the all-encompassing chaos that shrieked about his ears" (158). The final blow comes when Tony discovers that Brenda, in her demands for increased alimony, has willingly agreed to force Tony to sell Hetton. His disillusionment is now complete: "A whole Gothic world had come to grief. . . the cream and dappled unicorns had fled. . ." (173 - 74). On a technicality (the presence of the repulsive child during the Brighton weekend), Tony refuses a divorce to Brenda.

He takes refuge from these horrors by escaping to the jungles of South America in company with an archaeologist, Dr. Messinger, searching for a fabulous lost city, a place that soon becomes for Tony the city of his lost Gothic dream fantasy. Messinger's description of the legendary city becomes for Tony a tapestried vision of "vanes and pinnacles, gargoyles, battlements. . .pavilions and terraces, a transfigured Hetton, pennons and banners floating in the sweet breeze" (184).

Once underway in South America, the expedition soon passes from physical, irritating discomfort to nightmare, and Tony's journey becomes penance as well as quest. For a period of time the party wanders in a maze of rivers. All external signs are useless, for even "the chart began to have a mythical appearance" (207). Set against Tony's aimless wandering in the jungles of the Amazon are Brenda's equally futile activities among London salons, for, no longer supported by Tony's money, she must cope with an increasingly restive Beaver. From this point, and to the end of Chapter 5, Waugh cuts back and forth between the jungle and London. By means of this movie technique, Waugh makes his reader increasingly aware of the void in the lives of Brenda and Tony. Their marriage wrecked, neither one has any inner resources or religious faith to sustain them.

Approaching the land of the fabled Pie-wies, the superstitious Macushi guides refuse to go on. Fatuously trying to appeal to their childlike curiosity, Dr. Messinger dumps on the ground a bag of dime-store goodies containing celluloid combs, pocket knives, glass beads—all the gimcrack products of English civilization. When these objects fail to overcome the Indians' dread of the unknown he produces his ace, jingling mechanical mice. But the mice are too much for the simple Indians. Routed by these mechanical devils, they fade back into the jungle. Attempting to find help, Messinger leaves Tony, only to drown when his canoe overturns in rapids.

Racked with fever, Tony has a phantasmagoric dream of Brenda, Mrs. Rattery, the mechanical green rats, and Mrs. Beaver's chromium-plated walls. He gets up from his hammock, plunges on into the jungle, and finally staggers into a clearing. His idealized dream world lies before him as gates open, trumpets sound, and showers of almond and apple blossoms carpet "the way, as, after a summer storm, they lay in the orchards at Hetton. Gilded cupolas and spires of alabaster shone in the sunlight" (233 - 34). The destruction of Tony's ordered life, which has really had no true order from the start, has now reached bottom, for Tony has stumbled onto the ramshackle home of the demonic Mr. Todd. Unable to confront reality in his earlier, and more sane existence in England, Tony becomes a prisoner of his dream and of Mr. Todd.[34]

His clothes torn, and his body battered, Tony has lost almost all vestiges of humanity. Still delirious from fever, he lives in the wild lucidity of his fantasy world: "There is no City. Mrs. Beaver has. . .converted it into flats. . . . Very suitable for base love" (238). As Brenda, at an earlier period, had become slowly smothered in the isolation of Hetton Abbey, so Tony is now trapped, and infinitely more horribly, by the crazy Mr. Todd. At the request of the illiterate Todd, Tony begins to read aloud from a set of Dickens.

In the novel's climactic irony, Tony becomes drunk, possibly drugged, at a native celebration, and passes out just hours before an English search party arrives. Todd shows the party the spot where Tony is presumably buried and gives them Tony's watch as proof of his death. Literally and symbolically, time stops for Tony. With firmly controlled irony Waugh has Todd speak Tony's epitaph:

I do not suppose they will visit us again, our life here is so retired. . .no pleasures except reading. . . . Your head aches, does it not?. . . We will not have any Dickens today. . .but tomorrow, and the day after that, and the day after that. Let us read *Little Dorrit* again. There are passages in that book I can never hear without the temptation to weep. (249)

This shocking conclusion must rank as the most ghoulish touch in all of Waugh's fiction, and in its absolute finality it is the most terrible fate to be endured by any of Waugh's hapless antiheroes. Chapter 7, "English Gothic III," provides the epigraph for this most sparely written of all of Waugh's novels. Hetton Abbey has now been given over to fox-farming by an impoverished branch of the Last family, wistfully hoping to restore Hetton to its former glory. In the description of the foxes, and especially of "the vixen who had had her brush bitten off" yet "seemed little worse for the accident" (254), there is a parting thrust at Brenda's devious vixenlike behavior, behavior suggested by the note of animality on which the novel concludes.

For the revised edition of *A Handful of Dust*, Waugh appended an alternative ending, originally written for the proposed American serialization. It introduces a jarring note, for it is difficult to conceive of a conclusion in which Tony is rescued, comes back to England and Brenda, and then unbeknownst to Brenda, rents her flat in London, presumably to install a mistress. Such an ending would have left the reader totally unprepared for the sudden shift in Tony's behavior.

Brenda may represent the Guinevere-like betrayer, tainted by the code of this world, but she also partially enlists our sympathies, for Tony's taciturn reserve isolates her from her husband. She is not as hard-boiled as Margot Metroland, nor as worldly-wise as Angela Lyne, but is a woman alienated from a husband who lives in a world of make-believe. What is more difficult to accept is her rapidly increasing bitchiness after leaving Tony, for Waugh provides no clues to account for this in the early scenes of the book. She shares some degree of the amorality of other heroines of the same era, notably Huxley's Myra Viveash, or Ford Madox Ford's Sylvia Tietjens, but perhaps most closely resembles Daisy Buchanan of Fitzgerald's *The Great Gatsby* in her dual attractiveness and destructiveness.

We become drawn into the lives of Tony and Brenda because they have some complexity and are not stock figures of satire in this novel in which, as Peter Quennell acutely observed, "tragedy and comedy are interdependent"[35] and the plight of the hero becomes more than a target for satiric derision. Only occasionally, as in the wild parody of British divorce proceedings, is our attention diverted from Tony and Brenda to the broader institutional targets of satire, for in *A Handful of Dust* satire is subordinated to character, to the pathos of a central figure who assumes at least a degree of human dimension in his virtues and weaknesses. While one might agree Rose Macaulay is justified in stating that *A Handful of Dust* is "a social novel about adultery, treachery, betrayal," from which most of the gaiety and wit of the early novels has disappeared, the work is far more than "the meaningless jigging of barbarous nit-wits" she would imply.[36] In the novels that preceded *A Handful of Dust* liaisons are formed, dissolved, reformed, without wrenching personal dislocations (if we except the stagy shock effect of Prudence

Courteney's abrupt end), but Waugh in *A Handful of Dust* adroitly leads us to identify with Tony Last's increasing misery and isolation.

Paul Pennyfeather and Adam Symes do not suffer, no matter what indignities are inflicted upon them, but Waugh does not allow us this detachment in our response to the overbalance of suffering Tony Last must endure.

Although Waugh may have intended to delineate a character who has never grown up and whose value system fatally lacks a supportive religious faith, Tony is more sinned again than sinning. He has much in common with the antiheroes of Hemingway's fiction, with Jake Barnes and Frederick Henry, for like them he simply cannot accommodate his own outmoded code to the more flexible moral code of the society in which he lives.

Described by Waugh as "a betrayed romantic" (preface to the 1964 edition, 7), Tony remains a pathetic, near tragic character. Counter to the view that he is simply a case of arrested adolescence, the gaucheries of Tony are not to be weighed in the balance with his old fashioned adherence to honor, especially when his concept of honor has been betrayed so close to home in Brenda's actions. In his unquestioned and unthinking trust of others, Tony approaches the dimensions of tragedy. But the traditional norms of tragedy do not apply, for there is no final insight, no catharsis, no purgation. The central figures of Waugh's earlier fiction survive, either by sheer luck (Paul Pennyfeather), or by a shrewd eye to the main chance (Basil Seal). There is no easy out for Tony. He is his own fate in this relentless, severely economical novel, possibly Waugh's masterpiece.

Everything has gone down to ruin in a world that lacks love, charity and kindness, and is largely peopled with the barbarous newly rich ("Eliot's Sweeney with money," an undergraduate perceptively observed). As in *Black Mischief,* there is little to choose between the corruption of London society and the primitiveness of the jungle.

V   Scoop

Distinct from the savagery just under the surface in *Black Mischief, Scoop's* (1938) genial picture of the machinations of English, American, and European war correspondents caught up in a comic opera rebellion in the African kingdom of Ishmaelia is farcical rather than satirical. Based on Waugh's stint as Special Correspondent in Abyssinia in 1935, and drawing, in part, on his despatches to the *Daily Mail* and on *Waugh in Abyssinia,* the work lightly satirizes the glamourous 1930s trade of foreign correspondent, and to a lesser degree than in *Black Mischief* reveals a people ill equipped to cope with the dubious blessings of European civilization.

To set his train of misadventures in motion, Waugh begins in London, with the fashionable young novelist John Boot paying homage to Mrs. Stitch, wife of a high government official. This is the first of several appearances of Mrs. Stitch, an elegant and witty manipulator of men's lives. In *Scoop,* she is a charmer out of a drawing-room comedy; later, in *Sword of Honour* she protects the tarnished honor of the Establishment by betraying Guy Crouchback's confidences to her.

At the beginning of Chapter 2, Waugh introduces us to the Boot clan, including the decaying Edwardian Uncle Theodore, and Nanny Bloggs, for whom "the Bible and the Turf Guide were her only reading" (28), a reminder of the simple world of the nursery, so often repeated in Waugh's fiction. Through the arbitrary working of a capricious fate, it is William Boot, weekly contributor of a nature column for the *Daily Beast,* who is mistaken for John Boot and is inexplicably called up to London to be assigned as special correspondent to Ishmaelia. Unquestioningly accepting Lord Copper's orders peremptorily sending him off to Ishmaelia, William departs by special plane, but not before he is joined at the last minute by a bundled-up mystery figure later to play a pivotal role at the novel's climax.

Waugh's description of the first European contact with Ishmaelia in the nineteenth century recalls Captain Gulliver's account of his travels, and also implies the caustic tone of *Black Mischief*: "They came as missionaries, ambassadors, tradesmen, prospectors, natural scientists. None returned. They were eaten, every one of them; some raw, others stewed and seasoned—according to local usage and the calendar (for the better sort of Ismaelites have been Christians for many centuries and will not publicly eat human flesh, uncooked, in Lent, without special and costly dispensation from their bishop" (91). As in *Black Mischief,* if Waugh describes an African culture in which barbarism is thinly concealed, he also mocks with greater derision those Europeans, sublimely ignorant of Africa and equipped with "cuckoo clocks, phonographs, opera hats, draft treaties" (91), who supposedly represented the highest achievements of nearly nineteen hundred years of European civilization.

The true reality of Ismaelian politics turns upon the slightest of palace intrigue between members of the White Shirt faction and the ruling Jackson family, but elsewhere political theorists misread the palace revolt: "In Moscow, Harlem, Bloomsbury and Liberia, however, keener passions were aroused. In a hundred progressive weeklies and Left Sunday Circles the matter was taken up and the cause of the Jacksons restated in ideological form" (95). In such an artfully casual dismissal of leftist politics as this may be found one of the sources of the scathing attacks on Waugh by hostile critics in the 1930s and the 1940s.

Boot becomes caught up in the frenzied news-seeking activities of the foreign journalists, most of them American; they are given names that might have been coined by Charles Dickens: Corker, Pigge, Whelp, Shumble, Pappenhacker, and best of all, Wenlock Jakes, whose last name derives from a long scatological tradition in English literature. In his sly but unsuccessful efforts to land a scoop and his obsession for ugly mass-produced native souvenirs, Corker suggests Hooper in *Brideshead Revisited,* or Trimmer in *Sword of Honour,* those upstart schemers, both amusing and irritating, whom Waugh presents as the plebeian counterparts of his more aristocratic boobs.

With no visible revolt to be witnessed, and confined to Jacksonburg, the correspondents simply improvise on the spot. Wenlock Jakes questions Paleologue, his paid spy, about the arrival of the latest train:

"Who was on the train?"
"No one except the newspaper gentlemen and M. Giraud."
"Who's he?"
"He is in the Railway. He went down to the coast with his wife last week, to see her off to Europe."
"Yes, yes, I remember. That was the 'panic-stricken refugees' story. . . ." (104)

But later on, when William Boot chances upon the intrigues of a genuine Soviet agent, quite properly named Smerdyakov, a la Dostoyevsky, Corker tells him that Russian spies are no longer newsworthy.

William falls into the clutches of a wandering Madame Bovary named Katchen, goes on a picnic with her, and promptly falls in love for the first time in his life. Celibate and now far from his more manageable pastoral life in England, this naif is over his head, "submerged among deep waters, below wind and tide, where huge trees raised their spongy flowers . . . a lush place" (147).

Throughout this innocent dalliance, William is prodded by telegrams from the *Daily Beast*, ending with the stern message: LORD COPPER PERSONALLY REQUIRES VICTORIES (161).[37] When Katchen tips him off that the Communist faction, under the leadership of the demagogic Dr. Benito, has engineered a coup d'etat, William scoops all the other journalists. Katchen's lover, a German prospector, appears from the hinterlands, where he has been prospecting for gold, and escapes from the country with her. Lonely, William longs to return to the untroubled safety of the English countryside, and wonders, " 'Was there not even in the remorseless dooms of antiquity a god from the machine?' " (190). As he dimly broods, the deus ex machina suddenly materializes in the form of a parachutist, none other than the mystery man of the earlier pages, who asks that he be called "Mr. Baldwin."

For enigmatic reasons of his own, Mr. Baldwin begins to set the counterrevolution in motion. In his regard for the propagandistic force of language, he resembles George Bernard Shaw's sly munitions maker, Andrew Undershaft (*Major Barbara*). With exact concern, he coaches William as to the phrasing of a properly ambiguous telegram to be sent to the *Daily Beast*: " '*Might must find a way.* Not "Force" remember; other nations use "force"; we Britons alone use "Might" ' " (196).

Mr. Baldwin quickly capitalizes on the unrest in the city, whose name has been changed from Jacksonburg to Marxville. When an ordinarily mild-mannered Swedish missionary rides his motorcycle into Popotakis's Ping Pong Parlor in a drunken rage, Mr. Baldwin eggs him on to attack the Jackson's palace, now occupied by the Young Ishmaelites. As Mr. Olafsen runs amok ". . .the sequence unfolded itself with the happy inconsequence of an early comedy film" (201), concluding with the rout of Dr. Benito, who dives off the balcony from which he has been haranguing the Ishmaelites. But behind this Chalinesque scene Waugh denies any reasoned historical cause-effect; rather, he suggests that the overthrow of governments, at least in the unstable mid-twentieth century, is a matter of blundering, irrational fate, perhaps given a twist by the likes of Mr. Baldwin, and that beneath surface order, chaos always lurks. With the climactic action finished, Waugh briskly moves to the denouement via a series of mistaken identities, similar to those at the beginning of the novel.

Lord Copper (probably a composite of the overbearing newspaper tycoons Lord Beaverbrook and Lord Northcliffe) requests a knighthood for William, but it is given to the wrong Boot, John Boot, the novelist. Deputized to wrest William Boot out of the fastness of Boot Magna to be feted by Lord Copper, Mr. Salter, Copper's bilious subordinate, is set upon by farm dogs and receives the ultimate blow when his overnight bag becomes buried under a load of slag. The countryside has taken its drastic revenge in this reversal of the country mouse - city mouse fable. As the crowning touch, William refuses to appear for the banquet in his honor. With his job in peril unless he produce William Boot for Lord Copper's dinner, Mr. Salter's fortunes are saved when Uncle Theodore unexpectedly shows up at the newspaper office, exuding "Edwardian light and warmth in that dingy room" (246). The impasse is resolved: Uncle Theodore will be passed off as William Boot.

For once, Lord Copper dimly recognizes a gaffe has been committed, but at the banquet he resolutely covers up, and blandly ignores Uncle Theodore, who briskly converses with one of the guests, Bertie Wodehouse-Bonner. The latter's name provides a clue to the benign influence lurking in the background of this farcical and intricately complex novel: P. G. Wodehouse.

Victory his, William can now return to the writing of his weekly nature column, with its equally lush prose, "maternal rodents pilot their furry brood through the stubble. . ." (254). As was true of Paul Pennyfeather, William ends where he set out, unchanging and unchanged. Of him, Malcolm Bradbury remarks that "William. . . has preserved his standard of judgment, the standard of Nannie Bloggs. He is the most successful, least suffering of all Waugh's heroes: but he has lost his love and the 'new world' that went with it, and his victory is a small one."[38]

The novel contains several recurring motifs of Waugh's early work: the ingenuous central character mildly bemused, mildly irritated by the misadventures that befall him, who emerges serenely triumphant at novel's end; the shadowy minor character who appears, disappears, reappears, and whose true identity is never fully revealed—in this instance, Mr. Baldwin, the international financier, "possessor of the largest octopus in captivity" (69); the casual and contradictory operation of fate in which the wrong Boot is sent as correspondent to cover the revolt in Ishmaelia; the pervasive influence of *Alice in Wonderland* to be noted in the frequently repeated tag phrase of Mr. Salter, " 'O dear, oh dear, you're late Boot' " (49), and the anarchic semantic confusion, especially in the scene at the newspaper office when Salter explains to William Boot the intricacies of Ishmaelian politics, reminiscent of the logic-chopping trial in Carroll's work: ". . .The fascists won't be called black because of their racial pride, so they are called White after the White Russians. And the Bolshevists *want* to be called black because of their racial pride. So when you *say* black you mean red, and when you mean *red* you say white and when the party who call themselves black say traitors they mean what *we* call blacks, but what *we* mean when we say traitors I really couldn't tell you" (54 - 55).

Often dismissed by critics as not top-drawer Waugh because it lacks the fiercely acerbic observations and the glittering eye of the madman of the other novels, *Scoop* contains a wealth of farcical situations contrasting the frequent discrepancies between appearance and reality in the twilight world of newspaper reporting, and particularly so in the characterization of Lord Copper, whose newspaper, the *Daily Beast,* stands for " 'strong mutually antagonistic governments everywhere' " (23).

Although there are many situations in the plot that provided Waugh with the opportunity to exercise his gift for the macabre, he foreswears this completely. Sudden, grotesque death, the fate of many of his characters, is totally missing. It is a relaxed book, reflective of his contented frame of mind in 1937, the year of his second marriage.

Throughout *Scoop* the quietly persistent thought recurs that in William Boot's picking up the thread of his life where he had left off that the intrusive blaring of the "real" world is not real at all. In this escapist, Wodehouse-style novel, Waugh quixotically suggests that if one is sturdy enough to deny the presence of the urban world that perhaps it will go away and not trouble those few civilized beings left to their own devices in their rural retreats.

VI   Put Out More Flags

Put Out More Flags, published in 1942 and dedicated to Randolph Churchill, examines the shadowy unreality of the early months of World War II—the world of grandiose strategy, bureaucrats, and evacuees from London. A diverting mixture of far-cical lampooning of bureaucratic types who thrived before the fall of France and of pathos in those lives irrevocably altered or even destroyed by the war, *Put Out More Flags* may be read as prologue to the war trilogy, *Sword of Honour*.

Waugh introduces several characters from his preceding novels. The raffish hero, Basil Seal, described as "a kind of dilapidated Bull Dog Drummond" (37) and now in his mid-thirties (virtually the same age as Waugh), steps directly out of *Black Mischief*. Among other tattered holdovers from the more light-hearted, partygoing 1920s era are Alastair Trumpington, Peter Pastmaster, Margot Metroland, and Angela Lyne. They are, as Waugh notes in the preface to the 1942 edition, "a race of ghosts, the survivors of the world we both knew ten years ago . . . where my imagination still fondly lingers" (7). One by one, the lingering remnants of the Bright Young Things go off to war. So Alastair Trumpington signs up for army service but refuses a commission, perhaps, as Sonia Trumpington remarks to Basil " 'as a kind of penance' " (113) for having had too much fun in the 1920s.[39]

In the opening pages, Waugh emphasizes the narcissistic relationship between Basil and his sister, Barbara Sothill: "They had played pirates together in the nursery and the game was over. Basil played pirates alone. She apostatized from her faith in him almost with formality, and yet. . .there was still in her that early piety" (17). With the onset of the war, that "early piety" reasserts itself. At the moment her newly enlisted but stodgy husband makes love to her, Barbara envisions Basil as a romantic combination of Rupert Brooke and T. E. Lawrence. Miles away in London, Lady Seal, calmly awaiting an air raid, muses on the names of Crécy, Agincourt, Cadiz, and Blenheim, as if the ritual naming of these great victories of the past would somehow magically banish the harsh reality of the German bombers.

We next meet Agnela Lyne, Basil's mistress. Impeccably dressed, aloof, separated from her dilettante husband, and dependent upon Basil's unsteady affection: "She watched herself moving in the mirrors of the civilized world as a prisoner will watch the antics of a rat" (29). Absorbed in the contemplation of death, she first thinks of Basil as one of the Greeks nobly dying in the pass at Thermopylae, then considers the prospect of his dying as giving her release from an intolerable situation. But like the public face of Evelyn Waugh, all remains hidden beneath "a calm and pensive mask" (32).

Waugh quickly sketches in the arty crowd Basil hobnobs with, notably Ambrose Silk, an archaism out of Beardsley or Wilde, an aesthete unswervingly dedicated to an unfashionable ivory-tower integrity in the service of art. Looked upon by his peers as a survivor from the days of the *Yellow Book*, Ambrose articulates Waugh's attitudes toward art. Essentially the outsider, Ambrose draws a melancholy contrast between past and present, from "these coarse and tedious youngsters. . ." (47) with their interminable arguments about aesthetics and the politics of the writers Parsnip and Pimpernell (translated: Auden and Isherwood, about whom Waugh was often derisive) to the more exuberant days of Diaghilev, Cocteau, and Gertrude Stein.

At the opposite pole from Basil, Ambrose nevertheless recognizes in him that idiosyncratic individual who will have no place in a future workers' state. Further, traditional views of Heaven and Hell do not satisfy Ambrose, for his ideal heaven would be a Limbo, containing wine and conversation. He resignedly asks himself, " 'Am I baptised into this modern world?' " (64). Just as Basil's amoral rapacity has every right to succeed in a world ripe for the taking, so Ambrose, possessed of the dispassionate creative integrity of the artist, has no place in this system of shifting values, and finally becomes the pathetic victim of Basil's scheme to implicate supposed fascist sympathizers, a scheme crassly designed to advance his pointless military career.

Waugh pillories the utterly futile blossoming of bureaucracy that marked the early months of the conflict. Lunatic inventors carrying bombs in suitcases are shunted around from office to office until the bombs inevitably go off; Alastair Trumpington's platoon commander attends a lengthy Court of Enquiry investigating the theft of a swill tub; Ambrose Silk gets a job with the religious department of the Ministry of Information as representative of Atheism. He shares his quarters with "a fanatical young Roman Catholic layman," a Nonconformist minister, and an Anglican clergyman. The last three spend most of their time in pointless argument, while Ambrose counts up "the number of times the word 'God' appeared in Hitler's speeches" (116 - 17).

Refused enlistment because of his failure to butter up a pompous lieutenant-colonel, Basil gravitates back to the home counties, where he supervises resettling London slum children. He takes in tow the three Connollies, excessively repulsive in appearance, "one leering, one lowering, and one drooling" (86), forces them onto a succession of reluctant households, and then retrieves them by blackmail. In describing some of these homes and their inhabitants, Waugh satirizes pretentious urban primitives who fancy going "rural." Typical are the Harknesses, whose hand-woven rugs, prints, and hearth fire of billowing peat smoke imply a fraudulent antiquity, the English equivalent of a *Better Homes and Gardens* layout. Responding to Mrs. Harkness's newspaper ad for boarders of a cultivated turn of mind, Basil readies his symbolic hand grenade (the Connolly children): "Count seven slowly, then throw" (101). The Connollies are successfully passed off from one home to another until Basil meets his match in the equally cunning Mr. Todhunter, who threatens to expose Basil.

His talent for fraud temporarily used up, Basil drifts back to London and is casually launched on a career of counter-espionage, which reaches its apotheosis in the implication of Ambrose Silk as a dangerous Fascist. Ambrose innocently begins to weave his downfall when he tells Basil "to the Chinese scholar the military hero was the lowest of human types" (186) (the remark refers back to the extended quote from Lin Yutang's *The Importance of Living* cited immediately before Chapter 1). Given the incongruous opportunity to publish a government-sponsored "little magazine," the *Ivory Tower*, Ambrose prepares a lead article describing his friendship for a German, Hans, a friendship that fell victim to anti-Semitism "in a world where only the mob and the hunting pack had the right to love" (198). Basil cunningly persuades Ambrose to edit certain passages, and having done so, sees to it that Scotland Yard is alerted to the presence of a Nazi sympathizer! Suffering a mild twinge of conscience, and reluctant to let the full weight of authority fall on Ambrose, Basil, like Mr. Baldwin in *Scoop*, functions as the deus ex machina, arrives ahead of the police, provides Ambrose with a priest's vestments (including the lightly ironic touch of a racing form), and spirits him off to exile in Ireland. Set down amongst an alien people whom history had seemingly passed by, Ambrose thinks of the artists it had spawned, Swift, Burke, Sheridan, T. E. Lawrence, and of the Irish in general, those lucky escapist islanders, "who have seen the gold lace and the candlelight and left the banquet before dawn revealed stained table linen and a tipsy buffoon" (231). Like Tony Last, Ambrose is trapped in a dream world.

Angela and Cedric Lyne's deteriorating marriage situation is nearly as important as Silk's helpless plight. Obsessed with images of death, and deserted by Basil, Angela holes up in her apartment, her jaw stiffened like the face of a corpse. When Basil temporarily returns to her she has "an abstracted little smile; the inwardly happy smile of a tired old nun—almost" (196). Nor is the life of her estranged husband any happier. Assigned to overseas duty, Cedric Lyne takes leave of his estate's grottoes and caves—all artificial and bought with Angela's money, yet no more artificial than the pretense of marriage he keeps up at a distance with Angela. The real cave of his battalion headquarters in France takes the place of his artificially created stalactites, but the reality of the war seems just as insubstantial; sent to warn of a threatened Nazi enveloping action, Lyne walks out alone onto the hillside,

exhilarated with the sense of being one man, one pair of legs, one pair of eyes, one brain, sent on a single, intelligible task; one man alone could go freely anywhere on the earth's surface; multiply him, put him in a drove and by each addition of his fellows you subtract something that is of value, make him so much less a man; this was the crazy mathematics of war. . . . He did not know it but he was thinking exactly what Ambrose had thought when he announced that culture must cease to be conventual and become cenobitic." (220)

Like Hemingway's Francis Macomber, he has suddenly experienced, for the first time, a near physical sense of wholeness and of his own worth; but in less melodramatic circumstances than those surrounding the death of Macomber, he meets his fate alone "in a crazy world where he was an interloper" (222), and is killed wandering across the field of battle, in a death as useless as that of Brigadier Ritchie-Hook in *Sword of Honour*.

Not the community of the convent, but the singular, lonely existence of the cenobite in the desert is what Waugh himself appeared to be turning to as he commenced to grow older. Waugh's exaltation of the lonely, singular individual was diametrically opposed to all official propaganda about "the Common Man" and would be stated with increased force in his post - World War II fiction.

The novel concludes with none of the characters truly aware of the horrors of war lying ahead. Lured by the childlike masquerade of the rope ladders and special knives of the commandos, Alastair Trumpington leaves his pregnant wife. For Alastair and Basil, the war becomes a clubby affair, summed up by Peter Pastmaster: " 'Most of war seems to consist of hanging about. . . . Let's at least hang about with our own friends' " (233). From the billeting of the repulsive Connollies to the glamour of the commandos, the tone remains the same—an immense throwback to the games of childhood. *Put Out More Flags* is, then, a properly fitting, ironic forerunner to the increasingly disillusioned world of *Sword of Honour*.

The breakup of an older value system in a chaotic world which has never escaped the simplistic claims of the nursery and in which madness rides triumphant dominates the action of *Put Out More Flags* just as in the earlier work, but in the earlier fiction the wildly inventive, demonic farce, inextricably mingled with satiric jabs at one target after another, did not (with the exception of *A Handful of Dust*) attempt any complexity of characterization. The satiric cutting edge is maintained in *Put Out More Flags*, especially in Basil Seal's buccaneering among the suburban intelligentsia and in the exquisitely inaccurate prognostications of Sir Joseph Mainwaring that the Nazis would shortly sue for peace. On one level simply another of Waugh's Establishment boobies ineffectually meddling in high government circles, Mainwaring blindly holds to a witless belief in a British mystique of superiority that would cause the Nazi threat to evaporate. The attitudes he clings to, including the reworking of the Dunkirk debacle into victory, also may be read as Waugh's criticism of a blind complacency among civilians and politicians more willing to listen to propaganda, however spurious, than to recognize that they were involved in a desperate struggle for survival.

In the cuckolded, anachronistic Cedric Lyne, and in Ambrose Silk, whose angle of vision points up the inanities of the "phony war" (as commentators later designated the early months of World War II), Waugh moves beyond sketching one-dimensional satiric types to draw characters who are flawed human beings, half makers, half victims, of their fate. The quietly futile life of Cedric Lyne is the prototype of Waugh's more complex, extended characterization of Guy Crouchback in *Sword of Honour*. Ambrose Silk becomes metamorphosed into Anthony Blanche, the waspish commentator on the Marchmain family in *Brideshead Revisited*, but reverts to a satiric type in the latter novel.

At times, Ambrose's dual function as clown and commentator threatens to usurp Basil's role. The incongruously comic scene describing the transformation of Ambrose, a Jewish intellectual, into a disguised priest is certainly the climactic point of the novel, and may even be a send-up of the 1930s vogue for spy movies and novels of international intrigue, but also suggests the episodic quality of *Put Out More Flags*. Waugh was not entirely successful in sub-ordinating the activities of his minor characters so as to focus on Basil's joust with muddle-headed authority. However, in common with the flamboyant Ambrose, Basil remains "an obstreperous minority of one in a world of otiose civilians" (53).

There are many vignettes of minor characters, complete with en-trances and exits, which help illustrate the confusion of national purpose during the months when England was sliding into full-scale conflict, but this material is only loosely related. Waugh obliquely acknowledged he had written a novel lightly stitched together in the preface written for the 1967 edition of *Put Out More Flags*. He wrote that he followed his characters "with no pre-conceived plan, not knowing where I should find them from one page to the next" (7). He also commented that he wrote the book for fun while en route back to England on a troopship in 1941. Late in the novel, an unjustly imprisoned publisher named Rampole discovers the pleasures of reading the works of a lady novelist who regularly published a novel a year. It is quite likely that Waugh had Angela Thirkell in mind for there is the same spirit of fun in *Put Out More Flags* that one finds in novels such as *The Brandons* and similar potshots at the sacred cows of modern art, politics, the Establish-ment, and the military.

The work received good reviews, especially in the United States, but some critics insisted on reading it simply as an extension of the early novels. The *New York Times* reviewer clearly implied that Waugh ought to have taken a more serious attitude toward his sub-ject matter: "It is the mixture as before, Mr. Waugh's Second World War. It is very smart and snobbish. . .a book of characters, not a book of character."[40] Like so many other reviewers of Waugh's fiction, the *New York Times* critic refused to take the book on its own terms and seemed to imply that Waugh ought to have written a novel more appropriate to the taste of the critic. The review in *Time* contained the most judicious appraisal, for it pointed out the balance of farce and underlying seriousness, and recognized the novel as an important fictional document of Britain in crisis.[41]

Because of its increasing emphasis on character development, *Put Out More Flags* suggests that Waugh's fiction was heading in a new direction. Further evidence for this may be noted in the incomplete *Work Suspended*, published as a fragment in 1942, and later republished in 1949 in a collection of Waugh's short stories (*Mr.

Loveday's Little Outing). In the chapters that Waugh completed, he introduces a narrator-observer-author, the detective writer John Plant who both lives in, and is isolated from, society. Plant's rootless life is contrasted with the more rooted existence of Lucy Simonds, expecting a baby, and her husband, Roger, an old college friend of Plant's. What Waugh would have made of the increasing bond of affection between John and Lucy, as the latter helps him search for a permanent home in the country, is conjecture. Perhaps, for once in his career, he had reached an impasse and could go no further. But the fragment is valuable for its expression of the life of the artist and for its introduction of an eccentric character named Mr. Thornton, alias Mr. Long, alias Mr. Norton, but in reality plain Arthur Atwater, destined for failure, who "looked as though he had come to sell some hopelessly unsuitable commodity and had already despaired of success" (51), who recalls Philbrick of *Decline and Fall* and is a preliminary sketch for the many faces of Apthorpe in *Officers and Gentlemen.* Despite the tantalizing possibilities of *Work Suspended,* Waugh's readers had to wait until 1945, and the publication of *Brideshead Revisited,* to learn whether his fiction would remain satiric in form, with satire's emphasis on character types, or would move toward full-scale character development.

CHAPTER 3

The Catholic Novels

". . .a twitch on the thread"
G.K. Chesterton

WRITING in Life magazine in April 1946 in response to letters from admirers of *Brideshead Revisited*, Waugh flatly asserted that "in my future books there will be two things to make them unpopular: a preoccupation with style and the attempt to represent man more fully, which to me means only one thing, man in his relation to God."[1] The statement was unintentionally misleading, for Waugh had always been concerned with style, and *Brideshead Revisited* was not his first effort to consider "man in his relation to God," even though it was his most overt, extended treatment of the subject. In the early novels, the loss of moral values also implied the absence of a religious belief that might have provided an element of stability in the unstable lives of Waugh's characters. Again and again he scores off a Protestant ethos that is both inadequate and meaningless. Prendergast, the diffident Modern Churchman of *Decline and Fall*, has agonizing doubts as to why God had made the world, and when he becomes the prison chaplain of Blackstone Jail, the grisly facts of his death are interspersed between the lines of a hymn being sung in the chapel. Mrs. Ape (*Vile Bodies*) makes a rousing commercial success of her brand of evangelism. Tony Last (*A Handful of Dust*) goes through the motions of attending weekly Anglican services, but his ritualistic churchgoing fails him at his time of crisis. On occasion, Waugh can even introduce a lightly mocking touch: Father Rothschild (*Vile Bodies*) is a broad parody on Jesuitical intrigue (Waugh had not yet turned Catholic); Mrs. Ape is fun, if deplorably crass; Ambrose Silk (*Put Out More Flags*) has his racing form; and the Catholic layman in the Ministry of Information (*Put Out More Flags*) is a cantankerous intellectual. However, in none of these works is there any direct indication of Waugh's Catholicism, or suggestion that he was soon to write a carefully developed apologia for Catholic dogma.

I   Brideshead Revisited

Waugh wrote *Brideshead Revisited* in the winter and spring of 1944 while on leave from army service. Written under conditions of severe wartime austerity, its luxuriant prose and nostalgic recollections of the past were a form of escape for him. In the preface to the revised edition he acknowledges that *Brideshead Revisited* was "infused with a kind of gluttony, for food and wine, for the splendours of the recent past, and for rhetorical and ornamental language." He also defended the work's major concern: "Its theme—the operation of divine grace on a group of diverse but closely connected characters—was perhaps presumptuously large, but I make no apology for it" (9).

The novel's subtitle, *The Sacred and Profane Memories of Captain Charles Ryder*, also names the opposed qualities that shape, in a slow but progressively defined form, the statement of theme. While the sacred eventually sweeps all before it, in the beginning it is mute, for the profane, epitomized in the pastoral Oxford scenes and the early scenes at Brideshead, is dominant. The intertwined operation of these opposed elements is gradually worked out through the complex relationships that bind Sebastian Flyte,[2] his sister Julia, his mother and father, and the agnostic observer-participant, Charles Ryder.

Waugh probably did not intend any easy symbolism in the name he chose for his aristocratic, ages-old recusant family, but *Brideshead Revisited* is, nevertheless, filled with images of escape, of literal flight. In a despairing effort to escape the demanding bonds of both family and religion, Sebastian successively takes refuge in alcoholism and in running away to North Africa, where he finds sanctuary in a monastery. Julia, in unconscious rebellion against the dictates of her faith, takes flight in marriage to the amoral and power-hungry Rex Mottram, an aspiring politician of the Chamberlain years. The mother, a less charming Julia Stitch, drives her husband into adultery, apostasy, and exile in Venice. Through these varied yet closely related situations, the novel traces the slow, convoluted journey, the "twitch of the thread," from rebellion to a slow, sometimes painful reaffirmation of belief.

To give the novel a sense of Proustian distance,[3] Waugh encloses the action within the frame of Charles Ryder's wartime experiences at training camp, beginning with a slowly unfolding prologue describing Ryder's immersion in the purgatorylike life of an encamped army bogged down in monotonous routine. He imagines archaeologists digging into the rubble of the camp and discovering a culturally advanced people "capable of an elaborate draining system. . .over-run by a race of the lowest type" (15), symbolized by the uncouth lower-middle-class Lt. Hooper, Ryder's subordinate, the epitome of the mid-twentieth-century "common man." Shiftless, living only for the moment, he has no sense of continuity with past British history.

When ordered to a new encampment, Ryder discovers that it is Brideshead, a place of memories for him, "couched among the lime trees like the hind in the bracken" (25), as if in a medieval tapestry. This stylized, but quite romantic longing for a departed, Arthurian past (he also thinks of Oxford as "irrecoverable as Lyonness" (29)), contrasts with the drabness of a quite unchivalrous modern army, filled with Lt. Hoopers.

Book One of *Brideshead Revisited*, "Et in Arcadia Ego," is, in part, a pastoral reminiscence. Young Ryder, searching for love, perhaps in an "enclosed and enchanted garden" (39 - 40) beyond his reach,[4] accepts Sebastian's invitation to lunch at his rooms. The aesthetes gather, and Anthony Blanche recites passages from *The Waste Land* through a megaphone to students passing by on the road below.

Sebastian drives to Brideshead with Ryder. They stop to picnic on strawberries and wine "on a sheep-cropped knoll" (32), a truly Arcadian, pastoral setting. Although a homosexual idyll may be suggested by the passage, of greater significance is Sebastian's wish to escape to an idealized, timeless world. For him, the sunny knoll is a place "to bury a crock of gold" so that he can some day come back and "dig it up and remember" (32).

At Brideshead, the most imposing of Waugh's country houses, images of the nursery world, a familiar motif in Waugh's fiction, reappear in Nanny Hawkins, who has preserved beyond middle age an innocently limited experience of life. It is a closed world to the outsider, rendered even more complex to the nonbelieving Ryder by the family's Catholicism.

There follows, in Chapter 3, a battle of wits between Ryder, home on vacation, and his widowed father. A crotchety eccentric, who combines the civilized ferocity of Mr. Todd with some of the irritability of Arthur Waugh, the father tries to get his son out of the house so that he can return to the quiet of his figurines and the book propped in front of him at every meal. The dialectics of misunderstanding are highly entertaining and rather like the comedy of cross-purposes at the track meet in *Decline and Fall*, but also reveal the total absence of love in Ryder's life.

Ryder returns to Brideshead to be with Sebastian, who is recovering from a cracked ankle-bone. In mannered, deliberately overwritten prose, Waugh describes in full the terraces, lakes, and baroque fountains of the estate. The Arcadian organ-tones continue to be sounded in Sebastian's revery: "If it could only be like this always—always summer, always alone, the fruit always ripe and Aloysius [Sebastian's teddy-bear] in a good temper" (91). Amidst this idyll, rounded off with the daily rite of wine tasting, Sebastian's chance remarks about religion seem whimsical to Ryder, like the affectation of the teddy bear, but his still limited understanding of the Marchmains is jolted when Sebastian suddenly blurts out, ". . .It's very difficult being a Catholic" (98). Sebastian finally learns that temporal happiness bears small relationship to the tenacious demands of his belief. Except for this passing, but foreshadowing remark, the family's Catholicism remains enigmatic. Sebastian's older brother, Bridey, an unimaginative, stolidly dogmatic individual, is balanced off by the younger sister, Cordelia, refreshingly untroubled by dogma, who has a pig named Francis Xavier!

Waugh shifts the scene from Brideshead to Venice, where Sebastian and Ryder vacation with Lord Marchmain, Sebastian's father. In dispassionately analyzing the hatred consuming the Marchmain family, Cara (Lord Marchmain's mistress) tell Ryder:

"When people hate with all that energy, it is something in themselves they are hating. Alex is hating all the illusions of boyhood—innocence, God, hope. Poor Lady Marchmain has to bear all that. A woman has not all these ways of loving. . . . Sebastian is in love with his own childhood. That will make him very unhappy. His teddy bear, his nanny. . .and he is nineteen years old. . . ." (116)

Sebastian has a lot in common with those other cases of arrested development, Tony Last, William Boot, even Basil Seal, but Waugh's detachment has gone, for through Cara's monologue we are told *how* to think about Sebastian.

In the final chapter of Book One, life closes in on Sebastian in the form of a tutor, Mr. Samgrass, whose unannounced duty is to act as a warder for Sebastian, now become a secret drinker. His downward spiral into drunkenness is further complicated by his mother's absolutely rigid, stiflingly earnest adherence to the tenets of doctrine, complete to the blue walls of her sitting room, the color of the Virgin.

At the heart of Sebastian's rebellion (Book Two, "Brideshead Deserted") is the vexing matter of belief, which takes its most relentless form in conversations between Ryder and the elder son. Talking with Brideshead, Ryder is in ". . .a dead world. . .a moon-landscape of barren lava, a high place of toiling lungs" (185), where all doctrine is reduced to sterile theology. Hovering in the background is Rex Mottram, another of Waugh's opportunists, who proposes a thoroughly secular, easy rehabilitation of Sebastian—a *Brave New World* cure in a sanatorium at Zurich.

Paradoxically, with the Marchmain honour and fortune in disarray, Rex Mottram's star begins to rise. He is committed to the main chance, which includes plans for marrying Julia, and displays a breezy willingness to turn Catholic, especially if it means an exclusive guest list for the wedding. As Ryder looks back in retrospect, Julia appears as "the heroine of a fairy story turning over in her hands the magic ring" (202) rather wishing for a romantic attachment, but the reality is the amoral Rex who has given up his mistress, Brenda Champion, for Julia. They are married, but not in the fashion he had planned for, as it is discovered that he had been divorced in 1919.

Chapter 2 further contributes to the novel's sense of period in its recreation of the confused atmosphere of the General Strike of 1926, in which Rex thrives. Amidst this social and political turmoil, and with Lady Marchmain dying, Ryder agrees to go to North Africa to search for Sebastian, who had escaped enroute to the Zurich sanatorium. He discovers him in Fez, where he has in tow a young derelict German who had fled the chaos of Germany in the early 1920s, joined the Foreign Legion, and in despair shot himself in the foot. The two are oddly matched, as both have been running away, Kurt from a corrupt political system and Sebastian from a belief inexorable in its demands on the faithful. Sebastian stops running for the first time in his life, and devotes himself to nursing Kurt.

When Ryder returns to England, Bridey asks him to paint a series of canvasses of the Marchmains' London home, slated for the bulldozer. As he begins the project, a chance encounter with Cordelia foreshadows the tortuous return to the fold of both Julia and her father. Cordelia recalls the night her mother had read from G. K. Chesterton's wise priest-detective, Father Brown: " 'I caught him with an unseen hook and an invisible line which is long enough to let him wander to the ends of the world and still to bring him back with a twitch of the thread' " (245). Cordelia also remarks that when the chapel at Brideshead had been closed on the death of Lady Marchmain that it had become just another "oddly decorated room" (245). She quotes from the Mass: "Quomodo sedet sola civitas" (How doth the city sit solitary that was full of people). Although the Marchmains' falling off from the faith reaches its nadir in the closing of the chapel, the lines from Chesterton clearly indicate the direction of the rest of the novel.

At the outset of Book Three, Ryder's opening line, "My theme is memory, that winged host" (254), serves to keep the reader's attention focused on Ryder's retrospective piecing together, in the present, of the pattern of his life. We move ahead ten years to the time when Ryder has become a successful, if second-rate, artist who has made a specialty of painting country houses about to fall under the wrecker's hammer, a fitting vocation for a character who has never formed any lasting human ties. Occupying only a page or so, the passage describes a parallel, if less sensational, version of Sebastian's earlier evasion of individual responsibility. Reflecting on what he was then, from an understanding the reader cannot comprehend at this point in the novel, he realizes that something was missing, that he was "still a small part of myself pretending to be whole" (254).

He travels for two years to the jungles of South America to seek new perspectives, but he remains unchanged, "still a small part of myself trying to be whole" (254). At the end of his immersion in the jungle, he returns aboard ship with his ambitious wife, Celia. Julia Flyte is also one of the passengers; the three meet, and when Celia gets seasick during a violent storm, Ryder and Julia become secret lovers, perhaps because Julia is really Sebastian's alter ego, and hence appeals to Ryder. Although Julia seems to be an apostate, when she tells Ryder of her child born dead: " 'You, see, I can't get all that sort of thing out of my mind, quite—Death, Judgment, Heaven, Hell, Nanny Hawkins, and the catechism' " (286) she has felt the first "twitch of the thread" that ultimately draws her back to the fold.

Through the skillful maneuvering of Celia, Ryder's London exhibition of paintings done in South America is a success, but the artist knows what it is—empty technique, an understanding painfully underscored when Anthony Blanche unexpectedly flounces in to see the exhibit and sums it up for Ryder: " 'It was charm again, my dear, simply, creamy English charm, playing tigers' " (301).

With Julia and Ryder facing the prospect of a double divorce before they can marry, there follows (Chapter 3) one of the most incongruously dramatic scenes in the novel. Having done little in life other than to gather an immense collection of matchboxes, Bridey unexpectedly announces his engagement to a buxom Catholic widow, Beryl Muspratt. Earlier a ridiculous figure, he suddenly becomes a nemesis, for he will not bring his future wife to Brideshead as long as Julia lives there in adultery.

The phrase "living in sin," with its full theological condemnation, exerts its hold on Julia's conscience so that she must begin to weigh the conflicting demands of her Catholicism with her two-year affair with Ryder. Consistent with his failure to understand the depths of the Flyte clan's belief, Ryder fails Julia and can only respond in the cadences of an unfeeling agnostic, playing at psychology.

Using a technique he had employed so successfully in his novels prior to *Brideshead Revisited* Waugh contrasts Julia's private misery and futility by cutting directly to futility on a public scale in the machinations of Rex Mottram's political cronies, "the Brideshead set."[5] Vaguely aware of the impending Nazi threat to the peace of Europe, they are limited, grasping men whose fragmented conversation, solidly based on expedience, has the jazzy flavor of Eliot's "Fragment of an Agon":

"Peace Pledge."
"Foreign Office."
"New York Banks."
"All that's wanted is a good strong line."
"A line from Rex."
"And a line from me."
"We'll give Europe a good strong line. Europe is waiting for a speech from Rex."
"And a speech from me."
"And a speech from me. Rally the freedom-loving peoples of the world. Germany will rise; Austria will rise. The Czechs and the Slovaks are bound to rise."
"To a speech from Rex and a speech from me." (323 - 24)

Cordelia, now devoted to caring for the wounded in the Spanish Civil War, tells Ryder of Sebastian's fate (Chapter 4, "Sebastian contra mundum"). She describes Sebastian as something of the saint in the desert, through suffering becoming holy. With Kurt dead (forced to return to Germany, Kurt hangs himself), he has been taken in by the fathers at a North African monastery. Her remark that " 'no one is ever holy without suffering' " (340) is a reminder that Ryder, the detached artist-narrator, has remained, notwithstanding his affair with Julia, above human contact.

In the last chapter, Lord Marchmain comes home to die. With Sebastian sure to die childless, and with Brideshead marrying a woman beyond childbearing, the line will come to an end. At the moment of death, he crosses himself, and by this gesture repudiates the years of apostasy. The father's death ends the Julia-Ryder situation, phrased in Julia's words of renunciation: ". . .It may be a private bargain between me and God, that if I give up this one thing I want so much, however bad I am, he won't quite despair of me in the end" (373).

Waugh manages the plot so that the question of commitment to religious belief overshadows the importance of all other questions, public or private. Within this context, it is fitting that Julia, won back to the faith, should forsake Ryder. The foreboding image of a trapper's cabin, about to be overwhelmed by an avalanche on an Arctic mountainside, prepares the reader for her decision and for Ryder's conversion. The image flashes through Ryder's mind as he talks with Cordelia shortly before Julia breaks with him. At the moment when she renounces him the vision once more appears, but now "the avalanche was down, the hillside swept bare behind it" (373). Several critics have suggested (most notably David Lodge and Malcolm Bradbury) that the avalanche can be taken as symbolic of a destructive and purifying action, strongly Catholic in import, that combines both grace and anarchy in the destruction of the secure personality.[6]

In the Epilogue we return to the prosaic world of the soldiers encamped at Brideshead. Ryder discovers that of the former household, only Nanny Hawkins remains in residence, and we are back at the opening pages of the novel. Her continued sybillike presence may be taken as a reminder of the constancy of a simple, pious belief uncontaminated by a world at war, or as recollection of the childlike world of the nursery, happily insulated against the corruption of adulthood. But if the latter (a view clearly substantiated in the early pages when the adult Sebastian visits Nanny with his teddy bear tucked under his arm) this would undermine the positive resolution of the crisis of faith in the Marchmain family near the end of the work. On the surface, at least, Nanny Hawkins's conversation with Ryder serves as a chorus device whereby Ryder learns of the wartime fortunes of Bridey, Beryl (who has been bombed-out of a series of homes, seemingly in revenge for being so atrociously middle class), Julia, Cordelia, and Rex Mottram, whose political fortunes are at their height.

A recent convert, Ryder reflects on the slow growth of the mansion, generation after generation, "until in sudden frost came the age of Hooper. . .and the work all brought to nothing; Quomodo sedet sola civitas. Vanity of vanities, all is vanity" (380). Yet this is not the last word for Ryder. Neither the vacuousness of Hooper, nor the fierce tensions of the Flytes finally matter to him, for the altar lamp of the Brideshead chapel is once more relit, and the flame the Crusaders saw now "burns again for other soldiers, far from home. . ." (381).

For the first time, Waugh had rounded off a novel on an assured, optimistic note, rather than in the wryly ironic manner that had characterized all of his fiction before *Brideshead Revisited*. The deliberate shift toward a positive resolution and greater emphasis on characterization was not an entirely satisfactory achievement even though Waugh took great personal satisfaction in the work and fiercely defended it.[7]

As an apologia for Catholicism, the novel stresses grim obligation rather than the enfolding grace that Waugh envisioned as its chief concern. None of the Flyte family, with the exception of Cordelia, show any love for their religion. Sebastian rebels, Bridey becomes increasingly intransigeant on doctrinal matters. Lady Marchmain is a boring meddler in other people's lives, and Lord Marchmain's return to the fold, with its "will he or won't he" atmosphere, is contrived melodrama. For the Marchmains, religious belief becomes remembered duty rather than a faith to be cherished, an attitude partially attributable to Waugh's especially rigorous attitudes as a convert. Long before the publication of *Brideshead Revisited*, the uneasy position of the convert was summed up by Waugh's Oxford friend and contemporary Terence Greenidge: "The convert would in the nature of things be too proud to admit that anything could be wrong about the goal which he has attained after such expenditure of spiritual endeavor. Yet he does not give the impression of being pleased with it. . . . I can only describe his attitude by saying that he appears to submit passively to a discipline rather than joyously to accept a faith."[8] In this connection, Christopher Sykes has noted in his biography of Waugh that if he were not a Catholic, *Brideshead Revisited* would lead him "to regard the Catholic church as institutionalized fantasy. . . . The general reader is left rather in the cold."[9] O'Faolain provides the most trenchant analysis. He contends that the theme is poorly focused, for "the twitch on the thread" becomes so generalized in *Brideshead Revisited* that it could apply equally as well to patriotism or love, rather than to specific Catholic doctrine. With a shift in setting, the novel might conceivably have been written "by a fervent Congregationalist." The old Waugh detachment has gone, sold to loyalty, for there can be no loyalty in art.[10]

In 1946, when asked to summarize the theme of *Brideshead Revisited* for Hollywood movie producers who were considering adapting the novel to film, Waugh wrote a faintly patronizing memorandum in which he stressed the theology, and by implication, the use of the novel rather than its entertainment value: "Grace is not confined to the happy, prosperous and conventionally virtuous. . . . God has a separate plan for each individual by which he or she may find salvation. The story of 'Brideshead Revisited' seeks to show the working of several such plans in the lives of a single family."[11] Sykes believes that Waugh knew he had written a novel in which theology and story had not been successfully united, and that he was all the more impelled, therefore, to stoutly defend the work.[12]

Brideshead Revisited's limitations become more apparent when contrasted to the way in which Graham Greene's novels dramatize religious themes. For Greene, as for Waugh, love of God takes precedence over temporal, limited human love, but Greene's protagonists, caught up in these conflicting demands, must undergo an agonizing test of faith, as in the instance of Scobie in *The Heart of the Matter*, or of Sarah in *The End of the Affair*. Not only do Greene's characters suffer, but the intensity of their suffering mounts almost unbearably as they become more and more aware of their transgressions against the faith they cannot elude.

We can readily identify with the muddled lives of Greene's middle-class characters. It is difficult to be more than fascinated observers of the eccentric panache of Sebastian Flyte or to be convinced of Sebastian's return to the Church. His faith is not really tested, nor can we sense spiritual anguish in anything he says as we do in Scobie's troubled relationship to his wife, Louise, his mistress, Helen Rolt, and the betrayed servant, Ali. The focus of our interest in the early chapters, Sebastian fades out when our attention is shifted to the Ryder-Julia affair. His ultimate fate, described by Cordelia to Ryder, has the unreal quality of a scene viewed from a train window.

Critical consideration of the women in *Brideshead Revisited* has been contradictory. Sykes believes that Julia never comes to life and introduces an "ugly note of religiosity," while, paradoxically, only the calculating, self-serving wife, Celia, has any vitality.[13] Robert Heilman, in noting structural parallels between *Brideshead Revisited* and Hardy's *Jude the Obscure,* states that "there is almost no dramatic proof of clash and struggle in Julia. . . . It is as though her decision were made in advance, and Waugh were only filling in the pages."[14] Contra to these interpretations Bernard Bergonzi contends that "Waugh has invented an attractive female character of, for him, unusual depth and complexity";[15] "for him," however, is a quite limited qualifier apparently implying that Waugh had merely taken a few steps beyond sketching satiric types.

The fictional reality of Julia is only partially convincing because of a shift in characterization that does not match the flow of events in the novel. Julia's amused, detached restlessness, the restlessness of the wealthy young woman unsure of what to do with her life, is believable, but later in the novel when she weighs the claims of the sacred and the profane in her relationship to Ryder she becomes little more than a speaking voice for dry Church doctrine. That she will renounce Ryder seems inevitable well before the novel ends; what is not so credible are the series of scenes in which she rather mechanically voices her doubts, one by one. Brenda Last, of *A Handful of Dust,* is a far more credibly consistent portrayal. The victim of her husband's well intentioned but claustrophobic life in the country, she is also utterly heartless in abandoning her husband and her son to become the lover of John Beaver. We can believe in her plight, even if we may not be quite prepared for her callous self-absorption.

Beyond his unsure treatment of characterization, Waugh's presentation of scene and use of dialogue are uneven. The Oxford scenes, so romantic in tone, are recreated exactly as one might look back in nostalgic remembrance, and especially as Ryder tries to recall precisely how he felt and acted at the time, but in the later pages the recollections are contrived, almost as though Waugh had set himself to write a best-selling novel. Chapter 1 of Book Three, "Orphans of the Storm," describing the Ryder-Julia affair aboard ship, typifies the mixed tone of the later pages. Are we to read the title ironically, or to take it as part of the rather archaic romanticism that pervades most of *Brideshead Revisited*?

Ryder's description of the ship's interior, "its carpets the colour of blotting paper; the painted panels of the walls. . .like blotting paper, too—kindergarten work in flat, drab colours" (262) is perfectly in accord with his sharp-eyed, observant nature and with the morally neutral world inhabited by Mottrams and Hoopers. Then, a page or two later, Ryder mouths these treacly lines (written in a style Waugh had parodied in *Scoop*) describing Julia: "now approaching the zenith of her loveliness, all her rich promise abundantly fulfilled. . .this haunting, magical sadness which spoke straight to the heart" (265).

After pages of this posturing Waugh regains control of his material in his wonderful ticking off, in the old malicious vein, of a group of stuffed shirts including a movie producer, an Episcopalian bishop, and a U.S. Senator invited to the shipboard cocktail party given by Celia. One by one they unwittingly reveal themselves, the U.S. Senator by his obtuse incomprehensiveness, the bishop by his fatuously dim remark, " 'The speech of the coming century is in thoughts not in words. Do you not agree, Mr. Ryder?' " (273). In scenes such as this, and in others scattered throughout the book, the old anarchistic Waugh spirit asserts itself; its acidulous tone undercuts the overripe style that characterizes long stretches of the narrative and serves as a reminder that romanticism was not Waugh's forte, except when he is simultaneously skeptical and ruefully admiring as in, say, his description of the gathering of the old regime at Anchorage House in *Vile Bodies*, or in his carefully modulated humorous-pathetic characterization of Apthorpe in *Sword of Honour*.

Published at a time when Henry Wallace's phrase "the century of the common man" was echoing around the world, *Brideshead Revisited*, in its defense of the aristocracy, doomed to be killed off by the common man "so that things might be safe for the travelling salesman, with his polygonal pince-nez, his fat wet handshake. . ." (155),[16] alienated several influential critics, American and British. In a strongly critical review, Edmund Wilson wrote that Waugh's former unredeemed anarchic spirit (Ryder's "hot springs of anarchy") had been brought under control by Catholic doctrine. For Wilson, the loss of this anarchic spirit was disastrous, because

Waugh did not "allow it to raise its head—boldly courageously, hilariously or horribly. . .at the same time the religion that is invoked to subdue it seems more like an exorcistic rite than a force of regeneration."[17] Although he liked the Prologue and the Oxford passages, the novel was "a bitter blow" to the American critic, who had found in the earlier novels so much to admire. In its emphasis on religious belief exalted by remembrance of medieval knighthood, the concluding passages of *Brideshead Revisited* infuriated the usually tolerant Wilson, whose tolerance did not extend to the writers of novels of specifically religious themes. Wilson's strictures seem overstated, for where the novel fails is in its too frequent fine writing, its soap opera confrontations, as in Julia's hysterical accusation of Ryder: " 'Why must you see everything secondhand? Why must this be a play? Why must my conscience be a pre-Raphaelite picture?' " (320), and in Ryder's emotional distance from the lives of the other characters. He remains the same from beginning to end, the uncommitted observer, so much so that his offstage conversion rings hollow, though surely this was not Waugh's intent.

A few months after the publication of Wilson's diatribe, the British critic Rose Macaulay wrote a balanced and lengthy estimate of Waugh's career for *Horizon*, but sternly criticized *Brideshead Revisited* as flowering "too often into an orchidaceous luxury of bloom that, in a hitherto ironic wit, startles and disconcerts. Love, the English aristocracy, and the Roman Catholic Church, combine to liquefy a style that should be dry."[18] On the other hand, some of the reviews were highly laudatory; the remarks of Father Ronald Knox were typical: ". . .In the second half of *Brideshead* you emerged into a new world of imagination, as concrete as the world of Trollope. . . ."[19] Knox's remarks tempered the harsh outbursts of Wilson and Macaulay, but in these reviews and in many others, the praise or blame sprang from political or sectarian bias, rather than from a reasoned critical evaluation.[20]

Granted its limitations, *Brideshead Revisited* is significant for (1) its author's effort to move in a new direction in writing a novel with a religious theme, (2) its remarkably accurate evocation of English undergraduate life of the 1920s,[21] and (3) its gallery of sharply drawn minor characters. Hooper, Anthony Blanche, Mr. Samgrass, and Ryder's slyly malevolent father are nowhere surpassed in the novels Waugh wrote at the outset of his career.

II   The Loved One

The Loved One was the indirect result of Waugh's visit to Hollywood in 1947 to discuss the proposed adaptation of *Brideshead Revisited* for the movies. Despite the six-figure contract offered Waugh for the screen rights, he refused to allow any tampering with the novel, and the negotiations were broken off. The trip would have been spoiled for the Waughs "had we not been introduced by an Australian friend to the unsurpassed glories" (7) of that monstrously rococo cemetery, Forest Lawn Memorial Park, "Whispering Glades" of *The Loved One*. Waugh was so engrossed by everything he saw at Forest Lawn, including the canned music piped through loudspeakers hidden in the shrubbery, and the imitations of British literary shrines, that he recorded his observations for *Life* several months before the novel was first published in Cyril Connolly's journal, *Horizon*.

Both in the article and later in the novel, Waugh described a soulless, immature refusal by Americans to recognize death: "Even the names given to their various sections—Eventide, Babyland, Graceland, Inspiration Slope, Slumberland, Sweet Memories. . .are none of them suggestive of the graveyard. . . . Forest Lawn has consciously turned its back on 'the old customs of Death,' and grim traditional alternatives of Heaven and Hell, and promises immediate happiness for all its inmates. . . ."[22]

This tightly constructed short novel is audaciously gruesome from start to finish. Dennis Barlow, a young expatriate British poet quits his job at a movie studio to go to work in the less arduous surroundings of a pet mortuary, The Happier Hunting Ground. Like so many of Waugh's antiheroes, he moves from one horrifying scene to another without the flicker of an eyelash. Although not as passive as Paul Pennyfeather or William Boot, like them he is the observer of an incomprehensibly mad world. When Sir Francis Hinsley, former scriptwriter but now a fading publicity agent, commits suicide after being fired, Dennis visits Whispering Glades to make the funeral arrangements.

There he meets Aimee Thanatagenos (Greek for "love of death"), assistant cosmetician and a real decadent, her green eyes reflecting a "glint of lunacy." A Hollywood updating of Edgar Allan Poe's vampire women, she immediately attracts Dennis's interest. Torn between her love for the "ethical" head mortician, Mr. Joyboy, and the "unethical" Dennis, she consults a newspaper oracle, the Guru Brahmin (Mr. Slump, a seedy alcoholic). On discovering both the drab reality of Mr. Joyboy's private life, complete with domineering Mom and parrot, and the deception of Dennis's love poems that happen to be plagiarized lyrics of Keats and Poe, she again consults Mr. Slump, who tells her to jump out a window. Literally following his advice, she gives herself a lethal injection in Mr. Joyboy's embalming room. When Joyboy discovers the body, he appeals to Dennis to help save his reputation. Dennis imperturbably cremates Aimee at The Happier Hunting Ground, and then blackmails Joyboy into providing some of the money for his return to England.

Suggesting the closing passage of *A Handful of Dust*, the novel ends on an even more macabre note: every year on the anniversary of her death, Joyboy will receive a card from The Happier Hunting Ground stating, "Your little Aimee is wagging her tail in Heaven tonight" (128).

There are no distinctions in the burial customs; whether for animals or for human beings, the undertaker's sales spiel is the same. Dennis advises a client concerning the arrangements for the burial of a Sealyham terrier:

"And the religious rites? We have a pastor who is always pleased to assist. . . ."

"Mr. Barlow, we're neither of us what you might call very church-going people, but I think on an occasion like this Mrs. Heinkel would want all the comfort you can offer."

"Our Grade A service includes several unique features. At the moment of commital, a white dove, symbolizing the deceased's soul, is liberated over the crematorium." (21 - 22)

This grotesque passage is compounded in the parody of Scripture read at a pet's funeral: "Dog that is borne of bitch hath but a short time to live, and is full of misery" (97). We look back not to *Gulliver's Travels* but to *A Modest Proposal* for a similar expression of the horribly abnormal disguised as normality, of human dignity reduced to zero.

Almost unaccountably, we laugh, and frequently. In this throwback to *Decline and Fall*, *Vile Bodies*, and *Black Mischief*, conventional norms of behavior and thinking simply do not apply. As literary high-wire artist, Waugh precariously makes his way between revulsion and horror. The incongruities become so horrifying that they are removed into the realm of the fantastic, from "the orgiastic cremation of a nonsectarian chimpanzee" (24) to Aimee Thanatagenos's questions to Dennis about the embalming procedures to be used on Sir Francis Hinsley: " 'Did the Loved One wear his own hair? And the normal complexion? We usually classify them as rural, athletic and scholarly—that is to say red, brown or white' " (48), or to Joyboy's clinical professionalism in imparting a smile to the fixed countenances of the bodies he daily prepares for funeral rites.

In other instances, Waugh appeals to his reader's taste for word-play, as in " 'Normal disposal is by inhumement, entombment, in-urnment or immurement, but many people just lately prefer insar-cophagusment. That is *very* individual' " (38), or to the fooling around with allusions to the lines of Poe, Keats, Burns, Dowson, Yeats, and Shakespeare.

In the preface to the American edition of *The Loved One*, Waugh dryly advised any squeamish readers to "return their copies to the library or bookstore unread." Well chosen words, especially in the contrast between the ghastly reality of "the devil-mask Den-nis had found in the noose" and the even more ghastly, unreal parody of life in the product of the undertaker's art, "the face. . .as ageless as a tortoise and as inhuman; a painted and smirking obscene travesty. . ." (62).

While almost all of the earlier novels could be counted on for one or more macabre deaths, in *The Loved One* this concern relentlessly preoccupies the reader from the opening lines. In its rendering of the empty horrors of life in Hollywood it is in a class with Nathanael West's *The Day of the Locust*, and has some affinity with Aldous Huxley's *After Many a Summer Dies the Swan*. Cyril Connolly sums up the novel: "In its attitude to death, and to death's stand-in, failure, Mr. Waugh exposes a materialist society at its weakest spot, as would Swift and Donne were they alive today." [23]

But the novel consists of more than an attack on the materialistic grotesqueness of American funeral customs, for Waugh deliberately reverses, often in an immensely witty fashion, the Jamesian theme of American innocence vs. European experience. While in many of James's novels the innocent American morally triumphs over his or her corrupt European protagonist, in *The Loved One* the innocent and vacuous Americans are merely boorish pragmatists. In a typical scene, Dennis asks his employer for a raise:

"Through no wish of my own I have become the protagonist of a Jame-sian problem. Do you ever read any Henry James, Mr. Schulz?"

"You know I don't have the time for reading."

"You don't have to read much of him. All his stories are about the same thing—American innocence and European experience."

"Thinks he can outsmart us, does he?"

"James was the innocent American."

"Well, I've no time for guys running down their own folks."

"Oh, he doesn't run them down. The stories are all tragedies one way or another."

"Well, I ain't got the time for tragedies neither. Take an end of this casket." (97)

Not only do these innocents fear death and go to any length to disguise its presence in the midst of life, but their relationship to each other is a symbolic death, for they avoid the sometimes troubling communication necessary to define true human identity and remain imprisoned within their own egos. Sir Francis Hinsley says to Dennis, " 'They are a very decent generous lot of people out here and *they don't expect you to listen*. . . . Nothing they say is designed to be heard' " (10). Aimee Thanatogenos encounters Dennis resting in the shade on The Lake Isle of Innisfree. Vaguely remembering their conversation concerning the interment arrangements for the body of Sir Francis, she remarks, " 'Aren't you the friend of the strangulated Loved One in the Orchid Room? *My memory's very bad for live faces'* " [italics mine] (71). Expatiating on her move up the scale from the Beverly-Waldorf beauty parlor to the cosmetics room at Whispering Glades, Aimee confesses, " 'It's only in the last year that I've come really to love the work. Before that I was just glad to serve people that couldn't talk' " [italics mine] (76 - 77).

Aimee and her counterparts are the standard products of an impersonal assembly line packaged in cellophane. Even the lovemaking of the Los Angelenos is characterized by the same sterile emptiness. When the Charon-like ferryman to The Lake Isle of Innisfree is about to cast off, Dennis notices that "some young people had emerged from the bosky and stood waiting his summons to embark; oblivious Paolas and Francescas emerging from their nether world in an incandescent envelope of love. One girl blew bubbles of gum like a rutting camel but her eyes were wide and soft with remembered pleasure" (68). But Waugh does not limit himself to sneering at the crudities of American folkways, for he does not spare his countrymen. The members of the British colony in Hollywood, with their Cricket Club mannerisms and unconscious parody of proper British decorum among the natives are, in reality, lifeless publicists and actors who spend their lives in creating a false sense of identity. Failing in his assignment to transform Juanita del Pablo, née Baby Aronson, into an Irish colleen, and having lost both caste and job, Sir Francis (like Lord Balcairn in *Vile Bodies*) has no alternative but to commit suicide.

Underlying this sterility is a decadent romanticism, the end result of the death wish found in Keats and Poe (and later in *Sword of Honour*) a romanticism which has become an obsession with the oblivion of death. In the circumstances of her mindless, empty life, it is not surprising that Aimee is attracted by Keats's line "I have been half in love with easeful death," for life and death become one in the nirvana of Whispering Glades, where Mr. Joyboy, "sometimes laying his gentle hand on a living shoulder or a dead haunch. . .was a figure of romance" (81).

The Californians of *The Loved One* have attempted to weld a seamless bond between life and death, but as Waugh interprets this obliteration of the older, more traditional distinctions between life and death, heaven and hell, they may have damned themselves to living out their own hell in an empty, valueless world. In his wickedly bland description of Forest Lawn, Waugh conjured up an inverted contemporary version of the medieval dance of death.

III   Helena

Helena (1950), the story of the supposed discoverer of Christ's cross, was the fictionalized result of a biography of St. Helena that Waugh had begun in 1945, and then dropped. It veers between sly leg-pulling of British mythos in the characterization of Old King Coel, the father of Helena, and good-humored seriousness in Helena's steadfast pursuit of the holy relic. Experiencing no qualms about the novel's uneven tone, Waugh wrote to a correspondent, "I am glad you like *Helena*. It is my own favorite."[24]

With the storybook line "Once, very long ago. . .there sat at an upper window a princess" Waugh begins to unfold his reworking of the legends surrounding the life of Helena, the mother of Constantine. Her imagination stirred by her tutor, she dreams of discovering the remains of Troy, a dream that fades when she meets and marries the young Roman, Constantius, already lusting for power.

On their way back to the Empire, as they travel past the Roman wall near Ratisbon, Constantius thinks of the wall as protecting the

108 EVELYN WAUGH

peace, law, and arts of the "City" from the barbarians without, but to Helena the reverse is true, for she envisions the wall as encompassing the world, and all men, civilized and barbarian, sharing in it. This is one more reworking of Waugh's metaphor of the "City," which had been so imaginatively developed in *A Handful of Dust*. In Helena's version, it rather murkily suggests Rome as the center of Christendom.

Although attracted to the Mithraic cult, a cult that anticipated some aspects of Christianity, Constantius does not swerve from his drive for power, abstract, divorced from any true sense of grace. Reigning over the Empire for a year, he dies amidst a shifting social, religious, and political background in which the subversive activities of the Christians play a large part. His effete son, Constantine, successfully repeats his father's devious stratagems to gain power. His plotting forms part of his muddled relationship to his conversion to Christianity, a relationship directed to the maintenance of temporal power. For a time, his new wife, Fausta, inveigles him into murdering scores of alleged political enemies.

Wearing a green wig and behaving quite like Ambrose Silk or Anthony Blanche, Constantine evades Helena's queries about his son, Crispus, killed on Fausta's insinuations. Wavering in his belief, Constantine remains half pagan, half Christian. Finally coming to an understanding of Fausta's sinister intrigues, including a plot to implicate Helena, his solution is quite simple: he disposes of her by ordering that the heat be turned up when she is in her steam bath.

Not understanding and unable to accept the doctrine of redemptive suffering implicit in Christian doctrine, Constantine decides to relocate his capital in the East, for as he tells Pope Sylvester, he has no wish to be associated with catacombs and martyrdom. When the hill of Golgotha is rediscovered, Constantine reduces that stark reminder of suffering to a shrine ensconced in an ornate basilica, a testament to his civic might rather than to his new faith. In the words of Lactantius, he gave "the wrong form to the right thing" (116).

Helena's more simplistic actions are the reverse of her son's Byzantine sophistries: she sets out to find the true Cross. As she begins her task, she dreams of meeting an incense seller, whose eyes are "weary and old as a crocodile" (119). The Wandering Jew of medieval fable, supposed to have driven Christ away from his door on the road to Golgotha, he tells her where to dig for the Cross. A rather distressing stereotype that Waugh was at least partially to repudiate in *Sword of Honour*, he has an easy adaptability of belief, the accommodation for personal gain of Rex Mottram, that Waugh increasingly distrusted in mankind at large as he grew older. With dogged assurance, Helena commences her task, and finally discovers pieces of the Cross, in an undertaking not costing martyrdom, but to be completed only by the simple believer.

Recognizing that his more literal-minded readers would question his tampering with fact, Waugh stated, "The novelist deals with the experiences which excite his imagination. In this case the experience was my desultory reading in History and Archaeology. The resulting book, of course, is neither History nor Archaeology. Where the authorities are doubtful, I have often chosen the picturesque in preference to the plausible. . ." (ix).

Read uncritically as a freely rendered, lively historical novel, *Helena* presents no difficulties; but if we compare Waugh's efforts to recreate the Roman world to, say, G. B. Shaw's *Caesar and Cleopatra*, problems arise. Shaw successfully reduces the historically monumental figures of Caesar and Cleopatra to a paunchy, balding philosopher and an unsure, awkward young girl; he does so in order to develop a series of Shavian reflections on the nature of power, and simply uses the historical situation for his own purposes. But Waugh cannot do this, for the novel is also an apologia for specifically Christian foundations of belief. Helena's quest, late in life, to find the true Cross jars with his description of her as a bustling, rather dowdy British matron. In his commitment to the spiritual seriousness of Helena's search, Waugh is not as successful, as in other of his works, in combining comic incongruity with an unspoken didactic purpose. In his excellent short monograph on Waugh, Paul Doyle develops a similar observation: "Tragic occurrences abound and the theme of joy pervades the book, but the tragi-comedy is not blended or properly proportioned."[25]

The opening pages of the novel involve such a lively putdown of traditional classroom notions of British history that the non-Catholic reader, not schooled in the Catholic's often easy yet reverential attitude toward his belief, may find the latter part of the novel too pietistic. Among those novels developing specifically Christian themes, *Helena* is far better written than Lloyd Douglas's *The Robe* but lacks the stark power of Per Lagerkvist's *Barabbas*. Read in a relaxed frame of mind, as Waugh probably intended us to do, it is fun to read, and especially in its transposition of Waugh's comic gallery to the era of the Emperor Constantine. Rather than turning into a stately figure of hagiography, Helena combines Lady Circumference and Prudence Courteney, and Constantine, "dull when drunk and sly when sober," is another Basil Seal.

In one of the few studies praising *Helena*, Aubrey Menen maintains that *Helena* is baroque in tone. Menen astutely observes that Constantine is "Basil Seal turned middle age, gross, absurd, muddled," who distorts Christianity into a "Seal-religion of personal vanity,"[26] but when he begins to analogize from baroque art forms in his efforts to defend *Helena* as an unified aesthetic expression, his argument becomes weakened. In essence, he argues that "baroque art must be looked at in parts. The parts are joined together, but only by an intellectual effort on the part of the spectator. . .it is only the focal points which count."[27] Perhaps Menen is right in stating that Helena is a fine example of the baroque impulse, but it could be argued that the "focal points" are not focal points at all, but only a series of separate historical scenes, linked together in no especial pattern. And Menen does not demonstrate how three of the parts he mentions (the courting of Helena, the vagaries of the adult Constantine, and Helena's search for the Cross) form an aesthetic whole.

Despite Menen's admiration for the novel, *Helena* is an odd combination of a saint's tale for the true believer and exotic high-jinks, *Vile Bodies* style, at the imperial court of Constantine, for the comic world of Waugh's early novels has been superimposed on the historical, literal world of Constantine. The result is a sometimes contradictory effort in the recreation of a crucial historical epoch far removed from the present. As Waugh notes, the novel had a didactic purpose. Writing in *The Month*, he observed that we can learn from *Helena* "something about the working of God; that He wants a different thing from each of us, laborious or easy, conspicuous or quite private, but something which only we can do and for which we were created."[28] Only briefly suggested in *Helena*, "the different thing from each of us" that He wants is given extended emphasis in *Sword of Honour* when the disillusioned, humilitated Guy Crouchback gives the protection of his name to the illegitimate baby of Virginia Troy. *Helena* is a special case, a labor of love, that perhaps ought not to be too harshly evaluated against the rest of Waugh's fiction, for it has an artfully contrived simplicity that makes highly pleasurable reading.

IV   The Ordeal of Gilbert Pinfold

The Ordeal of Gilbert Pinfold occupies a unique niche in Waugh's fiction because of its deliberately autobiographical tone. In the introductory note to the American edition, Waugh addresses the reader through the guise of an impersonal third-person narrator: "Three years ago Mr. Waugh suffered a brief bout of hallucination closely resembling what is here described. It was an interesting experience for a man whose business is storytelling. Hallucination is far removed from the loss of reason. The reason works with enhanced power, while the materials for it to work on, presented by the sense, are delusions. A storyteller naturally tries to find a plot into which his observations can be fitted" (from the prefatory "Note" to the American edition). The effect of the hallucinations was far more traumatic than Waugh's explanation suggests. It must have been an overpowering experience, for during this period he ceased writing in his diary and did not pick it up again until June 1955. On Waugh's return to England a psychiatrist acquaintance who treated him suggested that he might write about his ordeal, possibly as therapeutic release.[29]

Pinfold is first described in the role of a ruddy-faced, testy old colonel. From all accounts of those who knew Waugh in the post - World War II years, the role of the eccentric crank, intolerant of faults in grammar or of a bad bottle of wine, was the mask he adopted to ward off an increasingly hostile world. Similar to the eighteenth century writers praised in his opening sentence, Pinfold considered his work in terms of form, of art objects, not as studies in "cosmic significance." Further, he maintained that "most men harbour the germs of one or two books only; all else is professional trickery. . . ." (2).

The picture Waugh sketches is of a man isolated, living a lonely, quiet life far removed from London, an older William Boot not involved in local politics and rather isolated from neighbors by the Pinfolds' Catholicism; yet in his religion there was little solace, for even as the Church was urging Catholics "to emerge from the catacombs into the forum,. . .Mr. Pinfold burrowed ever deeper into the rock" (6).

The autobiographical introduction is revealing in what it indirectly tells about Waugh himself, but not until we come to the description of Mr. Pinfold's use of sedatives and of an ominously prying radio interview, does the slight plot begin to knit. The leader of the interviewers (named Angel) is later to become one of the chief persecutors in Pinfold's bout with hallucination. His probing, relentless manner upsets Pinfold, and especially in the menacing voice, in which "there was the hint of the under-dog's snarl" (14 - 15). Continued and indiscriminate doses of medication cause Pinfold to become forgetful. The failures of memory begin to pile up, and reach their peak during Christmas. Frightened, and physically aching, he books a leisurely cruise to the tropics aboard the S.S. *Caliban* (appropriately named, for it suggests Caliban's riotous disorder in *The Tempest*).

Laboriously staggering aboard ship, "prayerless he got himself to bed" (42). This bit of information is important to later development of the novel, for Pinfold does not attend Mass on the Sunday before his departure, and does not resume his prayers until the voices he begins to hear have tormented him for three days. He becomes vulnerable to the powers of darkness, for the dog he hears snuffling at his stateroom door could suggest Goethe's *Faust*, in which the tempter, Mephistopheles, appears disguised as a black dog. Taken literally, and Waugh makes full allowance for literal interpretation here and later in *The Ordeal of Gilbert Pinfold*, the dog's presence may be subconscious recollection of a neighbor's dog left in the Pinfolds' barn during a church service. In quick succession he hears a babble of youthful voices (the characters in Waugh's early novels?) a jazz band that slides off into the rhythms of the Pocoputa Indians (*A Handful of Dust*?), and an evangelistic revival sermon (*Vile Bodies*?)—all of these disordered sounds apparently emerging from the wiring strung overhead in Pinfold's cabin. Later, the voices begin to assail him everywhere, from the lamps in the dining salon to the open decks. It would be pointless to trace out references to Waugh's private life or to the novels in all of the hallucinatory episodes, but it is clear that *The Ordeal of Gilbert Pinfold* records the turning back upon the novelist of all the satiric thrusts of the novels and the critical gibes he had been forced to endure for so many years. Many of the scenes, deliberate parody of melodramatic crime on the high seas, international intrigue, and shipboard romances contrast with Mr. Pinfold's surface calm and his reserved daily exchange of civilities with the other passengers.

Other hallucinatory encounters intermix passages from the earlier novels with episodes derived from Waugh's own life, as in the scene in which Pinfold imagines that he hears Captain Steerforth lecturing the crew concerning a sailor who had become entangled in some machinery: " 'I want you to understand,' he was saying, 'that a great deal of valuable metal was sacrificed last night for the welfare of a single man. That metal was pure *copper*' " (51). The italicized word and the pious rhetoric recall Lord Copper, the newspaper magnate, of *Scoop*. And the noise of the accident, ". . .a huge percussion of metal as though a hundred pokers and tongs had fallen into an enormous fender" (48 - 49), could very easily be read as recollection of the World War II plane crash in Yugoslavia which Waugh and Randolph Churchill miraculously survived.[30]

That the imaginative life of his novels was about to take temporary possession of Pinfold's subconscious being, crowding out all else, is suggested in a faintly hostile encounter with one of the ship's passengers, a German, who tells him she has just begun to read one of his novels:

"It is a humorous book, yes?"
"Some people have suggested as much."
"I find it so. It is not your suggestion also? I think you have a peculiar sense of humour, Mr. Pinfold."
"Ah."
"That is what you are known for, yes, your peculiar sense of humour?" (58)

Later, when Pinfold returns to his cabin, he overhears Captain Steerforth and his inamorata (who reminds Pinfold of Goneril in *King Lear*) torture and murder one of the stewards. A third female character, Margaret, behaves more compassionately, leading eventually to an attempted seduction of Pinfold. It is the omnivorously curious mind of the novelist which begins to save Pinfold. Where the average man would shrink in horror from what he hears, Pinfold takes it all in. Though only one day out on the trip, he begins to heal—externally, at least—for the blotched hands and red complexion begin to fade. For the moment, Pinfold is suddenly freed of the voices. He wonders whether it might not have been possible "that what he heard was a piece of acting—a charade of the bright young peoples? a broadcast from London?" (66).

"A broadcast from London" provides the key to the next hallucination. When Pinfold dresses for dinner, a radio broadcaster

damns his work: " '. . .conventionality of plot, falseness of
characterization, morbid sentimentality, gross and hackneyed
farce. . .cloying religiosity. . .' " (67 - 68). At a later time, other
and younger voices add successive charges: that he was a Jewish
refugee named Peinfeld, that he had shirked his responsibilities in
World War II, that he was a homosexual, that he had left his
mother to die a pauper, that he always thought of death, and that
he was a Catholic just because he thought it aristocratic. In sifting
through all of these charges against him, Pinfold recognizes that
many of them were preposterous and others inconsistent. What
matters, however, is that the charges had stung Waugh-Pinfold and
pursued him into his fantasies. By so grotesquely distorting all the
old innuendoes, perhaps Waugh revenged himself at the expense of
his detractors.

Matters take a sharp downward turn for Pinfold when he
believes, nearing Gibraltar, that the Spaniards will halt the ship to
take off a secret agent, and that he, Pinfold, will be substituted for
the agent. He rushes out on deck. All is quiet. Panicked, he cries,
" 'O let me not be mad, not mad, sweet heaven. . .' " (11) in the
voice of the agonized King Lear. The voices mock him, but are his
saving, for he suddenly realizes he has been deluded. The next
morning, when the ship steams into the Mediterranean, that great
ocean, full of memories for him, works its healing effect ". . .of
work and rest and battle, of aesthetic adventure and of young love"
(114).

Though he slowly mends, the voices continue to assail him; all of
the old charges are repeated in full, monotonously, by Pinfold's
fellow passengers:

". . .Were his books ever any good?"
"Never *good.* His earlier ones weren't quite as bad as his latest. He's
written out."
"He's tried every literary trick. He's finished now and he knows it."
(122)

When several of the voices refer to the "Rules" of the game, we in-
fer that Pinfold has been talking to himself throughout, and that he
has partially confused the real, physical world with the hallucinatory world. One of the voices (Margaret Angel's) chides him for
going to the captain with his imagined complaint that the
passengers have been reading his telegrams:

"We *must* all play by the Rules."

"I'm not playing at all."

"Oh yes, darling, you are. We all are. We can't help ourselves. And it's a Rule that no one else must be told." (145)

Expressed in the language of the Red Queen of *Alice in Wonderland*, the "Rules" of Pinfold's fantasizing effectively cut off Pinfold from human contact and prolong his dream condition.

He determines to get off the ship at Port Said and then fly on to Colombo; he writes his wife a rambling letter informing her that he had spent most of his time talking with people he had never seen and attributes his condition to the hypnotic effect of a quack medical device owned by a neighbor (Reggie Upton's "Box").[31] His voices try to persuade him not to send the letter—that they will cease to haunt him if he does not mail it, but he resists this final and subtle temptation. In turn, he begins to rout his oppressors in a manner that the mad trader of *A Handful of Dust* would have approved of—he exorcises their presence by reading *Westward Ho!* backwards hour by hour.

Although the voices follow him to Ceylon, he now begins to learn to live with their irritable, less threatening cadences. He writes another letter to his wife, and wonders "whether it is not literally the Devil who is molesting me" (171). In Ceylon, and for the first time since the voyage began, Pinfold attends Mass, pursued only by the more subdued voice of Margaret Angel, who accompanies Pinfold in making responses to the Mass.

On his return to England, the voices do not disappear until he is assured by Father Westmacott that no such thing as a "Box" described by Pinfold ever did exist. He wryly acknowledges to his wife that if he wanted to draw up an indictment of himself he " 'could make a far blacker and more plausible case than they did' " (181 - 82). With his ordeal behind him, Gilbert Pinfold sits down to write, and puts away the unfinished manuscript of his novel, for ". . .there was more urgent business first, a hamper to be unpacked of fresh, rich experience—perishable goods" (184).

It was a virtuoso performance, by which Waugh mastered his illness and whatever private demons may have possessed him at the time.[32] Although the novel's ironic subtitle, "A Conversation Piece," seemingly implies only idle talk, in actuality it indicates the artistic distance Waugh had won through to in his struggle with hallucinatory visitations. Pinfold-Waugh conveys to the reader that the artist's capacity for absorbing all experience was the force that truly helped him win out in the end, even when he was himself the Henry James - like malignant experience.[33] Although *The Ordeal of Gilbert Pinfold* concludes with priestly assurances that allay Pinfold's apprehensions about his fantasies, Waugh emphasizes the comparative success of the private struggle rather than a specifically religious redemption.

As with *Brideshead Revisited*, the novel received mixed critical reception, and evoked predictable responses, dividable into two categories: personal attacks on Waugh, balanced by a few genuine efforts to appraise the novel on its own merits and to place it vis à vis the earlier novels. Typical of the first was J. B. Priestley's article[34] in the *New Statesman and Nation*, following upon a friendly review by John Raymond in the same journal only a few weeks earlier.[35] Priestley remarks he "found the hallucination scenes aboard ship rather crude and tedious, quite without the nightmare quality I had expected to find in them. . . . What is on trial here is the Pinfold *persona*. This *persona* is inadequate. . . ." But Priestley the dispassionate critic and Priestley the moralist parted company in the malicious comment that ". . .Pinfold must step out of his role as the Cotswold gentleman quietly regretting the Reform Bill of 1832. . . . He must be at all times the man of ideas, the intellectual, the artist, even if he is asked to resign from Bellamy's Club."[36] The most trenchant criticism was that of a fellow Catholic, Gabriel Fielding, who considered *Pinfold* to be "heavy with the dead weight of a satire grown old, the gravest of Mr. Waugh's novels"[37] and felt that the novel reflected an effort to reconcile the anger and cynicism of satire with Christian belief. What Fielding describes as "the price of his satire" is a melange of scenes, characters, and tag ends out of the earlier novels that rise up out of Pinfold's subconscious to bedevil him. For example, the hallucinatory romance with Margaret Angel becomes parody of both the style and situation of the Julia-Ryder tryst in *Brideshead Revisited*. Fielding's is a perceptive reading, but *Pinfold* also is a record of all the attacks on Waugh's private life. Here he gets his own back.

Although *The Ordeal of Gilbert Pinfold* is an almost plotless roman à clef, Waugh successfully dramatized the especial nature of Pinfold's ordeal. What distinguishes the hallucinatory experience in this novel from its presence in other of the novels (notably in Tony Last's fever-ridden vision of "The City" in *A Handful of Dust* and in Guy Crouchback's nightmare fantasy of the whales and turtles in the escape by open boat from Crete in *Men at Arms*) is that in *Pinfold* the experience dominates the whole novel in its emphasis on malignant forces bent on driving Pinfold into madness by causing him, literally, to betray himself. The notion of betrayal is not a new theme, of course, but Pinfold is no gulled antihero, and emerges victorious at the end, although aware that it was a hard-won victory. Limited by its autobiographical tone, nonetheless *The Ordeal of Gilbert Pinfold* is the fitting culmination of the incipient madness that informs so much of Waugh's fiction, for in *Pinfold* reality, fantasy, and madness become, for a time, closely linked.

Waugh's expression of Catholicism in *The Ordeal of Gilbert Pinfold* is surprisingly underplayed in contrast to the more fully developed doctrinal approach in *Brideshead Revisited* or in *Helena*. Waugh's readers might well have speculated if his fiction would continue to be preoccupied with an interpretation and defense of religious doctrine. His Catholicism was always an intense personal matter, and we know, from the evidence of his own comment and that of his friends, that his conversion in 1930 was, outwardly, at least, an intellectual response to a belief that promised stability and an unbroken tradition of religious custom. Reticence about his religious beliefs carried over into his novels, for neither in *Brideshead Revisited* nor in *Helena* do we find the depth of characterization, the agonized questioning of the leading characters in Graham Greene's novels. Waugh's lapsed Catholics, converted agnostics, and pilgrims to holy places are all quite decorous (with the exception of Sebastian Flyte in *Brideshead Revisited*), but do not provide the stuff of individual drama, for it was not his forte to create inwardly tormented characters.

The direction he might take in combining character and belief would be found in the completion of the *Sword of Honour* trilogy in 1965. *Sword of Honour* sets forth Waugh's most compelling argument for Catholicism, in the creation of a hero in whom religious belief is more than simply an exhortation to believe. Guy Crouchback's sometimes troubled allegiance to his creed, amidst an increasingly secular betrayal of his impossibly idealistic code of honor, maintains a higher level of reader credibility than the editorial voice of Waugh in *Brideshead Revisited*.

CHAPTER 4

The World War II Trilogy

"Quantitative judgments don't apply"
(*Sword of Honour* [546])

W AUGH'S three novels about World War II, *Men at Arms* (1952), *Officers and Gentlemen* (1955), and *Unconditional Surrender* (1961), were published as one novel, *Sword of Honour*, in 1965. Although each of the novels is independent of the others, there are interconnecting thematic developments that receive greater emphasis when read as a single volume. As an isolated example, the mock ferocity of Brigadier Ritchie-Hook is high comedy in *Men at Arms*, but becomes pathos in *Unconditional Surrender* in Ritchie-Hook's futile, wasted death in a fake attack on a German held Yugoslav blockhouse, an attack that underlines the note of waste and frustration that marks the third volume.

Sword of Honour does not have the tight economy of language and spare effect associated with the prewar novels, for it is characterized by a more diffuse, leisurely pattern which first appeared in *Brideshead Revisited*. "Diffuse," however, is not necessarily pejorative as applied to *Sword of Honour*, for the novel encompasses both a large scope in time and in setting, the latter extending from England to the eastern Mediterranean. This was clearly an instance in which a complex subject (the public and personal reverberations of World War II) dictated a large canvas.

As distinct from the more naturalistic, gritty perspective of Norman Mailer's or James Jones's enlisted men, in which officers are often little more than complicit tools of "the system," the experience of World War II in *Sword of Honour* is seen from the narrative perspective of an upper-class protagonist, a citizen turned volunteer soldier, who interprets the war from the angle of vision of a highly amateur man at arms. The novels that make up the trilogy

118

are given additional unity by the working out, in a series of sub-plots, of the fortunes of several minor characters. In 1962 Waugh noted in an interview that "each volume had a common form because there was an irrelevant ludicrous figure in each to make the running"[1]—Apthorpe in *Men at Arms*, Trimmer in *Officers and Gentlemen*, and Ludovic in both *Men at Arms* and *Unconditional Surrender*. While these figures derive from the comic types everywhere present in Waugh's novels, their main function is to help define the shifting fortunes of Guy Crouchback. The over-arching theme was stated by Waugh, with his customary in-cisiveness, in commenting on the first novel of the series: "*Men at Arms* was a kind of uncelebration, a history of Guy Crouchback's disillusion with the army. Guy has old-fashioned ideas of honor and illusions of chivalry; we see these being used up and destroyed by his encounters with the realities of army life."[2]

Each of the three novels contains a major thematic statement about Waugh's experience of World War II, but becomes more meaningful, in Crouchback's movement from high optimism to dis-illusionment, when brought together in the recension. They are (1) the artificiality of the training camp routine, focused on the vendet-ta between Apthorpe and Ritchie-Hook, as parody of war; (2) the rout of the British forces in Crete involving horror, suffering, and the near complete loss of all chivalric honor; and (3) the betrayal of the Jewish war refugees, helpless pawns in the Yugoslav power struggle, as final abandonment of principle.

Intertwined with Guy's increasing disaffection with the war is the pervasive influence of his Catholicism. Catholic doctrine serves an important function in Guy's increasing meditation as to how to lead his own life by religious principles, and also plays an historical role, commencing in the opening pages with Guy's reflection on his medieval ancestor, Roger of Waybroke, who died a useless death in fighting in a local Italian war, en route to the Crusades.

I   *War as a Game*

Living alone at the Castello Crouchback in a secluded fishing village on the Italian Riviera, Guy Crouchback is isolated from both his countrymen and the Italians. Not "simpatico," but dry and reserved, "even in his religion he felt no brotherhood" (19). However, at the declaration of war everything had been clearly spelled out. "The enemy was at last in plain view, huge and hateful, all disguise cast off. It was the Modern Age in Arms. Whatever the outcome, there was a place for him in that battle" (15). Before leaving, the thirty-five-year-old Guy pays homage at the tomb of Roger of Waybroke, and attends confession, but cannot shake his spiritual dryness.

With Guy introduced, Waugh presents the history of the decaying Crouchback family. As in *Brideshead Revisited* there is a concern for family lacking in the early fiction. One brother had been picked off by a sniper in World War I; another had gone mad and had starved himself to death; Guy's marriage had broken up and his wife had left him to marry Tommy Blackhouse, later to become Guy's commanding officer; his sister had married a Protestant, Arthur Box-Bender. Set off against this breakup of family and religious ties "the sanctuary lamp still burned" (22) in the chapel at Broome as it had always done.

For Guy, walking in the London blackout, this is a grey, purgatorial world in which he lives, for at first, no branch of the services will accept him. At loose ends, neither soldier nor civilian, he has his immediate answer in the words of the Mass: *Domine, non sum dignus*. Waiting to enlist, Guy visits his father, an unembittered holdover from a more sun-filled age. Unlike the fathers in *Vile Bodies* and in *Brideshead Revisited,* Guy's father is sympathetically portrayed, and in a fashion almost too good to be true. A gentleman who would have admirably matched Cardinal Newman's description, he spends the war years filling in as a teacher at a Catholic academy. He serves as a sympathetic commentator who repeatedly sets Guy's dislocated world in meaningful perspective. The titular head of the Crouchback clan, he has links with the past, links that affect his reading of present history and allow him to take the longer view denied Guy. Archaic in his pride, he can accept the fact that his grandson may have been killed in honorable battle but feels an obscure taint on the family honor when he learns otherwise that Tony Box-Bender has been taken prisoner.

Purely by chance, Guy finally gets an appointment to the Halberdier Corps. The beginning of the war is a gentlemanly, clubby affair. Tommy Blackhouse remarks: " 'It's going to be a long war. The great thing is to spend it among friends' " (311). This offhand declaration (a repetition of a similar remark by Peter Pastmaster in *Put Out More Flags*) carries an unintended sting, for later events prove that not even Guy's circle of gentleman rankers is exempt from self-interest and even treachery. The life of the training camp has the whimsical, artificial quality of *The Pirates of Penzance*, including the ritual of the officers' mess (complete with silver candlesticks), the exactitude of rifle drill, and the niceties of saluting—all of which have an immediate adolescent appeal to Guy.

But what might have bogged down into a tedious account of the fortunes of a younger British George Apley is rescued by the appearance of Apthorpe, ex - East African planter, one of the more solemnly absurd characters in Waugh's gallery of the eccentric. A latter-day Grimes, he fabricates an upper-crust background for himself, complete with prep school, maiden aunts, and so on, but never once drops the mask; when drunk, he attributes his condition to "Bechuana tummy." Other characters are introduced: de Souza, later revealed as a Communist; Trimmer, the opportunist suggested by his name. One of the most significant characters is the commandant, Brigadier Ritchie-Hook, a ferociously beguiling combination of Captain Hook, T. E. Lawrence, and Orde Wingate (the erratic but audacious British general who served with great bravery in Burma and in Africa in World War II). Bereft of one eye and part of a hand, the maimed Brigadier has spent his life as a professional soldier in seeking out violence from Ireland to the Holy Land. At the outset of the trilogy he is a figure of high comedy envisioning war "as a prodigious booby trap" who engages in a mock-heroic feud with Apthorpe for ownership of Apthorpe's most prized possession, the "thunder-box," a portable field latrine. The episode, replete with ambush and surprise, is a burlesque parody of war games, and reaches its climax when the Brigadier blows up the shed containing both the device and the hapless Apthorpe.

The description of the training camp is typical of Waugh's dual intent. The ancient rituals and the strict discipline are couched in the language of fond nostalgia, but nevertheless, the ceremonious tradition of the Halberdiers, was far removed "from those secret forests where the trains were, even then. . .rolling east and west with their doomed loads" (87).

True of all of Waugh's novels, buildings contribute to the shifting mood of the novel. In one of several moves from one training camp to another, the Halberdiers are assigned to barracks that had formerly served as a dormitory for a nondescript prep school. But Guy begins to realize that romantic, adolescent prep-school values are done for, and that he and his comrades are helping to usher in the present age Guy so despises, "bringing the new world with them; the world that was taking shape everywhere all about him, bounded by barbed wire and reeking of carbolic" (105). Typical of the Waugh touch is the name of the room Guy is billeted in: Passchendaele, one of the most bloody stalemates of World War I.

Lamed in training, he becomes more and more set apart from his fellow officers, an aging, crippled figure whose slightly absurd appearance becomes even more distorted when Apthorpe returns to barracks, also lame and, like Guy, equipped with a cane. These parallel actions also suggest that Apthorpe may be the symbolic brother, the *doppelgänger* representing the other more ludicrous, suppressed characteristics of Guy.

On leave, Guy unexpectedly meets his ex-wife, Virginia Troy, a latter-day Helen. He smugly assures her he can make love to her because in the eyes of the Church they are still married. She rejects his bloodless casuistry and spurns him as a "pompous, sexless, lunatic pig" (149). Defeated, Guy returns to his quarters, but the barracks also serve as a buffer between Guy and the outside world; in this instance, the protecting limitations of prep school extend into the training camp.

The military routine continues in its monotonous round. The proprietor (and spy) of an Italian restaurant near the camp overhears Apthorpe and Guy using the phrase "thunderbox," assumes this is a code name for some high-placed official, and forwards the information to his superiors. In turn, the message is intercepted by British Intelligence, who associate "Box" with Box-Bender, Guy's brother-in-law, and by extension to Guy and his residence in Italy. Guy's name is added to the Most Secret files as of dubious loyalty. Thus, by a passing whim of fate spiraling outward from the "thunder-box" comedy, Guy becomes an unwitting victim of wartime bureaucracy.

With the fall of France, Guy's regiment is shuttled back and forth over the English countryside in anticipation of the expected German invasion. And the noble cause, which Guy had enlisted to defend, becomes forever tarnished when he first hears the phrase "fifth-columnist": "Suspect everyone—the vicar, the village grocer, the farmer whose family have lived here a hundred years, all the most unlikely people" (227). Finally, amidst much confusion, the brigade embarks for Dakar. Guy remains remote from any significant human contact. When his soldier-valet gets into a row with a Goanese deck steward (a fellow Catholic wearing a medal similar to Guy's) all that Guy can do in response is to overtip the steward—but he is too diffident to show him his own medal, and as in other episodes, in failing to reach out to others denies his own humanity.

The landing at Dakar unexpectedly called off, the Brigadier decides on an unauthorized night raid;[3] amidst the conspiratorial atmosphere of a prep-school prank, Guy is unwittingly conned into leading his company on the raid. Once ashore, he acts coolly, and on returning, discovers that one of the commandos is none other than Ritchie-Hook, in disguise, carrying with him the severed head of a native soldier.[4] Instead of being decorated for bravery, Guy barely escapes court-martial. The macabre quality of the episode, intermingling revulsion and black humor, is in keeping with the grotesqueness of the cannibal feast in *Black Mischief.*

The raid is followed by the malarial illness and death of Apthorpe, a death innocently brought about by Guy when he smuggles him a bottle of whiskey. Lying gravely ill in his hospital bed, Apthorpe reveals a pathetic humanity up to that moment hidden beneath several masks of middle-class respectability he had previously assumed. Earlier he resembled a comic Prendergast or pompous Captain Grimes of ambiguous identity; here, at the end of the road, giggling "slightly like Mr. Toad in *The Wind in the Willows*" (255), and with tears in his eyes, he confesses his deceptions about the impeccable family ties he had invented. He extracts a promise from Guy to turn over his gear to Chatty Corner, Apthorpe's comrade from his African days. Guy presently sets forth on this search in yet another of Waugh's inversions of the chivalric quest.

II *The Loss of Honor*

In the original one-volume series, the opening section of *Officers and Gentlemen* was entitled "Happy Warriors," but in the recension was changed to "Apthorpe Placatus," to indicate more appropriately Guy's ironic, graillike efforts to deliver Apthorpe's gear. Waugh wrote on the dust jacket of the American edition: "*Officers and Gentlemen* begins with the placation of his [Apthorpe's] spirit, a ritual preparation for the descent into the nether world of Crete. *Men at Arms* began with its hero inspired by illusion. *Officers and Gentlemen* ends with his deflation."[5] This "descent into the nether world of Crete," with its echoes of the legend of the Minotaur and portrayal of the horrors of the British defeat, contains the most expressive writing of the trilogy, for in this middle section, with its emphasis on betrayal, cowardice, and defeat, Waugh/Crouchback's disillusionment with Allied policy and an accompanying loss of honor reaches its nadir.

Returning to London from North Africa, Guy arrives at the height of the Nazi bombing. London is an inferno amidst the falling bombs; Guy describes it in the apocryphal language of the Bible: "a tremendous incandescence just north of Piccadilly; a pentecostal wind; the remaining panes of glass above them scattered in lethal splinters about the street" (266). Entering his club from this Judgment Day setting, he finds Air Marshall Beech cowering, animallike, under a billiard table. It is a comic scene but also foreshadows the terror of Major Hound's total collapse in the battle for Crete. Significantly, images of bestial animal behavior recur with increasing frequency. When Guy reports for duty, he meets a squad of fire fighters wearing gas masks, ". . .their faces transformed as though by the hand of Circe from those of men to something less than the beasts. . ." (274). Complaining about the food, the Adjutant tells him that they live like animals on the rations issued to them. In a later scene, Trimmer wanders into a Glasgow bar on the lookout for a woman, like "a mongrel among dustbins, tail waving, ears cocked, nose aquiver" (341).

Guy also discovers that the Halberdier battle flags and ceremonial swords have disappeared—all part of the erosion of tradition and identity. On leave, he sets out to retrieve and deliver Apthorpe's gear. New orders temporarily halting his quest, Guy is sent to commando training off Scotland. In the episode of the mad Scotch laird who maintains a cellar of dynamite to reshape his granite acreage and in the eccentricities of Dr. Glendenning-Rees, the survival expert who nearly kills himself and Trimmer's platoon in an effort to live off the land, Waugh again burlesques the training regime as he did in the parody of war-games in the "thunderbox" affair.

Several new characters are introduced: among them Ivor Claire, the "parfait knyghte" of medieval courtoisie. For the moment, he is simply a languid, English exotic, wearing embroidered slippers and sipping liqueur. Later, he is to be the last betrayer of Guy's ideal of chivalry. Trimmer reappears. Like Hooper (*Brideshead Revisited*), he lives by a code of pure expediency. But his instinct for survival is less damning than that of Ivor Claire, the aristocrat. By chance, Guy discovers Chatty Corner, who turns out not to be some mythic creature, but an ordinary mortal, down with a cold. "It was a holy moment. . . .the spirit of Apthorpe was placated" (324). Thus one phase of Guy's quest ends in solemn, mocking comedy.

Chapter 6, "Happy Warriors," opens with Trimmer on leave in Glasgow. At a bar, he recognizes Virginia Troy, whose coiffure he had often set when he was a ship's hairdresser aboard a luxury liner. Presuming on her memories of happier times crossing the Atlantic, he is an inadequate Paris for this latter-day Helen, but his brassy confidence triumphs, for he is a reminder of a lost 1930s life of elegance, of "days of sun and sea-spray and wallowing dolphins" (347).

Narrowly missing court-martial for posing as a major, Trimmer returns unscathed to the Hebrides training ground. The army routine goes on in its usual pattern until the arrival, aboard Mrs. Stitch's commandeered yacht, the *Cleopatra*,[6] of Brigadier Ritchie-Hook (now reinstated by Churchill) and his staff, including Ian Kilbannock, friend of Guy and public relations officer. Assuring Guy that World War I Rupert Brooke posturing is outdated he tells him, " 'This is a People's War. . . . The upperclasses are on the secret list. We want heroes of the People, to or for the People, by, with and from the People' " (375). Soon after, Ian is given a cynical opportunity to fabricate a People's hero out of whole cloth: Trimmer. To keep public attention on commando operations, military planners devise Operation Popgun, a raid on one of the Channel Islands. Accompanied by Ian, Trimmer's platoon is routed when a farm woman with a shotgun and a barking dog drives them off. Precipitously retreating, Trimmer falls and discovers he has ripped over a railway line: they have mistakenly landed in France. Working smoothly in tandem, the military and the public relations experts convert him into a national hero overnight. On reading of Trimmer's exploits, Mr. Crouchback reacts with unaffected John Bull patriotism, touched with an ingenuous snobbishness, that Trimmer was capable of leaving the beauty salon in carrying out his "daring" military exploit. The simple pieties of old Crouchback's generation are thus subverted in the whole network of complicity and half-truths agreed upon by the military, the politicians, and the press.

Abruptly, the soldiers are packed aboard ship and sent to Egypt, finally arriving at Alexandria in those months when the entire Near East front appeared to be collapsing. On Easter Sunday Guy attends Confession, only to discover, in the priest's close questioning, that he is dealing with a spy. No one is to be trusted, for betrayal has insinuated itself into Guy's most cherished inner life—his religious belief.

The description of the British disaster at Crete is the dramatic climax of the entire trilogy, and in the fiction of both World Wars is matched only by Hemingway's superb description of the retreat from Caporetto in *A Farewell to Arms*. In Waugh's description, as in the Hemingway novel, there is the same loss of general identity in the milling crowd of stragglers separated from their units, and the loss of personal identity under the unrelenting pressure of enemy shelling.[7] But if the forces in Crete have lost all identity in the scramble to retreat, Waugh implies that Western civilization has also reached a similar impasse, for at the same moment of Guy's despair in Crete, "the London crowd shuffled past, men in a diversity of drab uniforms, women in the strange new look of the decade—trousered, turbaned, cigarettes adhering and drooping from grubby weary faces. . ." (505). Guy becomes separated from his command and futilely attempts to join up with the shattered remains of other units. Before the war a passive observer of life, he must again, and unwillingly, remain an observer. Through his presentation of Guy as observer rather than as participant, Waugh can visualize for the reader a panoramic impression of the chaos of battle, similar to Stephen Crane's achievement in describing Henry Fleming's disoriented wandering through a Civil War battlefield in *The Red Badge of Courage*.

Crouchback remains unbelievably composed, if more and more physically fatigued. His composure is denied to Major Hound, in whose progressively downward spiral into a hell of his own Waugh creates an overwhelming sense of fear, of the loss of all order. When Hound breaks into a sweat at the thought of combat, Corporal Major Ludovic, a strange creature who keeps a daily journal of pensées, observes that he lacks "the Death Wish" (439). Reduced to an instinctive struggle for survival, Hound barters a few cigarettes for food meant to be shared with other troops, and as the nightmare of retreat heightens, takes refuge in an abandoned culvert where ". . .like a hunted fox, like an air marshall under a billiard table, he crouched in torpor. . ." (475). Like a bad dog "who had been off on his own, rolling in something nasty" (480) he reaches the Hookforce headquarters staff, holed up in a cave. But the staff isn't in any better shape than Hound, for they have all been reduced to primitive, animallike life, huddled "on their haunches like chimp n a zoo" (481). Leaving headquarters, Hound falls off a cliff and comes to rest, ironically enough, in an Arcadian, myrtle-covered vale next to a spring; but his traumatic hegira is not over. Coming to, he is robbed by an old Cretan shepherd, the antithesis of the Good Shepherd, and is finally picked up by Ludovic, who has cast his fortunes with a group of Spanish troops turned deserters, now looting the countryside.

In its unreal atmosphere Hound's sorry epic has something of the quality of Heller's *Catch-22*. War becomes total fantasy. Major Hound falls to his own private disgrace and destruction because he is no longer supported by the buoyant world of abstract regulations; with these removed, he cannot, in the Conradian sense, sustain himself in "the destructive element." But conversely, for Guy, likewise cut off from his unit, there is a feeling of freedom, of paradoxical release, "eased at last of the dead weight of human company. . ." (489), as was true of Cedric Lyne's battlefield experience in *Put Out More Flags* and Paul Pennyfeather's jail term in *Decline and Fall*.

Guy comes upon the dead body of a British soldier in a farmyard. Unable to bury him properly, he removes the soldier's ID tags, which designate him Roman Catholic, says a prayer, and moves on. This quietly honorable act has an ironic rounding off. Later in the novel when Guy recovers from his ordeal in an Alexandria hospital, he hands Mrs. Stitch an envelope containing the tags and asks her to turn it in at headquarters. Mrs. Stitch drops the envelope into an incinerator, believing it to contain incriminating evidence against her aristocratic friend, the deserter Ivor Claire.

At length, Guy encounters a group of Halberdiers still fighting a rear-guard action, but the same military code whose absence had helped to betray Hound only serves to thwart Guy, for strict army regulations prohibit his joining a new unit. Suddenly, the case is altered for him: ". . .all the deep sense of desolation which he had sought to cure. . .overwhelmed him as of old; . . . Philoctetes set apart from his fellows by an old festering wound; Philoctetes without his bow. Sir Roger without his sword" (495). Guy's blighting sense of his lack of human contact is quite in character, as is his remembrance of his frustrated Crusader ancestor and of the great bowman, Philoctetes, left behind at the outset of the Trojan War.

At this low point for Guy, Waugh moves the action to London. Guy's frustration at not being able to get into the action has become success for the equally inactive Trimmer, now transformed, Philbrick fashion, into Colonel McTavish, cast in the role of "the beauty parlor as the school of democracy" (503). To keep him happy, Ian Kilbannock inveigles Virginia Troy into becoming Trimmer's mistress, by whom she later becomes pregnant.

The fabrication of Trimmer as war hero magnifies the ever widening atmosphere of ironic melancholy when Guy's lingering illusions of honorable soldierly behavior are rudely dashed by the desertion of Ivor Claire. Months earlier, before going into action, he had thought of Claire as a perfect representative of the values England cherished. But it is this individual, seemingly resembling the medieval knight, who calmly deserts his men shortly before the Nazi forces overwhelm them. Ivor obliquely and ironically rationalizes the matter: "In the next war, when we are completely democratic, I expect it will be quite honourable for officers to leave their men behind" (508). Not until weeks later does Guy discover from Mrs. Stitch that Claire had escaped and had been very quickly packed off to India to avert public scandal.

With the enemy closing in on them, the British soldiers have no hope of a Dunkirk-like rescue. All semblance of military order disintegrates as they smash their weapons in a "symbolic farewell to their arms" (510). Guy happens upon Ludovic and they join some soldiers repairing a fishing boat in which they manage to escape to Alexandria. Recovering from his ordeal, mute, unable to talk to anyone, Guy now becomes totally solitary, turned in on himself. Lying in bed, he gropingly pieces together the wracking, hallucinatory days aboard the crowded fishing boat, and remembers his visions at night of whales and turtles, their blank faces staring up at him out of the water.

He slowly begins to mend "while the softly petulant north-west wind, which long ago delayed Helen and Menelaus on that strand, stirred and fluttered" (515). The naming of these great figures from *The Iliad* suggests the pairing of opposites, the duality of attitude that characterizes the entire pattern of betrayal and loyalty in *Sword of Honour*. As Helen adulterously betrayed the loyal but dim Menelaus, so Virginia Troy betrays the loyalty of Guy. Mrs. Stitch behaves more treacherously than Virgina, for she betrays the bond of friendship. Her unexpected and lively presence at the hospital breaks the spell of Guy's thralldom to combat fatigue, but the magical awakening quickly turns to bitterness when Guy, innocently questioning Julia about Ivor's desertion, learns of her efforts to cover up the scandal. For Mrs. Stitch, it is a simple matter of rallying around a friend. For Tommy Blackhouse (Guy's friend and commanding officer), whose military career might be tarnished by involvement, it is a question of never causing trouble unless for strong personal advantage. Colonel Blackhouse and Mrs. Stitch, representatives of the social class that Guy/Waugh would presumably look to for preservation of the older values, are as much betrayers as Ivor, for theirs is the betrayal involving tacit complicity in maintaining unbroken, at any cost, the social and political cohesion of the Establishment hierarchy.

The indirect collusion of two of Guy's friends in betraying one man's sense of honor is almost immediately overshadowed by a more colossal accommodation of values on June 22, 1941, the day Germany invaded the Soviet Union, and a totalitarian nation suddenly emerged on the side of the Allies. With the situation altered from that time at the beginning of the war when good and evil seemed to be clearly defined, Guy was at the end of his pilgrimage in a treacherous world in which "priests were spies and gallant friends proved traitors and his country was led blundering into dishonour" (531 - 32).

In a conscious act of renunciation, he burns up his battlefield diary, which would have incriminated Ivor. But this isn't the end of the affair; Mrs. Stitch's interest in protecting Ivor has further consequences for Guy. When she learns that he may rejoin Ritchie-Hook, a more ruthless defender of honor, she pulls strings to have him immediately shipped back to England. Like Margot Best-Chetwynde and Brenda Last, she is both charmer and betrayer. Waugh ends Chapter 8 (the conclusion of *Officers and Gentlemen*) with an appropriate description of Julia derived from Heredia's sonnet on Cleopatra's desertion of Marc Antony: "Her eyes were an immense sea, full of flying galleys" (536).

III *The Betrayal of Principle*

After the rich comedy of the "thunder-box" episode, the grim humor of the unauthorized night raid, and the dramatic intensity of the struggle for Crete, the events of the last years of Crouchback's military career are undramatic and drab, but they also match a general public malaise in the closing days of the European phase of the war. The occasional satiric thrusts at the inanities of civilian and military life in the two volumes that make up over half of the trilogy

130   EVELYN WAUGH

become increasingly somber in the pages of *Unconditional Surrender*, the third section of the trilogy.

The betrayal motif is expanded outward from the private betrayal of Guy by Mrs. Stitch to a sell-out on an international scale, in the too easy accommodation with Communism by the British government, both in high government circles in Westminster and in the field in Yugoslavia. Waugh describes this infiltration as occurring at every level in wartime Britain,[8] from the civilian machinations of the homosexual Sir Ralph Brompton, to Guy's fellow officer Frank de Souza, who furthers the Communist cause in Yugoslavia by making a cold-blooded sacrifice of his brethren, the displaced Jews Guy clumsily attempts to help.

This is the world of the "operator," ubiquitous, everywhere felt, from the black-market restaurant owner who never runs short of fresh fruit and eggs, to the American naval officer, Lt. Padfield, who, wraithlike, insinuates himself into top level social and political circles, and intrigues with Brompton's Communist cabal. The atmosphere of distrust, compromise and fear, of the purgatorial world of London is objectified in the gray bread, in Lt. Padfield, "face the colour of putty," in the oyster gray eyes of Ludovic, and the indiscriminate plaguelike destruction of the buzz-bombs.

It has become a world in which all traditional sanctions and beliefs are plunging into barbarism, as seen in the activities of a former African witch doctor and abortionist in a grubby district of London, who has been enlisted in the Allied cause to beat tomtoms and concoct a brew of scorpions and decapitated rooster heads so as to hex Hitler. When Virginia Troy seeks him out to perform an abortion as a result of her pregnancy by Trimmer, he indignantly refuses: " 'General Whale would not like it if I resumed my private practice. Democracy is at stake' " (622).

As in the opening chapters, the rear-echelon planning for war becomes a prep school game, especially in the activities of Hazardous Offensive Operations, whose staff make maps printed with invisible ink, noiseless booby traps, sand-castle models of enemy fortifications, "and other projects dear to the heart of the healthy schoolboy" (556). But these schoolboy games have had a deadly result, too, for they had culminated in the death of many Canadian soldiers when, at the height of General Whale's delirious planning, he had engineered the murderously disastrous raid on Dieppe.

With honor compromised and quantitative judgments in the ascendancy, most notably at the Teheran Conference, the closing years of the war are marked by the open parading of lunacy as good sense. Even the obtuse Peregrine Crouchback, Guy's uncle, knows this; he says to Guy: " 'It's a mad world, my masters' " (670). The disorder in political and military circles is paralleled by increasing disorder in the private lives of many of Waugh's characters. Despite his life-giving if anachronistic gesture in sticking to qualitative judgments in marrying Virginia Troy to protect her and her unborn child and in his efforts to see justice done to the displaced Jews, Guy sinks deeper into an obsession with death, a longed for death.[9] At Bari, awaiting orders, Guy tells the priest in the confession box that he wishes to die. Later, in Yugoslavia, he talks with Madame Kanyi (the spokesman for the refugees), concerning the plight of the refugees. Out of her wisdom acquired through suffering, she tells him:

Is there any place that is free from evil? It is too simple to say that only the Nazis wanted war. These communists wanted it too. It was the only way in which they could come to power. Many of my people wanted it, to be revenged on the Germans, to hasten the creation of the national state. It seems to me that there was a will to war, a death wish, everywhere. Even good men thought their private honour would be satisfied by war. They could assert their manhood by killing and being killed. They would accept hardships in recompense for having been selfish and lazy (788).

Appearing in the closing pages of the trilogy, Mrs. Kanyi's reflection forces Guy to recognize his own secret complicity in the matter—that it had been his way out, too. On a larger scale, Waugh implies a universal burden of guilt for the horrors of World War II.

This obsessive concern with death infects one character after another. General Whale, his nerve lost, broods in his air-raid shelter: " 'Why am I taking cover when all I want to do is to die?' " (741). Having sent her baby to safety in the country, Virginia stays on in the city. Waugh suggests that she, too, may have been infected with the death wish, for when the buzz-bombs descend over London she wonders if one of them will kill her. After the pathetic absurdity of Ritchie-Hook's death in an attack on a Yugoslav blockhouse, Hook's batman tells Guy what Hook had said to him at an earlier time: " 'Dawkins, I wish those bastards would shoot better, I don't want to go home' " (778 - 79). The same obsession also touches Ludovic. Back in England, with time on his hands, Ludovic writes a lush romance of the immediate past entitled "The Death Wish."

Certainly the action in the latter part of the novel is subordinate to the thematic concerns suggested above. Passed over as too old for combat, yet still hoping to get into action, Guy becomes part of the pool of unemployed officers in London, and sadly realizes that the war had lost the high sense of purpose which he had sworn to defend on Roger Waybroke's sword. The loss of purpose, both individual and public, is visualized in the neutral gray clothes of the listless crowd shuffling its way through Westminster Abbey to view a different kind of sword, the newly forged "Sword of Stalingrad," to be presented to the Soviets, the sword enshrined on a table in imitation of an altar.

With Guy's fortunes at low ebb, Waugh concerns himself with the further career of Ludovic, now advanced from enlisted man to Major Ludovic. Having little to do as commanding officer of an obscure paratroop training center, he works on his novel. Paradoxically, the more isolated he becomes from human society, the "more did words, printed and written, occupy his mind. Ludovic had become an addict of that potent intoxicant, the English language" (571). A startlingly rum character, Ludovic is parody of Waugh during that period of forced inactivity when he wrote *Brideshead Revisited*.

At a literary party, Ludovic is asked about the source of his motifs:

"—There is the Drowned Sailor motif—an echo of the *Waste Land* perhaps? Had you Eliot consciously in mind?—"

"—Not Eliot," said Ludovic. "—I don't think he was called Eliot."

"—Very interesting. And there was the Cave image. You must have read a lot of Freudian psychology.—"

"—Not a lot. There was nothing psychological about the cave.—" (585)

This byplay may have been deliberately intended to hold off Freudian reading of the repeated cave images throughout *Sword of Honour*, from the "etiolated cow" stabled in a cave near Guy's Italian villa, to Major Hound hiding in a culvert during the action at Crete. Ludovic's novel ends with the death of Lady Marmaduke, ". . .a protracted ceremonious killing like that of a bull in the ring. . . . He had feared sometimes that his heroine might be immured in a cave or left to drift in an open boat" (738). Waugh may have intended to parody the death of Lord Marchmain in *Brideshead Revisited*, as Gene Phillips suggests,[10] or to underline the continuing hold on Ludovic's mind, of the memories of hiding out in caves during the Cretan nightmare and the agonizing escape by boat. The immurement, with its faint echo of the tortuous labyrinth of the Minotaur, can also suggest the animallike entrapment of the British troops, and the escape by fishing boat an ironic, quite unromantic parallel to the drifting off of the boat containing the body of King Arthur in Tennyson's *Idylls of the King.* Waugh was generally contemptuous of such literary readings of his work, but nevertheless, *Sword of Honour's* repeated concern with themes of betrayal and labyrinthine treachery are given added emphasis by the many echoes of the Minotaur myth.

Much to Ludovic's intense horror, he meets Guy at the party. The latter's innocent questioning about the disappearance of Major Hound too much for him, Ludovic bolts. But he is not done with his memories for when Guy is assigned to paratroop training, naturally it is to the center commanded by Ludovic where, up until Guy's ghostly reappearance, he spends his time writing training reports and savoring the joys of new words in *Roget's Thesaurus.* With the reappearance of his nemesis, Ludovic sinks into paroxysms of recollected guilt:

To be struck twice in a month after two years' respite. . .was a disaster beyond human calculation. . . . Things had been done by him, which the ancients believed, provoked a doom. Not only the ancients; most of mankind, independently, cut off from all communications with one another, had discovered and proclaimed this grim alliance between the powers of darkness and justice. (626)

Fortunately for Ludovic, Guy sprains his knee in a practice jump, and is carted off to an Air Force hospital. Ludovic insists on referring to the absent Crouchback as "Captain A. N. Other." Dubbed "Major Dracula" by the trainees, and suspected of being certifiably mad, he buys a Pekinese puppy (for "love" as he tells his staff) named Fido, Major Hound's other nickname! At novel's end, Ludovic's epicene career comes full circle when he buys the Castello Crouchback and installs Lt. Padfield as his factotum.

Before assignment to Italy, Guy returns to Broome, the ancestral home of the Crouchbacks, to attend his father's funeral. As the funeral Mass proceeds, Guy thinks of his father, who had very clearly seen "the difference in kind between the goodness of the most innocent of humans and the blinding ineffable goodness of God. 'Quantitative judgments don't apply,' his father had written" (601 - 602). This thought leads Guy to reflect that contrasted to his father's simple humanity, his own great sin had been apathy. However he clings to his as yet undefined belief that he would find the opportunity to engage in "some small service, for which he had been created" (604).

This opportunity presents itself sooner than he anticipates. Recuperating from his training accident at Peregrine's flat, he is visited by Virginia Troy, unsuccessful in her efforts to secure an abortion. What Virginia really seeks is an ill-defined "normality" which Waugh, as omniscient narrator, sharply criticizes. To her, the word meant "power and pleasure. . . . Her power of attraction, her power of pleasing was to her still part of the natural order which had been capriciously interrupted" (694), for the waste and devastation of the war are as nothing to her. Guy accepts his humiliating role as cuckold, applies his father's counsel that "quantitative judgments don't apply," and marries Virginia, in the full knowledge that this is his first unselfish act, an idealistic deed of knight-errantry. After Virginia has given birth, and sent the child to the country to be cared for, she and Peregrine are killed by a buzz-bomb. Everard Spruce, editor of *Survival* (the characterization is a sly portrait of Cyril Connolly, wartime editor of *Horizon*), sums up, in prose as embroidered as Ludovic's, the role that Virginia played as the last embodiment of the Michael Arlen, Scott Fitzgerald, Aldous Huxley, and Ernest Hemingway heroines: " 'The ghosts of Romance who walked between two wars. . .' " (752). The tone is lightly self-mocking, and recalls Waugh's contributions to this gallery in the Margot Best-Chetwyndes and Brenda Lasts of his own fiction of that era.

In Italy, Guy finds his orders changed, for all of his earlier misadventures, including the "thunder-box" business, the spy disguised as a priest, and the fierce nationalist ranting of the Scotch laird's niece, have been duly recorded and misinterpreted in official government files. Considered a neo-Fascist risk, he is packed off to Yugoslavia.[11] Unexpectedly, amidst the dull routine of headquarters life, Guy's interpreter, Bakic (a faint shadow of Youkumian in *Black Mischief*), ushers into his presence a group of Jewish refugees, dressed in tatters.

This is the beginning of the second act of Guy's expiation, his redemptive act of mercy that only he can undertake. Pilate-like, at first he refuses to be drawn into their troubles. New to the phrase "displaced persons," he asks his squadron leader, " 'What are displaced persons?' " and receives the answer, " 'Aren't we all?' "

(728). Thwarted by the Communists in his well-meant but bungled efforts to assist the refugees in their flight to freedom, he becomes a more sadly victimized Paul Pennyfeather.

In his quantitative loyalty to the Communist cause, Frank de Souza, Guy's liaison superior, is quite willing to sacrifice the refugees' interests to political concerns including the staging of a fake attack on an enemy-held blockhouse (manned not by Germans, but by right-wing Croatian nationalists) in order to impress a high-ranking visiting American general with the partisans' fighting qualities. The plane carrying the general and his party crashes on landing, and incinerates most of its occupants; a few survive, including the general, Ritchie-Hook, Lt. Padfield, and Ian Kilbannock. Traumatized, Ian wanders about as in a dream, muttering to himself, " 'It's like the croquet match in *Alice in Wonderland*' " (766).[12] The maneuver commences with a bombing run by two planes, one of which accidentally fires into a column of partisans. Mysteriously disappearing before the attack, Hook suddenly materializes as the leader of the partisan soldiers. With the latter skulking at the edge of the battlefield, he attacks on his own, even though he knows the whole business is a put up job. Trailed by a magazine photographer who senses the publicity value in the inexplicably weird episode unfolding before him, Hook is killed as he attempts to climb the stone masonry of the blockhouse. Arriving on the scene, the puzzled Germans can only conclude that Ritchie-Hook is not Ritchie-Hook, that it was all part of an elaborate ruse. Orders fan out through Europe to "be vigilant for one-eyed men" (777).

For the last time in his fiction, Waugh once again demonstrates, with characteristic understatement, his verbal skill in spinning out an apparently illogical sequence of events, one absurdity leading into another, in which the irrational imposes a surreal surface order. It is an anarchic order accepted by the schemers (de Souza), the deluded (the American general, the Germans), and the driven (Ritchie-Hook), before which knowledgeable but innocent bystanders (Crouchback) are helpless—the pattern of all of Waugh's fiction. The filling of Ludovic's "abhorred vacuum" with such a sharply nihilistic view of life comes perilously close to upsetting the saving grace of Crouchback's distinctly religious acts of expiation intended to give meaning to Guy's life and to provide a stay against anarchy.

Guy's persistence in helping the refugees seems to prevail when orders are received for their removal to safety. His exultation is described with typical Waugh ambiguity, ruefully ironic, yet admiring: "That day Guy's cuckold's horns shone like the patriarch's, when he came down from the awful cloud of Sinai" (782). But Waugh denies him even this slight sense of achievement, for the weather shifts, the planes ordered to airlife the refugees cannot land, and the partisans herd the refugees off to a prison camp.

On his departure, Guy gives Madame Kanyi the remains of his supplies, including some magazines. Unfortunately, this generous act, and final irony of his military career, leads to a parallel repetition of the circumstances surrounding Apthorpe's death. Later, when most of the refugees have been rescued, the Kanyis are not among them. The real becomes the unreal, for Guy is told that Madame Kanyi had been seen with a spy and received counter-revolutionary propaganda (the magazines) and that both husband and wife had been tried by the People's Court. Persisting in his balked efforts to free the Kanyis, Guy is asked by the commandant of the refugees camp: " '. . .Aren't you making rather heavy weather of it? What do two more or less matter?' " (791).

With this grim twist of a malignant fate that has dogged Guy's steps throughout *Sword of Honour*, the novel ends, although a four-page epilogue follows, allowing Waugh to tidy up the loose ends, and to give his sadly quixotic hero a small measure of satisfaction for his efforts in belatedly sticking to the individual, qualitative judgement in his marriage to Domenica Plessington. Childless, Guy and Domenica have raised Virginia's son. This represents a significant change from the conclusion of *Unconditional Surrender*, for in the original version, the couple are described as having children of their own, including two boys. By denying Guy an offspring of his own, Waugh further dramatizes the sacrificial nature of Guy's action in engaging in an untainted qualitative act that gives Trimmer's child the protection of his name. There is an air of finality in the recension, for there would be no more of Waugh's innocents, unable to cope with a world not of their making.

IV   *Conclusion*

In *Sword of Honour*, and especially in the characterization of Guy Crouchback, Waugh wrote the definitive British novel about World War II, a novel comparable to Ford Madox Ford's reading of World War I from the viewpoint of his central character, Christopher Tietjens, in the *Parade's End* trilogy. Like Tietjens, liv-

ing by an outmoded chivalric code, Crouchback is totally unfitted
for soldiering in an army affected by politics of expediency. But
Sword of Honour is far more complex than the thematic concern of
idealistic honour versus a corruptive accommodation of honour to
win at any cost. For all its aristocratic tradition, Guy's beloved
Halberdier Corps is a microcosm of the larger world, and contains
its quota of brave men, misfits, and even deserters. It is part of
Guy's disillusioned awakening to the realities of military life that he
must recognize this levelling knowledge, even as he becomes increasingly isolated from his comrades at arms. Paradoxically, his
deepening isolation, setting him apart from his fellows, informs his
observations with a grim, sometimes terrifying detachment
analogous to the perspective of the psychically and physically impo-
tent Jake Barnes of Hemingway's *The Sun Also Rises*.

What saves Crouchback from the *nada* of Frederick Henry or
Jake Barnes is his growing acceptance, late in the novel, of his
father's serene mixture of religious belief and code of ethics that
offers more hope than the dry asceticism of Guy. At a particularly
difficult time in Guy's army service, when the father counsels his
son that "quantitative judgements don't apply," he expresses a
judgmental attitude that Waugh had voiced as early as 1929. In the
course of an article on the younger generation written for the
Evening Standard, he accused his contemporaries of lacking "any
qualitative standards."[13] What counts for Guy's father, then, is the
individual act of mercy, beyond mere *pietas*. Stopp reports an interesting conversation with Waugh concerning the elder
Crouchback: "The function of the father. . .was 'to keep audible a
steady undertone of the decencies and true purpose of life behind
the chaos of events and fantastic characters,' " and to show him as a
victim " 'in the war against the Modern Age.' "[14]

Looking back to the writing of the trilogy, Waugh maintained
that "*Sword of Honour* was not specifically a religious book" but
was "a document of Catholic usage of my youth."[15] This seems as
wrong-headed as Waugh's assertion, in another context, that satire
can only exist in a highly stable society. Surely it is not the Catholic
usage of Waugh's youth that is significant, but instead, the often
low-keyed but insistent presence of Catholic ritual and dogma that
adds up to a more telling apologia than the contrived dramatics of
Brideshead Revisited. *Sword of Honour* is, in part, the creation of a
writer who has come to terms with his faith, rather than that of the
somewhat uneasy, defensive convert.

Having recognized and shaken off his own subconscious death

wish, Crouchback's reaffirmation of a more positive belief takes on added meaning when we recall the strong undercurrent toward death running throughout the novel. Of the numerous characters who embody this wish, Ritchie-Hook is the most grotesque example. At rifle practice, early on, he quite literally engages in a dance of death as he skips about dodging the bullets of the trainees. Ironically, it is only the immediate presence of death that instils in him a convulsive kind of life. His enshrinement of the pickled head of the native soldier is a far more horrible *memento mori* than the skull in the bowl of flowers on Sebastian Flyte's dormitory table. Guy is a maddeningly inert creature in contrast to Ritchie-Hook, but he struggles to engage in life-giving acts, and in his often frustrated efforts to overcome the sin of *accidia*, is credible where Charles Ryder is not.

In addition to its description of Guy's redemptive acts, the closing pages of *Sword of Honour* strongly emphasize the saving grace of religious belief in other characters. Before her sudden death, Virginia becomes a convert. When she tells Peregrine Crouchback that " 'it's all so easy. . .I can't think what those novelists make such a fuss over—about people 'losing their faith.' The whole thing is clear as daylight to me' " (707), she speaks in the pragmatic voice of Helena (Waugh also satirizes the more self-conscious tone of *Brideshead Revisited*). Then on the last page of the novel we learn that Tony Box-Bender, taken prisoner early in the novel, has entered a monastery. Without the positive commitments to belief of Guy, Virginia, and Tony, however limited their actions may be, *Sword of Honour's* all encompassing movement toward the treachery and disorder of a Dantean inferno would be triumphant.

Because of its ambitious scope, *Sword of Honour* provided critics with the opportunity to reassess Waugh's achievement. Fortunately, most of the critics judged the trilogy on its own merits and in relationship to Waugh's earlier work, although there were a few rather strident dissenting voices. In evaluating the three novels as a single work, Andrew Rutherford noted in his very discriminating appraisal that ". . .we feel as we read that the author as well as the hero is achieving new self-knowledge, growing in moral insight, and we too are involved in the process: it is our own imaginative participation stage by stage in Guy's experience (including his illusions) that makes the conclusion so disturbingly effective." In recognizing that the satirist's angle of vision is narrow, intense, even prejudiced ("Heterodoxy is always the other man's doxy"), Rutherford reminds us that this is the way of all great satirists, and that it contributes to the sharpness of their perception. He finds the trilogy to be "a uniquely successful fusion of prejudice indulged with prejudices overcome. . .that Guy's final position (or Waugh's) is not ours need not disturb us, for it is the intensity of the process as much as the conclusions reached that gives it its validity."[16]

One of the most generous commentaries, combining criticism and tribute, was that by Anthony Burgess. Knowing that the barbarism of the age was irredeemable, in *Sword of Honour* Waugh recorded "the passing not merely of the religion of his youth but of the secular values that once sustained Western civilization. Unconditional surrender had to be made to the facts of history, but the new anti-values must be passively resisted." Like Rutherford, Burgess did not balk at the charges of snobbery leveled at Waugh: Critics who condemn alleged evidence of snobbery in his writing. . .missed something deeper even than the patrician pose that was inseparable from his comic technique: they missed the Shakespearian hunger for order and stability. . . ."[18]

Five years prior to the publication of *Sword of Honour, The Times Literary Supplement* devoted a lengthy review of *Unconditional Surrender* to a consideration of the third novel's relationship to *Men at Arms* and *Officers and Gentlemen*. The reviewer asserted that the trilogy "now clearly emerges as Mr. Waugh's main achievement to date, and the one piece of English fiction about the 1939 - 45 War which is certain to survive,"[18] an attitude that was restated in essentially the same form in its March 17, 1966, review of *Sword of Honour*. Although the later article regretted some of the bits of characterization omitted in the recension (old Crouchback's dry comments on the auctioning off of his furniture, Ritchie-Hook playing Bingo, the ancient and anachronistic General Miltiades), this did not alter the opinion that it was ". . .a large and very fine novel, whose scale and seriousness are offset by a remarkable lightness of texture." The reviewer also praised Waugh's illumination of "a wide swath of history as well as the individuals on all levels who made it" and concluded by affirming that *Sword of Honour* fulfills the test of first-rate fiction that subsequent rereadings should reveal new insights.[19]

Another critical approach was characterized by grudging praise. Writing in the *New York Times* Gore Vidal attacked Waugh's religious and political attitudes but concluded with praise of Waugh's craft and play of mind: "The wit endures: at full strength,

wit is rage made bearable, and useful."[20] Theological interpretation, although less critically valid, provides an additional dimension
in judging the achievement of *Sword of Honour*. Gabriel Fielding
felt that *Sword of Honour* marked a development in Waugh's fiction as important as *A Burnt-Out Case* in Graham Greene's. Just as
the despair in Greene's novel could be seen "as a consequence of
connivance in the novelist," the three novels by Waugh could be interpreted "as the outcome of a most subtle and retrograde romanticism. . .full of the medievalism the Roman Catholic Church is
forever trying to shake off."[21]

What was indefensible, however, were the reviews geared completely to the reviewer's own social and political bias. In judging
Unconditional Surrender, Kingsley Amis assailed Waugh from the
point of view of the class-ridden "red brick" writer, and devoted his
entire assessment to the building up of the carefully modulated
British literary insult, along the way gleefully disinterring all the old
charges of snobbism, Catholic "narrowness," and anti-Ameri-
canism. Of Guy's disinterested efforts to save the Jewish refugees,
Amis sneers, "Greeks or Turks, presumably, would not have given
him such a signal opportunity of showing how he can put duty
above prejudice."[22] Amis also took a few pot shots at the "souped
up traditionalism" of Mr. Crouchback's funeral. Equally subjective
was Joseph Heller's review of *The End of the Battle* published in
the *Nation*. Heller contended that Waugh writes of the closing
years of World War II "with an emotionless precision that borders
on indifference" and that "he organizes his incidents without any
feeling for the dramatic or tragic. . . . In Guy Crouchback,
Waugh has given to literature one of its biggest bores since J. Alfred
Prufrock."[23] Such facile dismissal tells more about the reviewer's
temperament (what Anthony Burgess termed "the underdog whine
that Mr. Pinfold's ear was quick to detect"), than it does of the work
discussed. Critics such as Heller would have been happier, we are
led to believe, if Waugh had written his three novels from the point
of view of his batman, ground down by the inequities of the
"system."

Although Mailer and Jones see World War II through the
enlisted man's observations of a caste-ridden military structure and
graphically describe the insensate, dehumanizing horrors of warfare, their orientation is rigidly limited by social, economic, and
political attitudes growing out of the proletarian novel. Waugh did
not concern himself with attacking a system (the military) that

many of his American counterparts felt was simply an extension of unjust institutions. It was the decay of values at the top that truly mattered. His upper class protagonist never questions the institutions themselves, but slowly and painfully recognizes their betrayal of the principles they were supposed to represent. Fortunately, *Sword of Honour* implies rather than states, and does so through its wealth of description that builds to an all-encompassing disillusionment. Waugh lectures us about the failure of British principle during World War II, but we are not as aware of the hectoring voice of the author as we are in reading the novels of his American contemporaries. Teeming with detail we would expect to find in the most naturalistic novel, *Sword of Honour* is not abstract tract, but in its large time span and in its broad frame of reference extending from initial idealism "with the enemy in plain sight" to the crass abandonment of principle to secure victory at any cost, it attempts far more than either *The Naked and the Dead* or *From Here to Eternity*.

Sword of Honour may be more profitably compared to James Gould Cozzens's *Guard of Honor*, written from Cozzens's experience as an U.S. Army Air Force officer in World War II. *Guard of Honor* traces out the consequences of a crash landing of a plane whose pilot, a commanding general of an Air Force base in Florida, loses his nerve. The consequences involve administrative stupidity, the assumption of authority by those ill-prepared to do so, the disruption of the hierarchical order of army command, and the complexities of racial tensions (one of the two planes that figure in the crash is piloted by a black crew). In this sudden disruption of order, Cozzens's leading characters, like Crouchback, experience disappointment, frustration, and discomfiture which, as Pierre Michel has pointed out, sharpen their "realization of man's limitations in dealing with the confusions of life."[24] This is a realization expressed in language by which Cozzens weighs, balances, and judges, roughly parallel to Waugh's technique in *Sword of Honour*, if far more overt. Both Cozzens and Waugh long for a stable, hierarchical world, informed by their own notions of what is a reasonable order. In *Sword of Honour* the movement (as distinct from the pattern of the early novels) is from order to disorder, to total disorder in which blundering, anarchic impulse rules the destinies of men. All that Guy Crouchback can salvage is some measure of spiritual solace at novel's end. In *Guard of Honor*, the pattern moves from order to disorder to the reestablishment of at least qualified order. As in all of his works, Cozzens seeks the middle course, the workable compromise necessary for the reinstitution of order. For the more stiff necked Waugh, compromise fatally corrupts.

Underneath the flashes of the old wit in the *miles gloriosus* behavior of Apthorpe, or in the antics of Hook, the folly of absurdity and madness solemnly parading as reason becomes accentuated in a more uncomfortable fashion than is true of any other of Waugh's novels, with the exception of *A Handful of Dust*. At least in the early novels the lives of the Bright Young things or the aberrations of emergent African nations did not, as a rule, have to be taken too seriously. But Waugh's purgatorial world of expediency and political treachery in which the Gilpins, Bromptons, and de Souzas thrive was not to be so readily dismissed as the product of Waugh's imagination. Guy Burgess's activity as a double agent of the Soviets during World War II, followed by his defection to Russia in 1951, and later repeated by Kim Philby in 1963, strongly indicated a network of conspiracy in high government circles. Burgess's defection was of additional significance for he belonged to an intellectual coterie of Waugh's friends including Cyril Connolly, Tom Driberg, and Graham Greene, whose 1978 spy novel, *The Human Factor*, appears to be based on Burgess's ambiguous career. Waugh's pessimistic reminder that consequences result from acts of betrayal hit close to home.

Sword of Honour is an impressive valedictory in its relentless piling up of one disillusionment after another, lightened only by the slight glimpse of Guy's happiness in the last few pages. For those who had read Waugh's fiction from the early novels to the last, it was perhaps not unexpected that this was to be the last work. He had always described a lunatic world posing as the reasonable order of things. The war trilogy pushed to its outermost limits, on an international scale, the consequences of such attitudes and behavior. Nothing remained to be done, for Waugh had traversed the entire landscape of unreason from the stylized farcical outrage of *Decline and Fall* and *Vile Bodies* to the weary disillusionment of the darkening pages of *Sword of Honour*. And perhaps for Waugh, the prematurely elderly private citizen as remembered by Nancy Mitford,[25] the final symbolic betrayal was the gradual abandonment of tradition within the castle keep itself, the saying of the Mass in the vernacular instead of the centuries-honored tradition of Latin.

CHAPTER 5

The Writer as Critic

"Never apologize, never explain"
Benjamin Jowett

UNLIKE many of his contemporaries, Waugh never published a collection of essays on the practice of fiction or thought of himself as a practicing critic, but nevertheless he held very cogently stated opinions as to what fiction should be and expressed them in many book reviews, radio and television broadcasts, the famous *Paris Review* interview, and in scattered but pointed remarks in his novels.[1] His critical standards were remarkably consistent, and did not change appreciably over the years, although on occasion he revised his estimate of individual authors.

He rather elaborately dissociated himself from any specific critical orientation, as we know from his jibes at F. R. Leavis and Edmund Wilson (the dismissal of the latter perhaps stemming from Wilson's altered opinion of Waugh after the publication of *Brideshead Revisited*), but was well aware of shifting critical trends in the literary world. Operating out of general principles of style and of what he felt to be good taste, like Samuel Johnson he refused to number the streaks of the tulip in his wariness of too detailed theories of criticism. For him, the jargon of contemporary criticism, and especially its use of such cant terms as "dialectic," "Normative," "experiential," and the like, was simply a cover-up for murky writing.[2] Despite his professed wariness of too theoretical considerations, he based his critical remarks on certain broad criteria by which he gauged a literary work of art.

In the first place, Waugh considered poets and novelists as craftsmen, engaged in the difficult business of shaping experience so as to create an art object external to the artist. In *Ninety-Two Days* Waugh stated that just as a skilled carpenter on "seeing a piece of rough timber feels an inclination to plane it and square it and put it into shape, so a writer is not really content to leave any experience in the amorphous, haphazard condition in which life presents it," and must put it "into communicable form."[3] According to his thinking, genuine artistic inspiration "slips in unsought and unobserved when the artist's conscious powers are most concentrated, when he is least thinking of himself. He is not the subject of his art."[4] This is rather broadly analogous to the critical stance expressed by Joyce in *Portrait of the Artist as a Young Man*. Indifferent, paring his finger nails, the artist refines himself out of existence, so that we are unaware of his controlling hand.

The creation of the well-made work of art, and the distancing of the artist's personality accurately describe the chief features of a Waugh novel, and are restated, with slight variations, in both his oral and written statements on the nature of literary creation. In *Work Suspended*, John Plant, Waugh's novelist-narrator, describes the act of writing: "To produce something, saleable in large quantities to the public, which had absolutely nothing of myself in it: to sell something for which the kind of people I liked and respected, would have a use. . . ."[5] Writing in 1949 on the morbid curiosity of American readers about the private life of novelists, he emphasized the functional: "The writer sweats to write well; the reader sweats to make dollars; writer and reader exchange books for dollars."[6] He told Harvey Breit, in the same year, that the entire process of writing simply involves an immense taking of pains, of rewriting each sentence several times " 'all from longhand. . .just push the words around and change them. . . .' "[7] In the same offhand tone, he said of Christopher Sykes, "He did not take a course in creative writing; he lived."[8] Bluff remarks such as these, implying the cultivated amateur's disdain for technique, exactly conform to the Waugh strategy of disconcertingly mixing straight talk and deliberate pose. Although Waugh fully believed that writers are artificers who shape an art object out of the chaos of experience and firmly held to this rather simplistic critical standard, it was also more than a trifle ingenuous, for it served to protect his elusive inner being from too close scrutiny by the critics and by the public at large. Thus when he warned against too much self-analysis, too much parading of the ego, he stated a critical principle and also, as in his own case, directed attention away from himself. His remark about Max Beerbohm's *Happy Hypocrite* that "the mask, the style, is the man"[9] perfectly illustrates both principle and a device by which the author's *persona* (a word Waugh detested) could be hidden.

Because he looked upon writing as a highly disciplined enter-
prise, he had little use for the "romantic agony" of the artist. When
his friend John Betjeman bewailed the lot of the artist in the drab
postwar years of the late 1940s, Waugh noted: "Who can fail to
sympathize? 'Why was I born when I was?' An heroic past, an
idyllic future—those are the alternatives, according to temperament, of the unhappy artist in any age. Never jam today. All the
agonies and annoyances of growing up, which may last a lifetime,
spring from the slow, necessary realization of the truth of the fall of
Adam, and the exiled condition of his progeny."[10] This bleak assertion, and especially "the truth of the fall of Adam," gives off a whiff
of pure Calvinism that Waugh's great-great-grandfather, the
Reverend Alexander Waugh, would surely have approved.

His most widely quoted statement about the duty of the writer
originated in remarks made to Julian Jebb. In his comment he
demolished the traditional and perhaps unthinking notion that the
artist reflects the culture in which he lives. For Waugh, the artist
"must be a reactionary. He has to stand out against the tenor of the
age and not go flopping along; he must offer some little opposition," and cannot give in to pressure to conform.[11] If he is to be
true to the writer's craft he can make only small allowance for the
more kindly virtues. He admired G. K. Chesterton's *Everlasting
Man* for its clarity of language, and praised Chesterton for his
humility and charity, but did not believe that these qualities enrich-
ed the world as much as the opposite qualities of "pride, emulation,
avarice, malice—all the odious qualities—which drive a man to
complete, elaborate, refine, destroy, renew his work until he has
made something that gratifies his pride and envy and greed."[12]
Coupled with his distrust of overly detailed theorizing about the
technique of fiction, was an abhorrence of writing too firmly wedd-
ed to a particular psychological or political orientation. He thought
psychology was a fraud, consisting of a made-up word like
slenderizing,[13] and disclaimed any interest in novels that probed too
deeply into character study. This may explain why D. H. Lawrence
was anathema to him ("Philosophically he was rot. . .and as a
craftsman he was frightful).[14] In one of his twenty-six book reviews
for *Night and Day* he succinctly reflected on the limitations of
Marxism:

I do not think any artist, certainly no writer, can be a genuine Marxist, for a
writer's material must be the individual soul (which is the preconception of

Christendom), while the Marxist can only think in classes and categories, and even in classes abhors variety. The disillusioned Marxist becomes a Fascist; the disillusioned anarchist, a Christian. A robust discontent, whether it be with joint stock banking or the World, the Flesh and Devil, is good for a writer. . . ."[15]

Waugh's affirmation of the writer's need to maintain a high degree of individuality, a need which he saw contradicted by Marxism, was consistent with his belief that the artist must stand apart from limiting political allegiances. Theologically, he was less consistent, for in setting off the individual soul as "the preconception of Christendom," he admitted religious considerations that sometimes qualified his literary judgment, and especially so in his troubled reflections on Graham Greene's flirting with apostasy in his later novels.

I Style

Clarity and brevity of expression were unwavering constants by which he evaluated good writing. At Lancing, when he was beginning to discover his own literary voice, he scribbled a master-disciple marginal notation on one of Dudley Carew's stories: "Don't put down thoughts at such length—be subtle, leave something to us readers. *Keep cutting out*—motto for artists of all sorts. Prune un-essentials."[16] By the time he had become a well-established writer his standards remained just as unqualified. On reviewing Somerset Maugham's *Christmas Holiday* he praised Maugham for "his virtues of accuracy, economy, and control."[17] He took Stephen Spender to task because he did not leave something to his readers: "Don't analyze yourself. Give the relevant facts and let your readers make their own judgments."[18] It is not enough, however, to let the reader make up his own mind, for the writer must also express himself so that he will be understood by his own and future generations. If he cannot do this, he "is a bad writer."[19]

Writing on "Literary Style in England and America," published in *Books on Trial* in 1955, Waugh began by lamenting the boredom of "the blank, unlovely facades" of buildings the world over de-signed by architects who have abandoned any concern for style, and warned against the same danger in literature: "Literature is the right use of language irrespective of the subject or the reason of the

itterance. . . . Style is what distinguishes literature from trash."
D. H. Lawrence "wrote squalidly" but was accepted as an artist
because his themes were of topical concern. James Joyce was
"possessed by style," but unfortunately his later work became so involved with mannerisms that "it lost all faculty of communication."
Perversely enough, Waugh maintained, Joyce was admitted into
academic respectability because of his difficulty in expression. He
failed to communicate in his later experimentations with fiction
because he forgot the "necessary elements of style. . .lucidity,
elegance, individuality." Having said this, Waugh will not be
trapped into a totally simplistic judgment, for he reminds us that
"lucidity does not imply universal intelligibility. Henry James is the
most lucid of writers, but not the simplest." He concluded with the
assertion that if a writer is to develop, he must increasingly concern
himself with style, because "style alone can keep him from being
bored with his own work."[20] Waugh was not at all happy with what
he conceived to be a distorted view of Christian martyrdom in Gibbon's great work of the eighteenth century on the Roman Empire,
but readily admitted that Gibbon's power lay in a prose style that
"held the Egyptian secret of the embalmers. It is not to be
despised."[21]

The source of Waugh's lifelong concern for style is not difficult to
find. It originates in Arthur Waugh's respect for language as an instrument of expression, and in Evelyn's childhood study of Latin
and Greek. His father's generation, Waugh tells us, worked to
master its "own language and to write it lucidly and elegantly"[22]
(using almost the same wording of his *Books on Trial* article). To
achieve a precise effect in writing, Arthur Waugh noted, one ought
"to write nothing, however brief, without considering the construction at least as much as the decoration: to follow form, as the one
more antiseptic of expression."[23] "To write nothing. . .without
considering the construction" has something of the same force as
the image of the carpenter shaping the unfinished plank of wood. In
both statements there is a similarity of intent that suggests the pervasive influence of the elder Waugh, an influence Evelyn did not
acknowledge, or even recognize (he called his father "Chapman
Hall" in the 1920s diary entries), until he was well along into middle age. As an adult, Waugh remembered no Greek, and never read
Latin for enjoyment, but did not regret his classical studies, for only
by them "can a boy fully understand that a sentence is a logical

construction and that words have basic inalienable meanings
departure from which is either conscious metaphor or inexcusable
vulgarity."[24]

Waugh's admiration for the precise, telling effect helps account
for his praise of Hemingway's *The Sun Also Rises* and *A Farewell to
Arms*. When writers whose work he admired showed a marked falling off in exact statement he let them know in pungently phrased
language, as in the case of Thomas Merton, for whom he served
through an exchange of letters, as a literary mentor. He told Merton
that his book *The Waters of Siloe* was too diffuse and urged him to
correct the fault: "It is pattern-bombing instead of precision bombing. You scatter a lot of missiles all round the target instead of con-
centrating on a direct hit. It is not art. Your monastery tailor and
boot-maker could not waste material. Words are our material."[25]

Among his contemporaries whom he admired for their stylistic
excellence were Elizabeth Bowen, Ivy Compton-Burnett, Graham
Greene, Henry Green, Anthony Powell, and P. G. Wodehouse.
While he favored those writers whose style was as crisp as his own,
he admitted a few who wrote in a more richly textured manner, as
in the work of Osbert Sitwell and Ronald Knox, and was delighted
to discover Leo Rosten's *The Education of Hyman Kaplan*, perhaps
because of its warmly sympathetic portrayal of an immigrant wres-
tling with the syntactical mysteries of American English.

In his eyes, the greatest enemy of clear writing was the almost
universal tendency of the mid-twentieth century to use the easy verbal abstraction, rather than the more difficult, precise word or
phrase:

One grows parched for that straight style of speech in the desert of modern
euphemisms, where the halt and lamed are dubbed "handicapped"; the
hungry, "underprivileged"; the mad, "emotionally disturbed."[26]

Mrs. Stitch's remark wittily illustrates Waugh's point; " 'Why
should I go to Viola Chasm's Distressed Area; did she come to my
Model Madhouse?' " (*Scoop*, 15). George Orwell's grim warning, in
"Politics and the English Language," is essentially the same argument as Waugh's: by hiding ugly realities under euphemisms, society and language are corrupted. Many of Waugh's naïfs (the
Emperor Seth, Sir Joseph Mainwaring, Aimee Thanatogenos) gladly
and innocently embrace the abstractions that mask an unpleasant
reality. Others, less innocent (Basil Seal, Ian Kilbannock), cold-
bloodedly manipulate words to self-serving private or public ends.

II   *Incident and Character*

Waugh's comments on incident and character are closely related
to his paramount concern for style. In considering incident,
Waugh's thinking is similar to Henry James's in "The Art of
Fiction." James, in remarking on the delicate interrelationship
between character and incident, stresses the importance of incident—that the slightest gesture of tone or voice may constitute
"incident." Likewise, Waugh held that murders, scandals, etc., the
regular fare of newspapers, have only limited importance in the
novel "according to their place in the book's structure and their
relationship to other incidents in the composition, just as subdued
colours attain great intensity in certain pictures."[27] For Waugh, as
for James, dialogue cannot exist apart from its function in the larger
pattern of the novel's total form, structure: "It cannot be said too
often that in a novel the interest of the conversations must not depend on the interest of the views expressed. No great novelist has
ever allowed this, nor ever will." Shifting time sequences, internal
monologues, and daydreams often keep the reader "rather busier
than was worth the effort expended."[28]

Preferring simplicity and directness in style, Waugh favored a
similar directness in characterization. To his way of looking at it,
characterization was the bold sketching in of brush strokes, as opposed to an ambiguous sounding of the depths of consciousness.
Writing should not be an "investigation of character," but "an exercise in the use of language. . . . I have no technical psychological
interest."[29] John Plant (*Work Suspended*) criticizes the efforts of
some novelists to describe true-to-life, in-depth characters:

The algebra of fiction must reduce its problems to symbols if they are to be
soluble at all. I am shy of a book commended to me on the grounds that the
"characters are alive." There is no place in literature for a live man, solid
and active. At best the author may maintain a kind of Dickensian
menagerie, where his characters live behind bars, in darkness, to be
liberated twice nightly for a brief gambol under the arc lamps; in they
come to the whip crack, dazzled, deafened and doped, tumble through
their tricks and scamper out again, to the cages behind which the real
business of life, eating and mating, is carried on out of sight of the
audience. "Are the lions really alive?" "Yes, lovey." "Will they eat us up?"
"No, lovey, the man won't let them"—that is all the reviewers mean as a
rule when they talk of "life." The alternative, classical expedient is to take
the whole man and reduce him to a manageable abstraction. Set up your
picture plain, fix your point of vision, make your figure twenty foot high or

the size of a thumbnail, he will be life-size on your canvas; hang your picture in the darkest corner, your heaven will still be its one source of light.
Beyond these limits lie only the real trouser buttons and the crepe hair with
which the futurists used to adorn their paintings.[30]

Plant's remarks are further reinforced in Waugh's diary entry for
May 9, 1962: ". . .We novelists should remember that our
'characters' and our 'dramas' are mere shadows compared with
those of the real world."[31] In this observation and in the passage
from *Work Suspended* Waugh looks not only to his own belief for
authority but also to classic theories of art as imitation of life, not as
life itself. Waugh's practice did not, however, entirely conform to
his theory. His theorizing about characterization certainly applies to
most of the one-dimensional figures in his novels (Paul Pennyfeather, Adam Symes, for example), but does not account for the
more subtle, multi-dimensional portraits of Tony Last, Sebastian
Flyte, or Guy Crouchback, who are not "abstractions" or "shadows" but characters of some depth and substance whose singular
identity interests the reader as much as their relationship to the
situation Waugh unfolds for us in each of the novels in which they
appear.

When Waugh wrote, "My problem has been to distill comedy
and sometimes tragedy from the knockabout farce of people's outward behavior," he was being perfectly true to his own critical
stance. This did not imply that character study was not worth
bothering with (Guy Crouchback's gradually changing consciousness is developed throughout three volumes) but clearly
suggested that novelists often try too hard to attain the "true to
life" verisimilitude most readers demand, and that when they "try
to represent the whole human mind and soul" they usually omit
(from Waugh's Catholic standpoint) its determining feature: "that
of being God's creature with a defined purpose."[32]

He was confident that Wodehouse's stylized characters would
live, but that the "half-real characters of the ordinary popular
novelist" would disappear. What signifies for Waugh, is that
characters in fiction must have credibility in their particular
ficitional world, no matter what the complexity of the characterization: "Literary characters may survive either through being
so real and round that they are true of any age or race, or through
being so stylized that they carry their own world with
them. . . . Mr. Wodehouse's characters live in their own universe
like the characters of a fairy story"; they are "purely and essentially

literary characters."[33] Waugh did not imply that *all* novelists ought to write like Wodehouse, or that the characters of any novelist ought to skitter along the surface of life like a waterbug. He did, however, quite clearly suggest that the novelist ought not to present a "slice of life," that he must not tell us everything about his characters, that he must be highly selective in emphasizing general character traits, and that his characters must be consistent, true to the situations in which they have their existence. In 1930, in writing a critique of Hardy's *Tess of the D'Urbervilles* for the *Evening Standard*, he attacked Hardy for writing a novel whose artificial dialogue was false to the life of its characters.[34] What he was arguing against was an inconsistent tone in the presentation of both character and action throughout the Hardy novel. To Waugh, *Tess* was neither consistently naturalistic nor imaginative in tone, and had no inner logic, an inner logic (no matter how fantastic) that is one of the major characteristics of Waugh's fiction.

Although Waugh could be savagely destructive in his reviews, as when he compared Stephen Spender's awkward use of language to the "horror of seeing a Sevres vase in the hands of a chimpanzee,"[35] his criticism usually stemmed from disappointment with botched work by a fellow craftsman, and was never tinged with sour envy of another writer's success. When Hemingway began to lose control of the clean, uncluttered style of his first two novels, and in its place substituted hardboiled melodrama in *To Have and Have Not*, Waugh felt that Hemingway had become a victim of arrested development, a widespread malady among American writers:

. . .Too often they are living and working at the stage of growth of prurient schoolgirls; Mr. Hemingway is a clean, strapping lad. . .house colours for swimming, etc. . . . he writes in an exuberant schoolboy slang and he deals with topics which. . .interest little chaps of his age; pirates, dagos, Chinks, plenty of bloodshed and above all the topic dearest to the heart of a healthy boy—How does it work? [36]

But in 1950, on reviewing Hemingway's *Across the River and into the Trees*, while recognizing that Hemingway had written a weak book, he asserted that he had been unfairly mauled by the critics ("smug, condescending, derisive,. . .some with an affectation of pity") and stoutly defended him. It was an entirely disinterested, charitable act, in which he extended his hand to a colleague down on his literary luck. Waugh retorted to Hemingway's detractors that he "is one of the most original and powerful of living writers. Even if he had written a completely fatuous book, this was not the way to treat it." Searching for the source of the hatred, Waugh concluded that the critics "detected in him something they find quite un-forgivable—Decent Feeling," including a "sense of chiv-alry—respect for women, pity for the weak, love of honor."[37]

Waugh's reviews of Graham Greene's work, beginning with *Lawless Roads* (1939), focus on Greene's skill in dramatizing agoniz-ing questions of religious belief, but unlike Waugh's emphasis on form and expression in his reviews of other writers, the subject of Greene's troubled faith made it increasingly difficult for Waugh to separate the writer from the work. In commenting on *Lawless Roads* (published in the same year as Waugh's *Robbery Under Law*, both books concerned with government persecution of the Church in Mexico), Waugh aptly describes what was to become the domi-nant tone of Greene's fiction: "Contemplation of the horrible ways in which men exercise their right of choice leads him into something very near a hatred of free-will."[38] In 1948 he wrote of the *Heart of the Matter* that Catholics would be scandalized, for "it not only portrays Catholics as unlikeable human beings but shows them as tortured by their Faith." Because they are part of our own ex-perience his characters are real, for they share "the same moral and spiritual predicament" of the rest of us. He praised Greene's skill in storytelling, ranking him with Georges Simenon and Somerset Maugham, and pointed out the neutrality of Greene's attitude in totally separating himself from his readers, an attitude equally descriptive of Waugh's practice in a succession of novels up to *Brideshead Revisited*. Both Greene's "Entertainments" and "Novels" are grim in style, but with the difference that the "Novels have been baptized, held deep under in the waters of life." He pondered Scobie's damnation in detail, decided that Greene "thinks him a saint," but that Scobie did not illustrate any special thesis. On the question whether we can separate Scobie's moral state from his spiritual state, Waugh dodged the issue by referring the matter to the theologians.[39] However, when Greene continued to explore "the dark fever-country on the unmapped borders of superstition and apostasy,"[40] Waugh became increasingly disturbed with his heretical philosophizing, and in his diary entry for 31 December - 1 January 1961, noted that he had to refuse to write a review of *A Burnt-Out Case*, for there was nothing in the "vexation of a Catholic artist. . .who cuts himself off from divine grace by sexual sin" that he could write about "without shame." He lamented that "it is the first time Graham has come out as specifically faithless—pray God it is a mood. . . . What is more—no, less—Graham's skill is fading."[41] Greene as literary artist had forsaken his earlier path and now almost openly identified himself with the leading character in the novel. This, clearly, would not do for Waugh.

As noted, many of Waugh's statements on the craft of writing, and especially on the role of the artist whose services are valued less and less in the modern age, can be interpreted as an ambiguous mix of dandified pose and underlying conviction. In the mid-1940s he began to believe that writers as a group, like the institution of the English Gentleman, were doomed. A few might find work as publicists, or as state functionaries in "Ministries of Rest and Culture." Some might turn to "anarchic bohemianism" and act as irritants to the bourgeoisie while a few others, the ascetics, the aesthetes, would produce the works of art that might save English culture. Not for Waugh were the equalities of the coming Socialist state, but an aristocratic ideal of patronage that shared its "freedom of thought and movement" with the artist. Only in a stratified society could language "be preserved as a vehicle for accurate and graceful expression."[42] Waugh knew full well that he was conjuring up a British Periclean Age that never did exist, but it is also true that his own generation was immensely concerned with style, and that his contemporaries wrote with a grace of expression only infrequently attained to by their successors after World War II. His ex cathedra critical pronouncements, sometimes abrasive, patronizing, and often maddeningly general, although clearly stated, belong to a very special critical orientation that deliberately provokes reaction, and forces a redefining of the reader's standards of judgment. In their abrupt, tendentious way, they lead us back to the texts, just as the abrupt finality of D. H. Lawrence's *Studies in Classic American Literature* or Leslie Fiedler's boldly speculative theorizing in *Love and Death in the American Novel* goads us into rereading and hence to a fresh and perhaps altered judgment of what we have read.

CHAPTER 6

Waugh's Achievement

Mr. E. A. St.J. Waugh. . .said that the only
thing certain was that the world was going to
the dogs. . . .
Lancing College Magazine, December 1920

I *Style*

IF Waugh develops no fully worked out philosophy in his
novels beyond suggesting general norms of what he believes to be
rational behavior, he achieves a fine blend of satiric farce and comedy, and occasionally pathos, expressed in language of artful
simplicity. Often a romantic in his public role-playing, especially in
his avowed distrust of organized political or social movements, he
was a classicist in his devotion to the precise, telling word combination.

Total commitment to an economical style shapes Waugh's distinctive blend of disgust and satiric comedy. In his meticulously
crafted art every word is exactly placed so as to build to a
cumulative, devastating situation or remark. Evidence for Waugh's
concern for the right word in the right place may be found in recent
studies of interlinear changes in the manuscripts of the novels, and
in changes between the manuscripts and the printed versions.[1]
Curiously enough, only in the last few years have scholars begun to
examine how Waugh manipulates verbal patterns. As Paul Farr has
observed in an illuminating essay, Waugh's elegant style is
characterized by simple sentences (often quite short), elliptical
clauses, parallelisms, appositives, occasional periodic sentences for
balance and variety, active verbs, sparing use of metaphor, and as a
bonus for the reasonably well-read, literary allusions (always in
ironic context) found everywhere in his fiction.[2]

The opening lines of *A Handful of Dust* illustrate how Waugh, in
a seemingly innocent, detached manner, builds to a climactic state-

ment that suddenly, and quite paradoxically, makes us laugh at the same time we experience revulsion. The avaricious Mrs. Beaver describes to her son, in a bored, flat tone of voice, what happened when her interior decorator shop caught on fire:

> "Was anyone hurt?"
> "No one, I am thankful to say," said Mrs. Beaver, "except two housemaids who lost their heads and jumped through a glass roof into the paved court. They were in no danger. The fire never reached the bedrooms, I am afraid. Still, they are bound to need doing up, everything black with smoke and drenched in water, and luckily they had that old-fashioned sort of extinguisher that ruins *everything*." (9)

In style and effect, this passage is similar to, if not quite so morally indignant as the lines in *The Adventures of Huckleberry Finn* when Aunt Sally Phelps questions Huck about a steamboat accident:

> "Good gracious! Anybody hurt?"
> "No'm. Killed a nigger."
> "Well, it's lucky; because sometimes people do get hurt."[3]

Through skillfully contrived detachment, both Evelyn Waugh and Mark Twain cloak their disgust under an apparent surface callousness that this is the way of the world. What we feel in these representative instances is pent-up anger at the absence of common humanity. Compassion may also be suggested, but the satirist's glaring eye takes precedence.

Where George Bernard Shaw or Aldous Huxley often stepped forward to the footlights and directly lectured, Waugh followed the more difficult path, especially in his early fiction, of deceptively simple understatement in gambling on his readers' intelligence to understand and to take pleasure in his verbal pyrotechnics. The high pitched audaciousness did not remain constant in Waugh's later fiction, and it is not coincidence that in the more relaxed, leisurely descriptive tone of *Brideshead Revisited*, the satiric voltage falls off, as with the exception of a few scattered passages, is true of *Sword of Honour*.

II *Fantasy*

Waugh's deliberately artless style achieves its most barbed effect when totally removed from any overt effort to score a point. By working out his satiric purpose through indirect means of description or dialogue, Waugh suggests an absurd, chaotic world posing as an ordered world, in which no one communicates or wants to communicate. This becomes evident when his characters start to talk. The moment they begin to do so, they damn themselves out of hand. Living in a fantasy world intolerant of clear expression, they cannot abide rational, civilized discourse. If it were otherwise, the cloud-capped towers of their fantasies would abruptly dissolve. Certainly it is not happenstance that references to *Alice in Wonderland* appear and reappear as motif in novel after novel, for words correspond to the inner reality of the character speaking them, and bear little relationship to outer reality. Only infrequently, as in Lady Circumference's bellowing deflation of Mrs. Ape's evangelistic pulpit rhetoric, are these fantasies shattered. Like the Nestorian priests in *Black Mischief*, most of Waugh's characters dance to an "interior melody."

Sir Joseph Mainwaring's witlessly fervent belief in nonexistent weapons that would instantly destroy the Nazis, or Prime Minister Outrage's highly colored dreams of Baroness Yoshiwara are harmless. More often, however, the fantasy lives of Waugh's characters have lethal consequences, as in Lucas-Dockery's unthinking mouthings of penological theory which bring about the death of the unfortunate Prendergast. Locked into his vision of the ideal country gentleman, Tony Last cannot reach out to his wife, Brenda, and for this failure in discourse his creator metes out to him a most dreadfully appropriate punishment. Emperor Seth's logorrheic infatuation with words and phrases such as "ectogenesis," "communal exercising," "autogyros," and "Surrealism" implies a pathetically fantastic confidence that the speaking of these words will exorcise the barbarism of Azania. His Merlin is Basil Seal, the juju magician who somehow will give shape and form to the abstract cant terms of post - World War I European "culture."

Unlike Seth, Basil knows how words can be manipulated. When the Lord Chamberlain informs him that Seth has forbidden raw beef to be served to Wanda chieftains at a banquet, Basil tells him, " 'Call it steak tartare' " (*Black Mischief*, 130). But not even Basil can foresee the confusion over the publicity for the Birth Control Program, the natives preferring the poster graphically illustrating the poverty-stricken, diseased lot of a family of eleven children, some deformed and mad (" 'Very holy' "), to the one picturing a healthy model couple with one child. Usually a quick study, Basil misreads the natives' reaction to his propaganda campaign and, caught up in his own rhetoric, he writes an article in Fleet Street journalese that Lord Copper, that arch fantasist, would have envied: "Once more, the people of the Empire have overridden the opposition of a prejudiced and interested minority, and with no uncertain voice have followed the Emperor's lead in the cause of Progress and the New Age" (*Black Mischief*, 149 - 50). As occurs so frequently throughout Waugh's novels, one semantic confusion has opened into another. Later, in *Put Out More Flags*, Basil becomes a more subtle adept in the semantic game, and skillfully employs the vaguely threatening language of bureaucracy to serve his own nefarious ends.

In *Vile Bodies*, Lord Metroland refuses to confront his wife's lover, "young Trumpington," but instead takes refuge in his library where he is comforted by the physical reality of "the *Encyclopaedia Britannica* in an early and very bulky edition, *Who's Who*, Burke" and "a safe in the corner painted green, his writing table, his secretary's table. . ." (134). As is true of Seth, he has his own stratagems to avoid painful communication. Waugh then cuts to another home, and to the bedroom of Lady Ursula, daughter of the Duchess of Stayle. The girl tells her mother she does not want to marry Edward Throbbing, who has just proposed to her, but the mother grandly sails ahead, quite oblivious to her daughter's anguish:

"But, Mama. . ."
Not another word, dear child. It's very late and you've got to look your best for Edward to-morrow haven't you, love?"
The Duchesss closed the door softly and went to her own room. Her husband was in his dressing gown.
"Andrew."
"What is it, dear? I'm saying my prayers."
"Edward proposed to Ursula to-night."
"Ah!"
"Aren't you glad?"
"I told you, dear, I'm trying to say my prayers."
"It's a real joy to see the children so happy." (136)

Emperor Seth, Lord Metroland, and the Duchess of Stayle and her husband are exemplars of an almost limitless number of

characters who cannot communicate, do not listen, and don't want
to listen. Seth is imprisoned by abstractions, the Duchess by her
blindly narrow view of the proper scheme of things, to be kept in
tact at all cost whatever the amount of suffering involved.

A much smaller group, including Philbrick, Fagan, and Captain
Grimes (*Decline and Fall*), Colonel Blount (*Vile Bodies*), Mr
Baldwin (*Scoop*), the elder Ryder (*Brideshead Revisited*), and
Apthorpe (*Sword of Honour*), use words with Elizabethan richness
in playing out the various masquerades they so readily assume. For
these characters, and especially for Philbrick and Baldwin, role
playing is fantasy exalted to its highest pitch. They know they are
living a dream, and revel in its gorgeousness. Creatures of their im
agination, they quite successfully circumvent the irrationalities of
the world in which they live.

III   *Burlesque*

Although Waugh's customary satiric stance was one of apparent
detachment, expressed through dialogue in which his characters un
wittingly reveal their folly and ignorance, he was equally sure in his
use of other of the satirist's weapons, notably the overstatement of
burlesque. In *Vile Bodies*, the circular, dangerous auto racing frenzy
parallels an even more catastrophic aimlessness in the lives of the
1920s younger generation; in *Scoop*, war correspondents spy and in
trigue like schoolboys; in *The Ordeal of Gilbert Pinfold*, the
narrator describes himself as an exaggerated caricature of the
figures in his novels: "he gradually assumed this character of
burlesque. . .a combination of eccentric don and testy colonel" (9).
Some of the most telling instances of satiric distortion may be
found in the least satirical of Waugh's fiction, the *Sword of Honour*
trilogy. They include the mock-epic struggle between Brigadier
Ritchie-Hook and Lt. Apthorpe for possession of Apthorpe's field
lavatory, the dreadful efforts of the nutritional expert, Dr
Glendenning-Rees, to teach the army how to live off the land, and
the conspiratorial, gleeful planning of the unauthorized night raid
on the coast of North Africa. In these and in other episodes, war
becomes a wild parody of children's games. Waugh focuses his
burlesque on certain attitudes of the military in Ritchie-Hook,
wonderfully fantastic distortion of the professional soldier. Hook
successively emerges as comic, grotesque, and pathetic, for Waugh

denies to him any of the configurations of tragic dimension. In *Scoop* and those who surround him, Waugh creates satiric types to illustrate confused general attitudes found in all mankind—here a series of attitudes about the nature of warfare.

Whatever the mixture of detachment or burlesque Waugh provides for his readers' delectation, it is the audacity of the satiric thrust in his novels which gives pleasure to his audience, rather than any suggestion of utilitarian remedies for the madness and betrayal confronting us at every turn. Leonard Feinberg remarks "the satirist has work to do but planning the ideal society is not part of that work. . .satires are read because they are aesthetically satisfying as works of art, not because they are (as they may be) morally wholesome or ethically instructive."[4] Waugh's aphoristic remarks on satire bear out Feinberg's contention that its principal function is to expose human folly rather than to offer solutions. Writing in *Life* magazine he said that satire "is aimed at inconsistency and hypocrisy. It exposes polite cruelty and folly by exaggerating them. It seeks to produce shame."[5]

IV *Ambiguous Detachment*

Even though they were entertained, many of Waugh's critics misunderstood the satire underlying the farce, and mistakenly believed that he lacked any humanitarian impulse. At the time of his death, a *Newsweek* editorial stated "Compassion for him was yet another foible of an absurd age."[6] The *New York Times* followed a similar line: "All the elementary decencies are spoofed. The world's cruelties are accepted, never protested against."[7] Admittedly the inhabitants of Waugh's fictional world are quite indifferent to the incongruous demise of his characters (Little Lord Tangent quite literally dying by inches, or Agatha Runcible's death brought on by the wild party at her bedside). While many of Waugh's innocents blind themselves to the pitfalls of an animallike world that is callous and devoid of compassion, this does not suggest that Waugh lacks compassion. To the contrary, its apparent absence implies disgust that human beings can be so heartless to each other. We can accept Waugh's indifference to the dreadful misfortunes of Paul Pennyfeather or Adam Symes, because for the most part these characters are no more than stick figures propelled through a series of situations Waugh wishes to inspect and satirize. But not even the unblinking Paul remains a completely stoic observer of the absurd cruelties of his world. When the rioting members of the Bollinger Club have torn off his pants, and he is then expelled from Scone College, he allows himself one quick, but telling protest: " 'God damn and blast them all to hell,'. . .and then he felt rather ashamed because he rarely swore" (*Decline and Fall*, 19). In *A Handful of Dust*, although Tony Last evades responsibility by escaping to the jungle, he has also been driven to this action by a society that has no standards of common decency. In *Sword of Honour*, Crouchback's redemptive but futile efforts to save the refugees are received with bored indifference by his military superiors.

The critics who so readily pigeonholed Waugh as a remarkably successful deviser of black comedy lacking any compassion for his characters missed his ambiguous detachment. Many of his characters, and especially William Boot, Emperor Seth, and Apthorpe are simultaneously ridiculous and likable. Victimized, yet bearing no ill-will to anyone, they elicit our sympathy. Differing from Swift or Huxley, the satirists most comparable to him, Waugh does not hate his characters. For a few unfeeling opportunists such as Rex Mottram or Gilpin, he reserves a feeling of contempt or disgust, but as in Dickens's characterization of Pecksniff, these figures have a repulsive vitality in their failure to be decent human beings. If Waugh had not had a high degree of tolerance for human weaknesses he could not have continued to write so many novels exposing our pretensions, nor could he have written that remarkable piece of self-parody, *The Ordeal of Gilbert Pinfold*. An acute observer of English life from the late 1920s to the mid 1950s, he does not loathe social and political institutions as Sinclair Lewis loathed small-town America in *Main Street*, or the business world in *Babbitt*.

V *Conservatism*

Accused of being heartless, he was also criticized for the extreme conservatism of his political and religious views, criticism that Waugh often brought on himself, as when he taunted his more ideologically oriented critics that he had never voted. However, in accounting for Waugh's doctrinaire attitudes, Christopher Sykes maintains that his comedy "grew from deep roots of conviction and belief, and if these sometimes made for excessive conservatism in his opinions, the fact should not obscure from anyone that the ideals by which he lived were noble ones which gave sustenance to a mind of astonishing power and agility."[8]

Paradoxically, in mingling freely with all manner of politicians both right and left, while at the same time keeping clear of any party label, he was more alert to the cross-currents of English politics than many of his literary contemporaries. Political life provided him with a never diminishing source of satiric material, yet the conservative views that inform his novels are reflective of an ingrained patriotism, love of tradition, and sense of historical process. The latter is especially important, for if Waugh's bureaucrats have no understanding, no grasp of the historical forces that shape their lives, his younger generation caught up in giddy inanities, have completely lost contact with their heritage. Malcolm Bradbury, in remarking on Waugh's travel books of the 1930s, points out the curious mixture of conservative satiric attitudes and love of country expressed in Waugh's novels:

A sense of the failure of liberal humanism, coupled with a sustained interest in it, runs through the work of this period; a suspicion of the nonconformist conscience, a distrust of all earthly regimes, a conviction that things decline and fall as we move away from a Catholic imperium, a view of the world as a place where the gates of the madhouse are periodically thrown open. . .are mixed with a patriotic ideal about his native land and those who have nourished it and sustained its traditional values.[9]

VI *Conclusion*

Throughout thirteen novels and several shorter works of fiction, Waugh's encompassing eye skewered all institutions and theories in which he detected humbug, including both democratic and socialistic forms of government, education, penology, newspapers, the idiocies of generals and university dons, funeral customs of the United States, social attitudes of the British establishment, the misguided efforts of emergent African nations in imitating European governments, and the dangers of outmoded romanticism. The malicious gusto of the novels, essentially conservative in their implied value system, did not always endear him to his readers, for satirists run the risk of being prophets without honor in their own country. Although his novels were translated into many languages, and at the time of his death he was acknowledged as a satirist of the first order, he was never accorded the full public recognition that he so richly deserved. Perhaps too many sacred cows had been gored along the way. Disdainful of the critics' jibes, he went his own way, and stated a modest valedictory for himself in the *Paris Review* interview: " 'I have done all I could. I have done my best.' "[10]

Years from now, readers may encounter Waugh for the first time with the same sense of shocked delight that the uninitiated often discover in a first reading of Twain, Swift, or Pope. Delight in absurd, if sometimes horrifying, incongruities provides a large measure of our enjoyment of Waugh, but his work is also to be read as a series of contemporary morality tales, Waugh's unblinking judgment on a mad world always teetering on the edge of chaos. With variations, the pattern remains consistent throughout Waugh's fiction.

Allowing for his cranky attack on Waugh's Catholicism, Edmund Wilson's evaluation in 1944 that "Waugh. . .is likely to figure as the only first-rate comic genius that has appeared in England since Bernard Shaw"[11] still holds true. Waugh continues to be invoked again and again in popular journal reviews as *the* model for satirists working the same vein. It is possible that with time's passage his unique mixture of high comedy and satire will outlast the more pretentious moralizing of Huxley.

In their efforts to estimate his achievement, not all of Waugh's critics have shifted their attention from his private life to the works of his imagination. No doubt he brought some of this misdirected attention on himself, for in Walt Whitman's phrase, he was "both in and out of the game," both clinically detached observer and delighted role-playing participant in the foibles of his world. Perhaps too much has been made of the latter at the expense of Waugh's astringent powers as observer. When critics focus more directly on the form and verbal patterns of his work, as they have now begun to do, it appears highly probable that Waugh's surrealistic farce, his skilful pillorying of fools and the illogical, and his precisely effective rapierlike style will rank him as one of the major English satirists of the twentieth century.

Notes and References

Chapter One

1. "Aspirations of a Mugwump," *Spectator* 203 (October 2, 1959): 435.
2. *A Little Learning* (Boston, 1964), p. 11.
3. Arthur Waugh, *Tradition and Change* (London, 1919), p. 3.
4. Dudley Carew, *The House is Gone, a Personal Retrospect* (London, 1949), p. 94.
5. As an undergraduate, Waugh remarked on this unease in "Oxford and the Next War," *Isis,* March 12, 1924, p. 10.
6. As reported in *Cherwell,* May 25, 1922, p. 43.
7. *Oxford Magazine,* March 1, 1923, p. 259.
8. Waugh's evaluation of the story. See *A Little Learning,* p. 189.
9. *Oxford Broom,* June 1923, p. 15.
10. Harold Acton, *Memoirs of an Aesthete* (London, 1948), p. 126.
11. "Oxford Revisited," *Sunday Times,* Weekly Review, November 7, 1965, p. 53.
12. Charles E. Linck and Robert M. Davis, "The Bright Young People in *Vile Bodies,*" *Papers on Language and Literature* 5 (1969): 80 - 90, contains a lively account of this group. See also Martin Green's study of the English dandy, *Children of the Sun* (New York, 1976), pp. 205 - 10.
13. *Rossetti* (London, 1928), pp. 13 - 14.
14. *Memoirs of an Aesthete,* p. 204.
15. Alec Waugh, *My Brother Evelyn and Other Profiles* (New York, 1967), pp. 191 - 92.
16. "Come Inside," in *The Road to Damascus,* ed. John O'Brien (Garden City, 1949), pp. 20 - 21. Also see "Converted to Rome: Why It Happened to Me," *Daily Express,* October 20, 1930, p. 10.
17. *Labels* (London, 1930), p. 44.
18. *Edmund Campion,* Third Edition (London, 1961), p. vii.
19. "Fan-Fare," *Life,* April 8, 1946, p. 53. He noted that he lived

in a shabby stone house. . .where nothing is under a hundred years old except the plumbing and that does not work. I collect old books in an inexpensive, desultory way. I have a fast-emptying cellar of wine and gardens fast reverting to the jungle. I am very contentedly married. I have numerous children whom I see once a day for ten, I hope, awe-inspiring minutes.

20. "Through European Eyes," *London Mercury* 36 (June 1937): 149.

21. "The Soldiers Speak," *Night and Day*, July 29, 1937, p. 24.

22. Statement in "Authors Take Sides on the Spanish War," answers to a questionnaire issued by the *Left Review* (London, 1937), n.p.

23. Eric Linklater, *The Art of Adventure* (London, 1948), p. 48.

24. Diary entry for May 7, 1945 quoted in "The Private Diaries of Evelyn Waugh," Part 6, ed. Michael Davie, *Observer,* April 29, 1973, p. 14.

25. *Scott-King's Modern Europe* (London, 1947), p. 39.

26. "The Jesuit Who Was Thursday," *Commonweal* 45 (March 21, 1947): 561.

27. "What to Do with the Upper Classes," *Town and Country*, September 1946, p. 260.

28. "P. G. Wodehouse, an Act of Homage and Reparation" (London: BBC, July 15, 1961). Recorded Programmes Permanent Library, BBC archives.

29. In a television interview in 1964, he remarked, "The particular quality of being comic. . .is a function of youth." "Evelyn Waugh Talks to Elizabeth Jane Howard," edited extracts from Monitor (London: BBC TV, February 16, 1964, unpublished).

30. *Love Among the Ruins* (London, 1953), p. 8.

31. Diary entry for November 17, 1955, quoted in "The Private Diaries of Evelyn Waugh," Part 7, *Observer*, May 6, 1973, p. 34.

32. Auberon Waugh, "Death in the Family," *Spectator* 216 (May 6, 1966): 562.

33. "Frankly Speaking," Evelyn Waugh answers questions from Charles Wilmot, Jack Davies, and Stephen Black (London: BBC radio, November 16, 1953, unpublished).

34. "Awake My Soul! It is a Lord," *Spectator* 195 (July 8, 1955): 36.

35. Diary entry for June 21, 1955, quoted in "The Private Diaries of Evelyn Waugh," Part 7, *Observer,* May 6, 1973, p. 30.

36. Frances Donaldson, *Evelyn Waugh: Portrait of a Country Neighbor* (Philadelphia, 1968), p. 48.

37. Interview with Julian Jebb, in *Writers at Work, The Paris Review Interviews*, Third Series (New York, 1967), pp. 109 - 10.

38. Howard interview, February 16, 1964. Ref. footnote 29.

39. Diary entry for December 8, 1960, quoted in "The Private Diaries of Evelyn Waugh," Part 8, *Observer,* May 13, 1973, p. 45. This observation, slightly altered, also appears in *Basil Seal Rides Again or The Rake's Regress* (Boston, 1963), p. 9.

40. "Face to Face," Waugh interviewed by John Freeman (London: BBC TV, June 26, 1960, unpublished tape in BBC archives).

41. Speech at Royal Society of Literature (London: BBC, June 26, 1963, unpublished tape in BBC archives).

42. "Passport into Spring" series, *Daily Mail*, March 28, 1960, p. 8.

43. "Sloth," in *The Seven Deadly Sins* (New York, 1962), p. 64.

44. Arnold Lunn, "Evelyn Waugh Revisited," *National Review* 20 (February 27, 1968): 190.

45. "Fides Quaerens Intellectum," *Tablet* 219 (July 31, 1965): 864.

46. Dom Hubert Van Zeller, "An Appreciation of Evelyn Waugh," *Downside Review* 84 (July 1966): 286.

47. "Death in the Family," 562.

48. Prefatory remarks to "The Private Diaries of Evelyn Waugh," Part 8, p. 44.

49. *My Brother Evelyn*, p. 166.

50. Graham Greene, Note to Waugh obituary, *Times*, April 15, 1966, p. 15.

51. "The Beauty of His Malice: Evelyn Waugh (1903 - 1966)," *Time*, April 22, 1966, p. 84.

52. "The Private Diaries of Evelyn Waugh," Part 8, p. 53.

53. Christopher Sykes, "Evelyn Waugh—a Brief Life," *Listener* 78 (August 24, 1967): 229. Reprinted in *Good Talk: An Anthology from BBC Radio*, ed. Derwent May (New York, 1979), pp. 11 - 34.

Chapter Two

1. Sean O'Faolain, "Huxley and Waugh," *The Vanishing Hero* (Boston, 1957), p. 26.

2. Among these few may be included Martin Green, "Meaning and Delight in Evelyn Waugh," *Tuftonian* 21 (February 1965): 79 - 89.

3. As quoted in Robert M. Davis, "Textual Problems in the Novels of Evelyn Waugh," *Papers of the Bibliographical Society of America* 62 (Second Quarter 1968): 263.

4. *Wine in Peace and War* (London, 1947), pp. 38 - 39.

5. Alvin Kernan, "A Theory of Satire," in *Satire: Modern Essays in Criticism*, ed. Ronald Paulson (Englewood Cliffs, N.J., 1971), p. 262.

6. Waugh remarked of *Decline and Fall* that "it was in a sense based on my experiences as a schoolmaster, yet I had a much nicer time than the hero." Quoted in Julian Jebb, "Evelyn Waugh," *Writers at Work: The Paris Review Interviews*, Third Series (New York, 1968), p. 108.

7. Ref. Edward C. McAleer, "*Decline and Fall* as Imitation," *Evelyn Waugh Newsletter* 7: 3 (Winter 1973): 1 - 4.

8. As quoted in "The Nature and Value of Satire," *A Treasury of Satire*, ed. Edgar Johnson (New York, 1945), p. 19.

9. "Marriage a la Mode—1936," (Review of Anthony Powell, *Casanova's Chinese Restaurant*), *Spectator* 204 (June 24, 1960): 919.

10. David Daiches, *The Present Age after 1920* (London, 1958), p. 110.

11. Anthony Burgess, *The Novel Now* (London, 1967), p. 55.

12. Arnold Bennett, "Books and Persons: Turning Over the Autumn Leaves. . . ," *Evening Standard*, October 11, 1928, p. 5.

13. Cyril Connolly, "New Novels," *New Statesman,* November 3, 1928, p. 126.

14. Rebecca West, "Evelyn Waugh," *Ending in Earnest: A Literary Log* (New York, 1931), pp. 220, 221.

15. *Times Literary Supplement,* September 27, 1928, p. 685.

16. *Paris Review Interviews,* pp. 108 - 109. See also the preface to the revised edition of *Vile Bodies* (London, 1967), p. 7.

17. In the preface to the revised edition of *Vile Bodies* Waugh acknowledges that Lottie is based on Rosa Lewis, the proprietress of the Cavendish Hotel. See also Daphne Fielding, *The Duchess of Jermyn Street: The Life and Good Times of Rosa Lewis of the Cavendish Hotel,* Preface by Evelyn Waugh (Boston, 1964), and Charles E. Linck, Jr., and Robert Murray Davis, "The Bright Young People in *Vile Bodies,*" *Papers on Language and Literature* 5 (Winter 1969): 80 - 90.

18. *Vile Bodies* (London, 1930), p. 123.

19. Heinz Kosok, "The Film World of *Vile Bodies,*" *Evelyn Waugh Newsletter* 4:2 (Autumn 1970): 1 - 2, points out the cinematic quality of *Vile Bodies.* Also valuable is Jeffrey Heath's article, "*Vile Bodies* a Revolution in Film Art," *Evelyn Waugh Newsletter* 8: 3 (Winter 1974): 2 - 7.

20. Patrick Balfour, *Society Racket, A Critical Survey of Modern Social Life* (Leipzig, 1934). With surprising perspective, Balfour defines the rootlessness of his own generation. Further corroboration of this rootlessness may be found in Nancy Mitford, "Nancy Mitford's Commentary," *Evelyn Waugh Newsletter* 1:1 (Spring 1967): 1 - 2. She writes, "We hardly saw daylight, except during the small hours of the morning; every night there was a costume ball: the White Party, the Circus Party, the Boat Party, etc." (translated from the French of the original communication to *EWN*).

21. See Bradbury's introduction to *Evelyn Waugh* (Edinburgh, 1964). One of the studies in the "Writers and Critics" series, Bradbury's work contains perceptive insights.

22. From the Preface to the standard edition of *Vile Bodies* (London, 1965): "I began under the brief influence of Ronald Firbank, but struck out for myself." Representative of Firbank's arch, delicately wrought novels are *The Flower Beneath the Foot* (1923), and *Concerning the Eccentricities of Cardinal Pirelli* (1926). See James Douglas Merritt, *Ronald Firbank* (New York, 1969). In "Ronald Firbank," *Life and Letters* 2 (March 1929): 194, Waugh describes Firbank's writing practice in language that closely describes his own technique: ". . .There is the barest minimum of direct description; his compositions are built up, intricately and with a balanced alternation of the wildest extravagance and the most austere economy, with conversational nuances."

23. V. S. Pritchett, "Fiction: Warnings," *Spectator* 144 (January 18, 1930): 99.

24. L. P. Hartley, "New Fiction," *Saturday Review*, January 25, 1930, p. 15.

25. Arnold Bennett, "Books and Persons: Laughter and a Lobster Supper," *Evening Standard*, January 30, 1930, p. 9.

26. "A Recent Novel," *Tablet* 161 (February 18, 1933): 213.

27. Martin Green, "British Comedy and the British Sense of Humour: Shaw, Waugh, and Amis," *Texas Quarterly* 4 (Autumn 1961): 223.

28. As quoted in Frederick J. Stopp, *Evelyn Waugh: Portrait of an Artist* (London, 1958), p. 32.

29. James Agate, "Extravaganza," *Daily Express*, October 6, 1932, p. 6.

30. William Maxwell, *Books*, October 9, 1932, p. 7.

31. Christopher Sykes, *Evelyn Waugh: A Biography* (Boston, 1975), p. 138.

32. Richard Wasson, in "A Handful of Dust: Critique of Victorianism," *Modern Fiction Studies* 7 (Winter 1961 - 62): 327 - 37, develops parallels to Tennyson's *The Holy Grail* and *Idylls of the King*. The Tennysonian echoes are also noted in A. A. DeVitis, *Roman Holiday: The Catholic Novels of Evelyn Waugh* (New York, 1956), p. 31.

33. "Fan-Fare," *Life*, April 8, 1946, p. 58.

34. Mr. Todd's name may be of some significance, at least for readers of Beatrix Potter, who will recall the sinister fox, Mr. Tod, in *The Tale of Mr. Tod*. "Tod" is also the word for death in German.

35. "New Novels," *New Statesman and Nation* 8 (September 15, 1934): 329.

36. Rose Macaulay, "Evelyn Waugh," *Horizon* 14: 84 (December 1946): 367.

37. The revolt in Ishmaelia and the exchange of telegrams between William Boot and Lord Copper can be paralleled to the unrest in Cuba in the 1890s. William Randolph Hearst sent Frederic Remington to illustrate the news stories. Remington cabled Hearst: "EVERYTHING IS QUIET. THERE IS NO TROUBLE HERE. THERE WILL BE NO WAR. I WISH TO RETURN." Hearst promptly retorted: "PLEASE REMAIN. YOU FURNISH THE PICTURES AND I'LL FURNISH THE WAR." Quoted in Ferdinand Lundberg, *Imperial Hearst: A Social Biography* (New York, 1936), pp. 68 - 69. Perhaps Waugh borrowed from the Remington-Hearst telegrams in *Vile Bodies*.

38. *Evelyn Waugh*, p. 73.

39. In *Ronald Knox*, p. 133, Waugh comments on a similar attitude found in undergraduates of 1914: "There was very little explicit patriotism about the mood of 'joining-up.' It was a fashionable craze with, behind it, a sense of private honour: of a debt on demand that had been incurred by privilege."

40. Peter M. Jack, "Waugh's War," *New York Times Book Review*, June 7, 1942, p. 7.

41. "Books," *Time*, May 25, 1942, pp. 90 - 92. The anonymous reviewer

stated, p. 90, that "everyone of his novels has its masked importance. History helps make *Put Out More Flags* his most important book so far."

Chapter Three

1. "Fan-Fare," *Life*, April 8, 1946, p. 55.
2. Sebastian's name suggests the martyred Roman soldier shot with arrows in the reign of Diocletian (A.D. 297 - 305). Anthony Blanche's leave-taking of Sebastian: " 'My dear, I should like to stick you full of barbed arrows like a p-p-pincushion. . .' " (*Brideshead Revisited*, 42) clearly implies the association. Charles Hutton-Brown in "Sebastian as Saint: The Hagiographical Sources of Sebastian Flyte," *Evelyn Waugh Newsletter* 11: 3 (Winter 1977): 1 - 6, develops the thesis that Sebastian's career closely parallels the life of St. Aloysius (the name of Sebastian's teddy-bear). In his characterization of Sebastian, Waugh appears to have drawn upon elements in the lives of both saints.
3. The reflective tone of *Brideshead Revisited* and the chapter headings in *A Handful of Dust* (Chapter I, "Du Cote de Chez Beaver," and Chapter VI, "Du Cote de Chez Todd") demonstrate Waugh's acquaintanceship with Marcel Proust's work, *Remembrance of Things Past*. An additional Proustian echo in *Brideshead Revisited* may be read in Mr. Samgrass's casual remark to Charles Ryder, "I have been spending a cosy afternoon before the fire with the incomparable Charlus" (139 - 40).
4. Note a similar passage in *Alice in Wonderland:* "Alice opened the door (a "low door" in *Brideshead*) and looked down a small passage, not larger than a rat-hole, into the loveliest garden you ever saw," *The Annotated Alice* (Cleveland, 1963), p. 30.
5. The political maneuvering of Rex Mottram's crowd suggests the intrigue associated with "the Cliveden set" during the late 1930s. See Christopher Sykes, *Nancy: The Life of Lady Astor* (New York, 1972).
6. Ref. David Lodge, *Evelyn Waugh*, Columbia Essays on Modern Writers, No. 58 (New York, 1971), p. 33, and Malcolm Bradbury, *Evelyn Waugh*, Writers and Critics Series (Edinburgh, 1964), p. 87.
7. Christopher Sykes, *Evelyn Waugh: A Biography* (Boston, 1975), p. 250.
8. *Degenerate Oxford?: A Critical Study of Modern University Life* (London, 1930), p. 142.
9. Sykes, p. 250.
10. Sean O'Faolain, "Huxley and Waugh," in *The Vanishing Hero* (Boston, 1957), pp. 37 - 41.
11. Quoted in Jeffrey Heath, "*Brideshead:* The Critics and the Memorandum," *English Studies* 56: 3 (June 1975): 226 - 27.
12. Sykes, pp. 250, 258.
13. Ibid., p. 257.
14. Robert Heilman, "Sue Brideshead Revisited," *Accent* 7 (Winter 1947): 125.

15. Bernard Bergonzi, "Evelyn Waugh's Gentlemen," *Critical Quarterly* 5: 1 (Spring 1963): 30.

16. Waugh gave further expression to his sometimes uneasy class consciousness in "What to Do with the Upper Classes: A Modest Proposal," *Town and Country*, September 1946, pp. 141, 260 - 61. Since the welfare state is about to finish off the upper classes, he suggests that special reservations be set up for the preservation of "The English Gentleman."

17. Edmund Wilson, "Splendors and Miseries of Evelyn Waugh," in *Classics and Commercials* (New York, 1950, reprinted 1962), p. 301. Similar animadversions are expressed in Diana Trilling's article, "The Piety of Evelyn Waugh," *Nation*, January 5, 1946, pp. 19 - 20.

18. Rose Macaulay, "Evelyn Waugh," *Horizon* 14 (December 1946): 372.

19. Ronald Knox, "The Reader Suspended," *Month*, New Series, 8:1 (January 1952): 237.

20. For a more balanced reading, see Marston LaFrance, "Context and Structure of Evelyn Waugh's *Brideshead Revisited*," *Twentieth Century Literature* 10 (April 1964): 12 - 18. At the time of his death, George Orwell was beginning to take notes for a long article on Waugh. Orwell unfavorably contrasted Graham Greene with Waugh in stating that Greene's characters, especially Scobie and Louise in *The Heart of the Matter*, are too highbrow, too intellectualized, but that ". . .Evelyn Waugh's *Brideshead Revisited* succeeds because the situation itself is a normal one. The Catholic characters bump up against problems they would meet with in real life; they do not suddenly move on to a different intellectual plane as soon as their religious beliefs are involved." From *In Front of Your Nose 1945 - 50*, Vol. IV of *The Collected Essays, Journalism and Letters of George Orwell* (New York, 1968), p. 442.

21. In *Four Studies in Loyalty* (New York, 1948), Christopher Sykes remarks on Waugh's success in *Brideshead Revisited* in describing the combination of tradition and modernity that characterized undergraduate life at Oxford during the 1920s. He states (p. 88), "People may believe that in this book he cannot be attempting a serious picture of that ancient seat of learning, but the picture is true." Also ref. Harold Acton, *Memoirs of an Aesthete* (London, 1948).

22. "Death in Hollywood," *Life*, September 24, 1947, pp. 74, 83.

23. Cyril Connolly, Introduction to *The Loved One*, *Horizon* 17 (February 1948): 76.

24. As recorded by Paul Doyle in "Some Unpublished Waugh Correspondence III," *Evelyn Waugh Newsletter* 5: 1 (Spring 1971): 4.

25. Paul Doyle, *Evelyn Waugh: A Critical Essay* (Grand Rapids, 1969), p. 35.

26. Aubrey Menen, "The Baroque and Mr. Waugh," *Month* 5 (April 1951): 230.

27. Ibid., p. 233.

28. "St. Helena Empress," *Month* 7 (January 1952): 11.

29. Sykes, *Evelyn Waugh*, pp. 365 - 66.

30. Cf. *Sword of Honour* (London, 1964), p. 765: "A great door slammed in his mind."

31. In his diary entry of February 29, 1956, he writes, "Laura was taken. . .to consult a witch about the health of a cow. This witch not only diagnoses but treats all forms of disease, human and animal, by means of an object called 'the Box' — an apparatus like a wireless set, electrified, and fitted with dials." From "Waugh Goes Slightly Mad," in "The Private Diaries of Evelyn Waugh," Part 7, *Observer*, May 6, 1973, pp. 36 - 37.

32. Frances Donaldson, in *Evelyn Waugh: Portrait of a Country Neighbor* (New York, 1967), Chapter 4, "The Real Mr. Pinfold," attests to the highly autobiographical tone of the novel.

33. Malcolm Bradbury has astutely commented on *The Ordeal of Gilbert Pinfold* that "its art. . .is precisely not external, but the product of irrationality and chaos within himself." The barbarism and anarchy of Waugh's novels are not simply an external matter. They are also "within and to be shaped and organized." ("America and the Comic Vision," in *Evelyn Waugh and His World*, ed. David Pryce-Jones [Boston, 1973], p. 171).

34. J. B. Priestley, "What Was Wrong with Pinfold?" *New Statesman and Nation* 54 (August 31, 1957): 244.

35. John Raymond, "Mr. Waugh on Deck," *New Statesman and Nation* 54 (July 20, 1957): 88.

36. Priestley, p. 244.

37. Gabriel Fielding, "Evelyn Waugh: The Price of Satire," *Listener* 72 (October 8, 1964): 542. In 1956, Fielding sent Waugh page proofs of Muriel Spark's hallucinatory novel, *The Comforters*. Later, in reviewing the novel, Waugh stated: "It so happens that *The Comforters* came to me just as I had finished a story on a similar theme and I was struck by how much more ambitious was Miss Spark's essay and how much better she had accomplished it." Quoted from "Something Fresh," *Spectator* 198 (February 22, 1957): 256.

Chapter Four

1. Julian Jebb, *Writers at Work*, pp. 112 - 13.

2. Ibid., p. 112.

3. See Waugh's article "Commando Raid on Bardia," *Life*, November 17, 1941, pp. 63 - 66, 71, 72, 74. Of the commandos Waugh says, "There was something of the spirit which one reads in the letters and poetry of 1914" (p. 64). But even in this highly factual account the Waugh touch is evident. The planning for the raid "reminded me of the scene in *The Wind in the Willows* where Badger prepares the attack on Toad Hall" (p. 71).

4. Waugh may have known of a similar incident involving Lord Kitchener. After the battle of Omdurman, in 1898, Kitchener stole the severed head of the Mahdi, as a trophy of war. "Queen Victoria was deeply shocked," notes Alan Moorehead in *The White Nile* (New York, 1960), p. 338.

5. The Dedication of *Officers and Gentlemen* reads: "To Major-General Sir Robert Laycock that every man in arms should wish to be." The dedication indicates Waugh's respect for Laycock, under whom he served, and for the soldier's profession.

6. Mrs. Stitch suggests Lady Diana Cooper, an old friend of Waugh's married to Duff Cooper, First Lord of the Admiralty, 1937 - 38. Cooper served on diplomatic missions in North Africa during the latter part of World War II. Mrs. Stitch first appears in *Black Mischief* and in *Scoop*.

7. In his preface to Christie Lawrence's *Irregular Adventure* (London, 1947), p. 11, Waugh recalls the horror of the last days of the Cretan rout: "Hunger and exhaustion had by then produced a dream-night condition when people seemed to appear and disappear inconsequently and leave unconnected fragments of memory behind them."

8. Concerning Communist infiltration in high government circles, both English and American, Waugh noted in a judicious review of Richard Rovere's *Senator Joe McCarthy* that "in England, between the outbreak of the Spanish Civil War and the Molotov-Ribbentrop treaty, there were numberless well-intentioned boobies who joined 'popular front' organizations, signed manifestoes, stood on platforms with Communist Party members while the 'Red Flag' was sung and politely raised their clenched fists in salute. America was farther away and its inhabitants have a natural inclination to 'join' whatever is presented to them as benevolent. These Americans were innocent and quite ignorant of the conspiracy" ("McCarthy," *Spectator* 204 [February 5, 1960]: 185).

9. Book Three of *Unconditional Surrender* is entitled "The Death Wish," but in the recension was changed to "The Last Battle."

10. Gene D. Phillips, *Evelyn Waugh's Officers, Gentlemen, and Rogues: The Fact behind His Fiction* (Chicago, 1977), p. 138. In another context (*The Loved One*) Waugh had earlier made ironic allusion to the myth. At her moment of crisis, Aimee Thanatagenos "had communed with the spirits of her ancestors. . .voices which far away and in another age had rung of the Minotaur, stamping far underground at the end of the passage" (116 - 17).

11. Unfortunately for the continuity of the one-volume recension, Waugh omitted several pages from *Unconditional Surrender* that further emphasized Guy's deepening sense of a mission gone astray: "He wore the medal which had hung around the neck of his brother, Gervase, when the sniper had picked him off on his way up to the line in Flanders. In his heart he felt stirring the despair in which his brother, Ivo, had starved himself to

death. Half an hour's scramble on the beach near Dakar; an ignominious rout in Crete. That had been his war" (*Unconditional Surrender,* p. 217).

12. In *The Diaries of Evelyn Waugh,* ed. Michael Davie (London, 1976), Waugh vividly describes the traumatic plane crash which he and Randolph Churchill miraculously survived. An excerpt: "then we suddenly shot upwards and the next thing I knew was that I was walking in a cornfield by the light of the burning aeroplane talking to a strange British officer about the progress of the war in a detached fashion and that he was saying 'You'd better sit down for a bit skipper' " (*Croatia,* Sunday, July 16, 1944, p. 573). See also Diana Cooper, *The Light of Common Day* (London, 1959), p. 205, for Churchill's account of the crash.

13. "Matter of Fact Mothers of the New Age," *Evening Standard,* April 8, 1927, p. 7.

14. Stopp, *Evelyn Waugh,* p. 168.

15. Preface to *Sword of Honour,* pp. 9 - 10.

16. Andrew Rutherford, "Waugh's *Sword of Honour,*" in *Imagined Worlds: Essays on Some English Novels and Novelists in Honour of John Butt* (London, 1968), pp. 456 - 57.

17. Anthony Burgess, "The Comedy of Ultimate Truths," *Spectator* 216 (April 15, 1966): 462.

18. "The New Waugh," *The Times Literary Supplement,* October 27, 1961, p. 770.

19. "Wartime Revisited," *The Times Literary Supplement,* March 17, 1966, p. 216.

20. Gore Vidal, *New York Times Book Review,* January 7, 1962, p. 1.

21. Gabriel Fielding, "Evelyn Waugh and the Cross of Satire," *Critic* 23 (February - March 1965): 55.

22. Kingsley Amis, "Crouchback's Regress," *Spectator* 207 (October 27, 1961): 581.

23. Joseph Heller, "Middle-Aged Innocence," *Nation* 194 (January 20, 1962): 62.

24. Pierre Michel, *James Gould Cozzens* (New York, 1974), p. 89.

25. Mrs. Mitford's recollections of Waugh (originally published in *Arts e Loisirs*) conclude: "One has the impression that he was a refugee in the Catholic Church from the ugliness of the world and that, suddenly, he found himself delivered to his executioners. During his last months he sank into a black melancholy; personally I am sure that he died of a broken heart" (translated from the French). *Evelyn Waugh Newsletter* I: 1 (Spring 1967): 1.

Chapter Five

1. A valuable summation of Waugh's attitude toward the practice of fiction may be read in Robert M. Davis, "Evelyn Waugh on the Art of Fiction," *Papers on Language and Literature* 3 (1967): 270 - 87. Also see

Frederick J. Stopp's analysis (Chapter 3, "War and the Settled Years") in *Evelyn Waugh, Portrait of an Artist* (London, 1958), pp. 47 - 59. *Evelyn Waugh: A Little Order*, ed. Donat Gallagher (London, 1977) makes available in one volume many of the essays Waugh wrote for newspapers and magazines.

2. "Chesterton" [review of Gary Wills, *Chesterton: Man and Mask*], *National Review* 10 (April 22, 1961): 251.

3. *Ninety-Two Days, The Account of a Tropical Journey through British Guiana and Part of Brazil* (New York, 1934), pp. 4 - 5.

4. "The Book Unbeautiful" [reviews of Truman Capote and Richard Avedon, *Observations;* Yousef Karsh, *Portraits of Greatness*], *Spectator* 203 (November 1959): 728. See also "Something Fresh" [review of Muriel Spark, *The Comforters*], *Spectator* 198 (February 22, 1957): 256.

5. *Work Suspended* (London, 1942), p. 5.

6. "Kicking Against the Goad," *Commonweal* 49 (March 11, 1949): 536.

7. Harvey Breit, "Evelyn Waugh," in *The Writer Observed* (Cleveland, 1956), p. 44.

8. From the introduction to Christopher Sykes, *Character and Situation* (New York, 1950), p. ix.

9. "Chesterton," p. 251.

10. "Mr. Betjeman Despairs" [review of John Betjeman, *First and Last Loves*], *The Month* 8 (December 1952): 374.

11. Interview with Julian Jebb in *Writers at Work: The Paris Review Interviews*, Third Series (New York, 1967), p. 113.

12. "Chesterton," p. 252.

13. Breit, p. 45.

14. Ibid.

15. "Art from Anarchy" [review of Arthur Calder-Marshall, *A Date with a Duchess*], *Night and Day*, September 16, 1937, p. 25.

16. As quoted in Dudley Carew, *A Fragment of Friendship* (London, 1974), pp. 18 - 19.

17. "The Technician" [review of Somerset Maugham's *Christmas Holiday*], *Spectator* 163 (February 17, 1939): 274.

18. "Two Unquiet Lives" [review of Stephen Spender, *World within World*, and John Miller, *Saints and Parachutes*], *Tablet* 197 (May 5, 1951): 357.

19. "Chesterton," p. 251.

20. "Literary Style in England and America," *Books on Trial* 14 (October 1955): 65 - 66.

21. *Helena*, p. 116.

22. "Father and Son," *Atlantic* 211 (March 1963): 49.

23. Arthur Waugh, *One Man's Road, Being a Picture of Life in a Passing Generation* (London, 1931), p. 49.

24. *A Little Learning*, p. 139.

25. "Waugh's Letters to Thomas Merton," ed. Sister M. Thérèse, *Evelyn Waugh Newsletter* 3 (Spring 1969): 3.

26. "The American Epoch in the Catholic Church," *Life*, September 19, 1949, p. 143.

27. *Remote People* (London, 1931), p. 52.

28. "Fiction," *Spectator* 160 (June 24, 1938): 1162.

29. From the *Paris Review* interview, p. 110.

30. *Work Suspended*, pp. 82 - 83.

31. "The Private Diaries of Evelyn Waugh," Part 8, *Observer*, May 13, 1973, p. 50.

32. "Fan-Fare," *Life*, April 8, 1946, p. 55.

33. "An Angelic Doctor; the Work of Mr. P. G. Wodehouse" [review of P. G. Wodehouse, *Week End Wodehouse*], *Tablet* 173 (June 17, 1939): 786.

34. "Tess—As a Modern Sees It," *Evening Standard*, January 17, 1930, p. 7.

35. "Two Unquiet Lives," p. 356.

36. "Edith Sitwell's First Novel" [reviews of Edith Sitwell, *I Live Under a Black Sun;* Ernest Hemingway, *To Have and Have Not;* Terence Greenidge, *Tinpot Country*], *Night and Day*, October 21, 1937, p. 28.

37. "The Case of Mr. Hemingway" [review of *Across the River and into the Trees*], *Commonweal* 53 (November 3, 1950): 97 - 98. Further comment on Waugh's attitudes toward Hemingway's style and choice of subject matter may be read in Calvin W. Lane, "Waugh's Book Reviews for *Night and Day*," *Evelyn Waugh Newsletter* 4 (Spring 1970): 1 - 3.

38. "The Waste Land" [review of Graham Greene, *The Lawless Roads*], *Spectator* 162 (March 10, 1939): 414.

39. "Felix Culpa?" [review of Graham Greene, *The Heart of the Matter*], *Commonweal* 48 (July 16, 1948): 322 - 25.

40. "Last Steps in Africa" [review of Graham Greene, *In Search of a Character*], *Spectator* 207 (October 27, 1961): 594.

41. *The Diaries of Evelyn Waugh*, ed. Michael Davie (London, 1976), pp. 778 - 79.

42. "The Writing of English" [review of Robert Graves and Alan Hodge, *The Reader Over Your Shoulder*], *Tablet* 182 (July 3, 1943): 8 - 9.

Chapter Six

1. See articles by Robert Murray Davis: "*Vile Bodies* in Typescript," *Evelyn Waugh Newsletter* 11:3 (Winter 1977): 7 - 8, and "Shaping a World: The Textual History of *Love Among the Ruins*," *Analytical and Enumerative Bibliography* 1 (Spring 1977): 137 - 54, and Jeffrey Heath: "Waugh's *Scoop* in Manuscript," *Evelyn Waugh Newsletter* 11:2 (Autumn 1977): 9 - 11, and "Waugh's *Decline and Fall* in Manuscript," *English Studies* 55: vi (December 1974): 523 - 30.

2. D. Paul Farr, "The Novelist's Coup: Style as Satiric Norm in *Scoop*," *Connecticut Review* 8 (April 1975): 42 - 54.

3. Samuel Clemens, *The Adventures of Huckleberry Finn*, Perennial Edition (New York, 1965), p. 193.

4. Leonard Feinberg, Chapter One, "Characteristics of Satire," in *Introduction to Satire* (Ames, 1968), p. 15. Alvin Kernan develops a similar view in "A Theory of Satire" in *Satire: Modern Essays in Criticism*, ed. Ronald Paulson (Englewood Cliffs, N.J., 1971), p. 256.

5. "Fan-Fare," *Life*, April 8, 1946, p. 55.

6. "Lower the Flag," *Newsweek*, April 25, 1966, p. 92.

7. "Evelyn Waugh, Satirical Novelist, Is Dead at 62," *New York Times*, April 11, 1966, p. 1.

8. Christopher Sykes, "Evelyn," *Sunday Times*, April 17, 1966, p. 12.

9. Malcolm Bradbury, *Evelyn Waugh* (Edinburgh, 1964), p. 11.

10. Quoted in Julian Jebb, "Evelyn Waugh," *Writers at Work: The Paris Review Interviews*, Third Series (New York, 1968), p. 114.

11. Edmund Wilson, " 'Never Apologize, Never Explain': The Art of Evelyn Waugh," in *Classics and Commercials* (New York, 1950, reprinted 1962), p. 140.

Selected Bibliography

Waugh's prolific output resulted in a complex publishing history. His work was translated into many languages, and several of them have different titles in the American editions. Eight of the novels have been published in a revised edition, and the three World War II novels published separately, have been brought together in a one-volume recension. The following listing contains the initial dates of publication in England and in the United States, and the publication dates of the revised editions. A full listing of Waugh source material may be found in *Evelyn Waugh: A Checklist of Primary and Secondary Material*, ed. Robert M. Davis, et al. (Troy: Whitston Publishing Co., 1972). A yearly bibliography is published in the *Evelyn Waugh Newsletter*, Paul Doyle, Editor, Nassau Community College, Garden City, New York. Both sources are a must for Waugh scholars. Alain Blayac's "Evelyn Waugh—A Supplementary Bibliography," *The Book Collector* (Spring 1976): 53 - 62, is an additional listing of more than eighty titles covering the period 1929 - 1942. Waugh's private library and the bulk of his correspondence are now deposited in the library at the University of Texas. The Division of Special Collections at Boston University, and the Fales Collection at New York University also hold some of Waugh's letters.

PRIMARY SOURCES

1. Books (chronologically arranged)

Rossetti, His Life and Works. London: Duckworth, 1928; New York: Dodd, Mead and Co., 1928.

Decline and Fall, An Illustrated Novelette. London: Chapman and Hall, 1928; New York: Doubleday, Doran, 1929. Revised edition, Chapman and Hall, 1962.

Vile Bodies. London: Chapman and Hall, 1930; New York: J. Cape, H. Smith, 1930. Revised edition, Chapman and Hall, 1965.

Labels, A Mediterranean Journal. London: Duckworth, 1930. Published in America as *A Bachelor Abroad, A Mediterranean Journal*. New York: J. Cape, H. Smith, 1930.

Remote People. London: Duckworth, 1931. Published in America as *They Were Still Dancing*. New York: Farrar and Rinehart, 1932.

Black Mischief. London: Chapman and Hall, 1932. New York: Farrar and Rinehart, 1932. Revised edition, Chapman and Hall, 1962.

Ninety-Two Days, The Account of a Tropical Journey Through British Guiana and Part of Brazil. London: Duckworth, 1934; New York: Farrar and Rinehart, 1934.

A Handful of Dust. London: Chapman and Hall, 1934; New York: Farrar and Rinehart, 1934. Revised edition, Chapman and Hall, 1964.

Edmund Campion: Jesuit and Martyr. London: Longmans, 1935; New York: Sheed and Ward, 1935. 3rd edition, London: Longmans, 1961.

Mr. Loveday's Little Outing and Other Sad Stories. London: Chapman and Hall, 1936; Boston: Little, Brown, 1936.

Waugh in Abyssinia. London: Longmans, Green and Co., 1936; New York: Longmans, Green and Co., 1936.

Scoop, A Novel about Journalists. London: Chapman and Hall, 1938; Boston: Little, Brown, 1938. Revised edition, Chapman and Hall, 1964.

Robbery under Law, The Mexican Object-Lesson. London: Chapman and Hall, 1939. Published in America as *Mexico: An Object Lesson.* Boston: Little, Brown, 1939.

Put Out More Flags. London: Chapman and Hall, 1942; Boston: Little, Brown, 1942. Revised edition, Chapman and Hall, 1967.

Work Suspended. London: Chapman and Hall, 1942.

Brideshead Revisited: The Sacred and Profane Memories of Captain Charles Ryder. London: Chapman and Hall, 1945; Boston: Little, Brown, 1945. Revised edition, Chapman and Hall, 1960.

When the Going Was Good. London: Duckworth, 1946; Boston: Little, Brown, 1946.

Scott-King's Modern Europe. London: Chapman and Hall, 1947; Boston: Little, Brown, 1949.

Wine in Peace and War. London: Saccone and Speed, Ltd., 1947.

The Loved One. London: Chapman and Hall, 1948; Boston: Little, Brown, 1948. Revised Edition, Chapman and Hall, 1965.

Work Suspended and Other Stories Written before the Second World War. London: Chapman and Hall, 1949.

Helena. London: Chapman and Hall, 1950; Boston: Little, Brown, 1950.

Men at Arms. London: Chapman and Hall, 1952; Boston: Little, Brown, 1952.

The Holy Places. London: The Queen Anne Press, 1952; New York: Queen Anne Press and British Book Center, 1953.

Love Among the Ruins. London: Chapman and Hall, 1953.

Tactical Exercise. Boston: Little, Brown, 1954.

Officers and Gentlemen. London: Chapman and Hall, 1955; Boston: Little, Brown, 1955.

The Ordeal of Gilbert Pinfold. London: Chapman and Hall, 1957; Boston: Little, Brown, 1957.

Ronald Knox. London: Chapman and Hall, 1959. In America, titled *Monsignor Ronald Knox.* Boston: Little, Brown, 1959.

Tourist in Africa. London: Chapman and Hall, 1960; Boston: Little, Brown, 1960.

Unconditional Surrender. London: Chapman and Hall, 1961. In America, titled *The End of the Battle.* Boston: Little, Brown, 1961.

Basil Seal Rides Again or The Rake's Regress. London: Chapman and Hall, 1963; Boston: Little, Brown, 1963.

A Little Learning. London: Chapman and Hall, 1964; Boston: Little, Brown, 1964.

Sword of Honour. The one-volume recension of *Men at Arms, Officers and Gentlemen,* and *Unconditional Surrender.* London: Chapman and Hall, 1965; Boston: Little, Brown, 1966.

2. Diaries and Letters

The Diaries of Evelyn Waugh. Ed. Michael Davie. London: Weidenfeld and Nicholson, 1976; Boston: Little, Brown, 1977. A tantalizing record, seldom dipping below the surface of Waugh's life, with some gaps notably at the time of his divorce from his first wife. The entries covering the years 1939 - 1945 provide a detailed and absorbing record of Waugh's checkered World War II experience. The entries from Waugh's later years sadly confirm his increasing moroseness as he grew older.

The Letters of Evelyn Waugh. Ed. Mark Amory. New Haven: Ticknor and Fields, 1980. The 840 letters in this volume contribute to a more thorough understanding of Waugh's ambiguous, role-playing nature and are a corrective to the frequent harshness of the diary entries. Amory notes that the letters reveal "a much nicer, kinder man. . . .talking to people he liked and respected—people he wanted to entertain." Not sparing of his own weaknesses, Waugh often figures as an absurd, incongruous, and even remorseful character.

3. Interviews

BREIT, HARVEY. "An Interview with Evelyn Waugh," *New York Times Book Review,* March 13, 1949, p. 23; reprinted in Breit, *The Writer Observed.* Cleveland: World, 1956, pp. 43 - 46.

BLACK, STEPHEN; DAVIES, JACK; and WILMOT, CHARLES, interviewers. "Frankly Speaking." London: BBC radio, November 16, 1953. Unpublished.

FREEMAN, JOHN, interviewer. "Face to Face." London: BBC TV, June 26, 1960. Unpublished.

JEBB, JULIAN, interviewer. "The Art of Fiction XXX: Evelyn Waugh." *Paris Review* 8 (Summer-Fall 1963): 72 - 85. Reprinted in *Writers at Work: The Paris Review Interviews,* Third Series. New York: Viking, 1967, pp. 103 - 14.

4. Reviews of Books

"Edith Sitwell's First Novel" [reviews of Edith Sitwell, *I Live Under a Black Sun;* Ernest Hemingway, *To Have and To Have Not;* Terence Greenidge, *Tin Pot Country*]. *Night and Day*, October 21, 1937, pp. 28 - 29.
"Present Discontents" [review of Cyril Connolly, *Enemies of Primise*]. *Tablet* 172 (December 3, 1938): 743 - 44.
"An Angelic Doctor, the Work of Mr. P. G. Wodehouse" [review of P. G. Wodehouse, *Week End Wodehouse*]. *Tablet* 173 (June 17, 1939): 786 - 87.
"The Writing of English" [review of Robert Graves and Alan Hodge, *The Reader Over Your Shoulder*]. *Tablet* 182 (July 3, 1943): 8 - 9.
"Felix Culpa?" [review of Graham Greene, *The Heart of the Matter*]. *Commonweal* 48 (July 16, 1948): 322 - 25.
"The Case of Mr. Hemingway" [review of *Across the River and into the Trees*]. *Commonweal* 53 (November 3, 1950): 97 - 98.
"The Heart's Own Reasons" [review of Graham Greene, *The End of the Affair*]. *Commonweal* 54 (August 17, 1951): 458 - 59.
"Mr. Betjeman Despairs" [review of John Betjeman, *First and Last Loves*]. *Month* 8: 6 (December 1952): 372 - 75.
"The Making of an American" [review of Leo Rosten, *The Return of Hyman Kaplan*]. *Spectator* 203 (October 16, 1959): 525.
"McCarthy" [review of Richard H. Rovere, *Senator Joe McCarthy*]. *Spectator* 204 (February 5, 1960): 185.
"Marriage a la Mode—1936" [review of Anthony Powell, *Casanova's Chinese Restaurant*]. *Spectator* 204 (June 24, 1960): 919.
"Chesterton" [review of Garry Wills, *Chesterton: Man and Mask*]. *National Review* 10 (April 22, 1961): 251 - 52.
"Last Steps in Africa" [review of Graham Greene, *In Search of a Character*]. *Spectator* 207 (October 27, 1961): 594.

5. Articles

Evelyn Waugh: A Little Order. Ed. Donat Gallagher. London: Eyre Methuen, 1977. A valuable collection of significant Waugh essays written mainly for newspapers and magazines throughout his career. Perceptive comment by Gallagher about Waugh's skills as a journalist.
"Oxford and the Next War." *Isis*, March 12, 1924, p. 10.
"Dante Gabriel Rossetti: A Centenary Criticism." *Fortnightly Review* NS 123 (May 1, 1928): 595 - 604.
"The Claim of Youth or Too Young at Forty; Youth Calls to Peter Pans of Middle-Age Who Block the Way." *Evening Standard*, January 22, 1929, p. 7.
"Ronald Firbank." *Life and Letters* 2 (March 1929): 191 - 96.

"Matter of Fact Mothers of the New Age." *Evening Standard,* April 8, 1929, p. 7.

"The War and the Younger Generation." *Spectator* 142 (April 13, 1929): 570 - 71.

"Converted to Rome: Why it Happened to Me." *Daily Express,* October 20, 1930, p. 10.

"Rough Life." *Virginia Quarterly Review* 10 (January 1934): 70 - 77. Part of *Ninety-Two Days.*

"Commando Raid on Bardia." *Life* 11 (November 17, 1941): 63 - 66, 71, 72, 74.

"Fan-Fare." *Life* 20 (April 8, 1946): 53, 54, 56, 58, 60. Abridged in *Catholic Digest* 10 (June 1946): 80 - 83.

"Palinurus in Never-never-land." *Tablet* 188 (July 27, 1946): 46.

"What to Do with the Upper Classes." *Town and Country* 101 (September 1, 1946): 141, 260 - 61.

"The Jesuit Who Was Thursday." *Tablet* 188 (December 21, 1946): 338 - 39; *Commonweal* 45 (March 21, 1947): 558 - 61.

"Why Hollywood Is a Term of Disparagement." *Daily Telegraph and Morning Post,* April 30, 1947, p. 4.

"Death in Hollywood." *Life* 23 (September 29, 1947): 73 - 74, 79 - 80, 83 - 84.

"Mgr. Ronald Knox." *Horizon* 17 (May 1948): 326 - 38.

"Foreword" to Thomas Merton, "Elected Silence." *Month* NS 1 (March 1949): 158 - 59.

"Kicking Against the Goad." *Commonweal* 49 (March 11, 1949): 534 - 36.

"The American Epoch in the Catholic Church." *Life* 27 (September 19, 1949): 135 - 38, 140, 143, 144, 146, 149 - 50, 152, 155; *Month* NS 2 (November 1949): 293 - 308.

"Saint Helena Empress." *Month* NS 7 (January 1952): 7 - 11.

"Literary Style in England and America." *Books on Trial* 14 (October 1955): 65 - 66.

"Anything Wrong with Priestley?" [article replying to J. B. Priestley's review of *The Ordeal of Gilbert Pinfold,* "What Was Wrong with Pinfold." *New Statesman* 54 (August 31, 1957): 224]. *Spectator* 199 (September 13, 1957): 328 - 29.

"Aspirations of a Mugwump." *Spectator* 203 (October 2, 1959): 435.

"An Act of Homage and Reparation to P. G. Wodehouse" (text of BBC broadcast, July 15, 1961). *Sunday Times Magazine Section,* July 16, 1961, pp. 21, 23.

"Oxford Revisited." *Sunday Times,* Weekly Review, November 7, 1965, p. 53.

SECONDARY SOURCES

1. Books about Evelyn Waugh

BRADBURY, MALCOLM. *Evelyn Waugh*. Writers and Critics Series. Edinburgh: Oliver and Boyd, 1964. A perceptive, clearly developed thesis by a critic and novelist. The "world of anarchy and disorder" Waugh describes is never brought under control in the novels, thus supporting Bradbury's contention that he is a truly modern novelist.

CARENS, JAMES F. *The Satiric Art of Evelyn Waugh*. Seattle and London: University of Washington Press, 1966. Carens relates Waugh "to significant literary, spiritual, and political tendencies of his period. . . ." The early novels are satiric romances, but the later works, especially the Crouchback series "are a satirical blend of novel and romance."

DEVITIS, A. A. *Roman Holiday: The Catholic Novels of Evelyn Waugh*. New York: Bookman Associates, 1956. DeVitis concludes that the religious theme is Waugh's "answer to the waste land which he had so admirably defined in his early novels."

DONALDSON, FRANCES. *Evelyn Waugh: Portrait of a Country Neighbor*. London: Weidenfeld and Nicholson, 1967; Philadelphia: Chilton Books, 1968. Chronicles the bitter-sweet nature of Waugh's relationship to his friends. Photographs.

DOYLE, PAUL A. *Evelyn Waugh*. Contemporary Writers in Christian Perspective Series. Grand Rapids: Eerdmans, 1969. Valuable for its perspective of Waugh as a writer of tragi-comedy. Doyle effectively applies this view to a balanced defense of *Brideshead Revisited.*

HOLLIS, CHRISTOPHER. *Evelyn Waugh*. Writers and Their Work No. 46. London: Longmans, Green, 1954. Hollis's brief study notes Waugh's emphasis on the dehumanizing effects of power.

LODGE, DAVID. *Evelyn Waugh*. Columbia Essays on Modern Writers. New York: Columbia University Press, 1971. An excellent short study. Points out the sense of comic anarchy, but also notes that Waugh remains objective—morally, emotionally, and stylistically. Waugh ridicules the modern, "but attempts to maintain or restore the traditional in the face of change are also seen as ridiculous."

PHILLIPS, GENE D. *Evelyn Waugh's Officers, Gentlemen and Rogues: The Fact behind His Fiction*. Chicago: Nelson-Hall, 1975. A good introduction to Waugh's novels, with special emphasis on religious elements present in the fiction. Makes use of correspondence with Waugh's family, the travel accounts, and so on.

STOPP, FREDERICK J. *Evelyn Waugh, Portrait of an Artist.* London: Chapman and Hall, 1958; Boston: Little, Brown and Company, 1958. The first full length critical study. Combines biographical insights with critical analysis. Chapter 8, "Comedy from Chaos," is especially good on Waugh's use of dialogue, and the clash of culture that produces comedy in the novels.

SYKES, CHRISTOPHER. *Evelyn Waugh: A Biography.* Boston: Little, Brown and Company, 1975. The authorized biography, by one of Waugh's close friends. Packed with factual, anecdotal detail, but makes no real effort to account for and explore the origins of Waugh's mercurial temperament. Impressionistic comment on the novels.

WAUGH, ALEC. *My Brother Evelyn and Other Profiles.* London: Cassell, 1967; New York: Farrar, Straus and Giroux, 1967. A generous tribute and revealing picture of Alec's relationship to his younger, more widely known brother.

2. Critical and General Studies

ACTON, HAROLD. *Memoirs of an Aesthete.* London: Methuen and Co., Ltd., 1948.
——. *More Memoirs of an Aesthete.* London: Methuen and Co. Ltd., 1970. In U.S.: *Memories of an Aesthete 1934 - 1968.* New York: Viking, 1970. Acton's two books provide detailed, colorful information on Waugh's changing moods and attitudes over the years. Highly valuable.

BERGONZI, BERNARD. "Evelyn Waugh's Gentlemen." *Critical Quarterly* V (Spring 1963): 23 - 36. In *A Handful of Dust* Tony Last's outmoded romanticism anticipates the more fully developed characterization of Guy Crouchback, "the doomed victim of the modern world."

BURGESS, ANTHONY. "The Comedy of Ultimate Truths." *Spectator* 216 (April 15, 1966): 462. Reprinted in *Urgent Copy: Literary Studies.* New York: Norton, 1969, pp. 21 - 29. Of *Decline and Fall,* Burgess remarks that it "would not have maintained its freshness for nearly forty years if it had not been based on the big theme of our Western literature—the right of the decent man to find decency in the world."
——. "War's Sour Fruits." In *The Novel Now: A Student's Guide to Contemporary Fiction.* London: Faber and Faber, 1967, pp. 48 - 58, "What Ford's tetralogy did for the First World War, Waugh's trilogy did for the second. . . . It is the whole history of the European struggle itself, told with verve, humour, pathos, and sharp accuracy."

COCKBURN, CLAUD. "Evelyn Waugh's Lost Rabbit." *Atlantic* 232 (December 1973): 53 - 59. Reminiscence by Waugh's cousin. Witty account of Waugh's enjoyment of role playing.

Davis, Robert Murray. "Evelyn Waugh on the Art of Fiction." *Papers on Language and Literature* 2 (1966): 243 - 52. Davis traces out Waugh's consistent praise, early and late in his career, for those writers who adopt "an 'objective' as opposed to a 'subjective' attitude to his material."

———. "Clarifying and Enriching: Waugh's Changing Concept of Anthony Blanche." *Papers of the Bibliographical Society of America* 72 (Third Quarter 1978), 305 - 320. A detailed analysis of Waugh's shifting characterization of Anthony Blanche ("the first and most consistent critic of the Flyte family") throughout the numerous versions of *Brideshead Revisited.*

Farr, D. Paul. "Waugh's Conservative Stance: Defending 'The Standards of Civilization.'" *Philological Quarterly* 51 (April 1972): 471 - 84. An examination of Waugh's "'conservative' vision as it appears in his non-fiction."

———. "The Novelist's Coup: Style as Satiric Norm in *Scoop.*" *Connecticut Review* 8 (April 1975): 42 - 54. Detailed, valuable study of how Waugh manipulates word patterns in "satirically exposing. . .the journalese which permeates the modern world."

Fielding, Gabriel. "Evelyn Waugh: the Price of Satire." *Listener* 72 (October 8, 1964): 541 - 42. Fielding reads *The Ordeal of Gilbert Pinfold* as an effort to reconcile the anger and cynicism of satire with Christian belief.

Graves, Robert, and Hodge, Alan. *The Long Week-End: A Social History of Great Britain 1918 - 1939.* The Norton Library. New York: W. W. Norton, 1963. Factual documentation of the period covered in Waugh's early satiric fiction.

Green, Martin. "British Comedy and The British Sense of Humour: Shaw, Waugh, and Amis." *Texas Quarterly* 4 (Autumn 1961): 217 - 27.

———. "Meaning and Delight in Evelyn Waugh." *Tuftonian* 21 (February 1965): 79 - 89. These two complementary articles are among the few that do justice to Waugh's humor. "Waugh is a major artist when he delights in the people and events he is presenting. . .and at the same time morally rejects them" (from "Meaning and Delight in Evelyn Waugh," 79).

———. *Children of the Sun: A Narrative of "Decadence" in England After 1918.* New York: Basic Books, 1976. A highly readable, opinionated account of the university dandies and aesthetes of the 1920s in rebellion against the mores of their fathers. Photographs.

Heath, Jeffrey. "*Vile Bodies*: A Revolution in Film Art." *Evelyn Waugh Newsletter* 8: 3 (Winter 1974): 2 - 7. "Mr. Isaacs' amateurs act out the history of amateurs in religion. . . . The real choice is between the entire City of Man (the film-world) and the City of God."

————. "Evelyn Waugh: Afraid of the Shadow." *Evelyn Waugh Newsletter* 9: 3 (Winter 1975): 1 - 4. Tony Last attempts to escape his other self, and in so doing fails to recognize his own responsibility for evil.

————. "The Private Language of Evelyn Waugh." *English Studies in Canada* 2: 3 (Fall 1976): 329 - 38. By indirect, allusive statement, Waugh "conveys values and meaning through what appears to be a prose of complete moral neutrality."

JOOST, NICHOLAS. "*A Handful of Dust:* Evelyn Waugh and the Novel of Manners." *Papers on Language and Literature* 12 (Spring 1976): 177 - 96. Thoughtful, detailed analysis of Waugh's use of (1) allusion (Eliot, Proust, St. Augustine), (2) contrasting scenes (jungle and London), and (3) metaphor (animal imagery).

KERMODE, FRANK. "Mr. Waugh's Cities." In *Puzzles and Epiphanies: Essays and Reviews 1958 - 1961.* London: Routledge and Kegan Paul, 1962, pp. 164 - 75. Kermode develops the thesis that "the great houses of England become by an easy transition types of the Catholic City. . . ."

KERNAN, ALVIN B. "The Wall and the Jungle: The Early Novels of Evelyn Waugh." *Yale Review* 53 (1963 - 64): 199 - 220. Kernan sees barbarism versus civilization as "a master image of life which underlies most of Waugh's novels."

————. "A Theory of Satire," in *Satire: Modern Essays in Criticism.* Ed. Ronald Paulson. Englewood Cliffs, N.J.: Prentice-Hall, 1971, pp. 249 - 77. A superb short introduction to the nature of satire. In the satirist's "vision of the world decency is forever in a precarious position near the edge of extinction, and the world is about to pass to eternal darkness" (p. 254).

LA FRANCE, MARSTON. "Context and Structure of Evelyn Waugh's *Brideshead Revisited.*" *Twentieth Century Literature* 10 (1964): 12 - 18. A balanced estimate of the most controversial of Waugh's novels. Notes the line of descent of the antihero from Paul Pennyfeather to Charles Ryder.

LANE, CALVIN W. "Evelyn Waugh's Radio and Television Broadcasts, 1938 - 1964." *Evelyn Waugh Newsletter* 9: 2 (Autumn 1975): 1 - 4. The broadcasts contribute to an understanding of Waugh's complex personality and to his beliefs about writing.

MACAULAY, ROSE. "Evelyn Waugh." *Horizon* 14 (December 1946): 360 - 76. High praise for the early novels but berates Waugh for his partisan religious views in *Brideshead Revisited.*

MECKIER, JEROME. "Cycle, Symbol, and Parody in Evelyn Waugh's *Decline and Fall.*" *Contemporary Literature* 20 (Winter 1979), 51 · 75. A thoughtful, carefully developed argument tracing out the failure of temporal values in *Decline and Fall.* Meckier sees Grimes as "a parodic Christ," and Prendergast as "a parody of spiritual man."

)'FAOLAIN, SEAN. *The Vanishing Hero: Studies in Novelists of the Twen-ties.* Boston: Little, Brown, 1957. "Waugh's detachment. . .is much more genuine than Huxley's." Good on the element of cruelty in Waugh's fiction.

RYCE-JONES, DAVID, ed. *Evelyn Waugh and His World.* Boston: Little, Brown, 1973. A fascinating potpourri of recollections and brief critical appraisals, including pieces by Peter Quennell on the Oxford years, Fr. Martin D'Arcy on Waugh's religion, and the Earl of Birkenhead on Waugh's involvement in World War II. Photographs and sketches.

UTHERFORD, ANDREW. "Waugh's Sword of Honour." In *Imagined Worlds: Essays on some English Novels and Novelists in Honour of John Butt.* Ed. Maynard Mack and Ian Gregor. London: Methuen, 1968, pp. 441 - 60. The best article on the World War II trilogy. Rutherford asserts that ". . .we feel as we read that the author as well as the hero, is achieving new self-knowledge, growing in moral insight, and we too are involved in the process" (p. 456).

PENDER, STEPHEN. "The World of Evelyn Waugh." In *The Creative Element: A Study of Vision, Despair and Orthodoxy among some Modern Writers.* New York: British Book Center, 1954. Reprinted in Folcroft Library Editions, pp. 159 - 74. Spender holds that Waugh says more in the "unconscious seriousness of his comedy" in the early novels, than in the consciously serious manner of his later work.

OGEL, JOSEPH F. "Waugh's *The Loved One:* The Artist in a Phony World." *Evelyn Waugh Newsletter* 10:2 (Autumn 1976): 1 - 4. "Illusions, deceptions, and false appearances" characterize *The Loved One.*

VASSON, RICHARD. "*A Handful of Dust:* Critique of Victorianism," *Modern Fiction Studies* 7 (1961 - 62): 327 - 37. The sham Gothic of Hetton Abbey in *A Handful of Dust* represents an attack on Victorianism and fake romanticism. Notes ironic parallels to Tennyson's *Idylls of the King.*

VAUGH, ARTHUR. *Tradition and Change.* London: Chapman and Hall, 1919. Arthur Waugh's concern for tradition and for style prefigure similar attitudes in Evelyn Waugh.

VEST, REBECCA. "Evelyn Waugh." In *Ending in Earnest: A Literary Log.* Garden City: 1931, pp. 217 - 26. Predicted that Waugh would be "the dazzling figure of the age as Max Beerbohm was of his."

VILSON, EDMUND. "Never Apologize, Never Explain: The Art of Evelyn Waugh," and "Splendors and Miseries of Evelyn Waugh." In *Classics and Commercials.* New York: Farrar, Straus and Co., 1950, pp. 140 - 46, 298 - 305. In the first article, Wilson hailed Waugh as a "first rate comic genius." But *Brideshead Revisited,* reviewed in "Splendors and Miseries of Evelyn Waugh," incurred his anti-Catholic bias.

Index